Legal Tales

International Studies in Law and Literature

VOLUME 4

The titles published in this series are listed at *brill.com/isll*

Legal Tales

Once upon a Time, the Law

By

François Ost

Translated from the French by

Mark Byrne

BRILL | NIJHOFF

LEIDEN | BOSTON

This book was originally published as *Contes de la rue Soufflot. Contes de la rue Soufflot.* © Éditions DALLOZ, 2024.

The Library of Congress Cataloging-in-Publication Data is available online at https://catalog.loc.gov

Typeface for the Latin, Greek, and Cyrillic scripts: "Brill". See and download: brill.com/brill-typeface.

ISSN 2773-191X
ISBN 978-90-04-73710-5 (hardback)
ISBN 978-90-04-73711-2 (e-book)
DOI 10.1163/9789004737112

Contents

Foreword VII

Introduction 1

A Law for Noah's Ark? 11

Ius et Agapè: The Trial of Jesus, or Impossible Justice 20

Me, Martin, the Five-Legged Bear: A Letter to My Judges 39

On the Way Back 49

On the Margins of the Palace 68

Fortuna Maris 84

3, 2, 1 … 109

Solange B., Infanticide? 120

The Liberated Library 148

By the Same Author 159
Index 161

Foreword

In the legal world at large – and in the field of Law and Literature in particular – the name François Ost is synonymous with excellence, originality, and the highest intellectual prestige. He is the author of an immense and remarkable body of scholarly work, so vast that any attempt to catalogue his achievements would only understate their true magnitude.

This is one of the reasons why writing the prologue to the English translation of a selection of his celebrated legal tales – published by Brill in the *International Studies in Law and Literature* series, of whose Editorial Board Professor Ost is a distinguished member – is, for me, a true honour. Yet this task is also a genuine pleasure, as my academic relationship and collaboration with Professor Ost extend far beyond this series and date back many years.

I first came into contact with him in 1991, during a six-month research stay as a grant-funded fellow at the *Facultés Universitaires Saint-Louis* in Brussels, under his supervision. That stay resulted in a monograph on *the validity of law* (published by Civitas), which he graciously prefaced with a beautiful introduction – something for which I shall always remain grateful. Some years later, over the course of two consecutive academic years, he invited me to deliver a seminar as guest speaker at the prestigious *Académie Européenne de Théorie du Droit* (Brussels), which he founded and directed for decades and which has since become a landmark European institution in the field.

Professor Ost also delivered a lecture on the topic of legal validity at the invitation of the Dean of the Faculty of Law at the Complutense University of Madrid, Professor José Iturmendi Morales, and he recently took part in the tribute to Professor Iturmendi on the occasion of his retirement – published in both Spanish (Tirant lo Blanch) and English (Brill/Nijhoff). Moreover, when I first began to explore the field of Law and Literature, my initial monograph on the subject (Marcial Pons) was once again graced by a generous preface from him. I shall never forget these gestures, nor cease to be grateful for them.

I should add, with regard to the Spanish-speaking world, that in addition to the many honours and distinctions awarded to Professor Ost both in his own country and internationally, he was named an Honorary European Academician by the *Real Academia de Jurisprudencia y Legislación* of Spain shortly before the pandemic.

When François published one of his collections of legal tales with Dalloz and kindly sent me a copy – which forms part of the basis for the book I now have the honour of introducing – I read it in a single sitting and found it simply 'magnificent'. At the time, I suggested that he consider publishing it in English.

He preferred, instead, to select nine of his most successful stories, which – as the reader will see – span a variety of literary genres, yet all share an exceptional level of literary and legal scholarship, a hallmark of all his work.

The volume before us adopts the perspective of Law through Literature, as distinct from other possible approaches such as Law in Literature or the Law of Literature. These stories were originally published in French by the prestigious publisher Dalloz and have already been translated into Brazilian Portuguese. An Italian edition is currently underway, as I recently learned from Professor Paola Mittica of the University of Urbino, who is also a member of this Editorial Board. Now that Dalloz and Brill/Nijhoff – represented respectively by Laurence Ballet and Bea Timmer – have reached an agreement regarding the English translation rights, the English-speaking world will likewise be able to benefit from the intellectual refinement of these writings.

I should also note that the French edition of these tales was reviewed in the Christmas 2024–2025 issue of *Le Soir*, a recognition of the distinguished place these works rightfully occupy.

I am confident that readers of this English edition will be captivated by the magic and *duende*[1] that pervade all of François Ost's work, and that mark him not only as a jurist of the first rank but also as a dramatist with a singular literary voice.

The *International Studies in Law and Literature* series was launched in January 2024 with a volume by Professor Martín Laclau of Buenos Aires. In 2025, two further volumes followed: the second by the legendary Richard H. Weisberg, and the third by the Spanish professor and renowned expert in Law and Literature, Pedro Talavera. This latest volume of legal tales by Professor Ost adds further distinction and mastery to this series from Brill, which – following its recent merger with De Gruyter – is poised to become the world's leading academic publisher in the social sciences.

María José Falcón y Tella
Professor of Legal Philosophy, Complutense University of Madrid
Editor-in-Chief, *International Studies in Law and Literature*

1 Translator's note: *Duende* is a Spanish term often used in literary and artistic contexts to describe a mysterious, ineffable power – an emotional intensity or soulful inspiration that moves both artist and audience.

Introduction

'Legal tales' – is the expression not a contradiction in terms? And if so, is writing Legal Tales not a futile, even illusory pursuit? That, no doubt, is what those who continue to oppose law and fiction would argue. On one side, they would say, is the 'as if' of the tale (it was as if ...): the vast realm of dreams, the play of imagination, the pleasure of fiction. On the other side, the 'because that's how it is!' of law: the empire of rules, the seriousness of constraint, the discomfort of sanction.

In contrast to these received ideas, this collection – and indeed the broader movement of Law and Literature, as well as the more recent development of narrative legal theory – takes up the challenge of dismantling that opposition. Law, it must be recognised, arises from fiction (*ex fabula ius oritur*), not from fact, contrary to what jurists are taught in university lecture halls. For there are no raw facts – only narrated ones. And law, once enacted, is immediately reappropriated by its addressees, who reshape it into a thousand singular stories. These are the stories that the courts are called upon to hear, giving rise to new rules – rules that will themselves be reinterpreted, retold, and reintegrated into new narratives.

As for jurists, centuries of positivism have made them forget that they are, at heart, storytellers. Yet, in their finest moments, they remember: litigators, who manage to evoke life beneath the letter of the law; professors, who recount to their students the historical genesis of an institution or the social relevance of a procedure; legislators, who persuade others of the need for reform by placing law back into its proper context.

After teaching law for decades and contributing to the development of the Law and Literature movement in French,[1] I eventually turned to writing legal fiction.[2] I have often been asked: 'Why write legal tales?' My first answer – and it may be reason enough – is: 'for pleasure'. This point is essential. The tales must stand on their own merits – that is, as works of fiction. Whatever other value they may possess (to which I shall return), it is of utmost importance that they bring pleasure to their readers – or to their listeners, if told aloud. This is the foremost criterion distinguishing fiction from other forms of writ-

1 F. Ost, *Raconter la loi: Aux sources de l'imaginaire juridique* (Paris: Odile Jacob, 2004); *idem*, *Sade et la loi* (Paris: Odile Jacob, 2005).

2 F. Ost, *Les Contes de la rue Soufflot* (Paris: Dalloz, 2024), boxed set comprising three previously published collections: *Si le droit m'était conté* (2019); *Nouveaux contes juridiques* (2021); *Le Congrès et autres contes juridiques* (2024).

 | DOI:10.1163/9789004737112_002

ing, as Aristotle already noted in his *Poetics*: 'all human beings delight in imitation'.[3] It is also the condition for the tale's success *as a tale*: its 'performativity' depends on it – it functions as a tale only if it delights.[4]

No doubt these stories serve many other functions, and they clearly partake of a form of knowledge – but it must be, as Nietzsche put it, a 'joyful science'. Jean de La Fontaine – the prince of storytellers, and a jurist himself – said much the same: 'a bare moral is tiresome / a tale carries the precept along with it'. And the great fabulist adds: 'in this kind of fiction, one must instruct and please / and storytelling for its own sake seems a paltry thing'.[5]

Once the ears are open, the heart receptive, and the mind alert – yes, the tale may also instruct. As Paul Ricoeur writes, the symbol – but also the narrative – 'invites us to think'.[6] For me, a legal tale 'invites us to think' about the law: to reflect on it more deeply, not merely to state it, like a code, or to describe it, like a textbook. This, then, is my second reason for telling legal stories: to reflect more deeply on the law through storytelling.

To reflect on the law is, first of all, to recall what should never have been forgotten: that law is, above all, a cultural construct. More than a system of norms, an arrangement of procedures, or a network of institutions, it is a representation of the world – of our world – as we would like it to be. It is an evaluative discourse, one that inspires practices and brings normative order to the world through a specific imaginary – foundational in nature, rooted in shared ethical convictions and factual intuitions.[7] Robert Cover powerfully underscored this through his concept of *nomos*, which he defined as a constellation of norms and narratives – a world we inhabit, and one that shapes our commitments. He writes:

> No set of legal institutions or prescriptions exists apart from the narratives that locate it and give it meaning. For every constitution there is an epic, for each decalogue a scripture. ... Every prescription is insistent in its demand to be located in discourse – to be supplied with history and destiny, beginning and end, explanation and purpose ... in the narratives that are the trajectories plotted upon material reality by our imaginations.[8]

3 Aristotle, *Poetics*, 48b20–24.
4 J.-M. Schaeffer, *Pourquoi la fiction ?* (Paris: Seuil, 1999), p. 327.
5 J. de La Fontaine, *Fables* (Paris: Presses Pocket, 1989), p. 175.
6 P. Ricoeur, 'Le symbole donne à penser', *Esprit*, July 1959, pp. 60ff.
7 C. Castoriadis, *L'institution imaginaire de la société* (Paris: Seuil, 1975).
8 R. Cover, 'Nomos and Narrative', *Harvard Law Review* 97 (1983), p. 5.

In this way, law – as a paradigmatic cultural production – contributes to giving meaning to our lives in both senses of the term: significance and direction. What matters in this regard is not so much the specific content of rules and procedures (which are often variable and sometimes negotiable), but rather the reflexes of legal thought, which constitute a particular culture: the culture of the *third*. In this culture, the relationship – whether public or private – between 'I' and 'you' is conceived of and adjudicated only under the aegis of the 'he' of the law and of the judge, who gives it voice.[9] Associated with this are principles such as publicity, the right to adversarial proceedings, the presumption of innocence, among others – principles that together define the regime of the rule of law (or *État de droit*, for civil law jurists): a society in which individuals are regarded not as subjects of the law, but as legal subjects – that is, as actors in the legal drama played out under the authority of the *third*.

What may seem highly speculative can be expressed simply through the tale – and to an audience far beyond the small circle of legal professionals. Too often, jurists, caught up in the necessary technicality of their discipline, have allowed themselves to be confined within the formalism of rules, leaving public debate to others – as if the law had nothing to say about society's choices, stepping in only *a posteriori* to cast decisions made elsewhere into normative form. If, on the contrary, one recognises the cultural nature of legal discourse, it becomes clear that law has an essential role to play in these debates – debates all too often conducted under the influence of other forms of normativity. And let us be clear: these are indeed normative systems – market rules, technical standards, numerical targets, health imperatives, religious precepts ...

To practise and teach law from this cultural perspective is to gain a deeper understanding of its underlying movements and living sources. It means drawing on centuries of experience through the history of law, and engaging with alternative solutions through comparative law – solutions practised by others, not by ourselves. This distancing – fostered by storytelling, which transports us elsewhere – is salutary, as it lends our legal practice greater flexibility and, no doubt, greater humanity. It also encourages what is referred to in academic jargon as the 'interdisciplinary approach' to law, which is nothing other than its social contextualisation – something legal professionals engage in every day, often like Monsieur Jourdain,[10] who had long been speaking prose with-

9 F. Ost, *Le droit ou l'empire du tiers* (Paris: Dalloz, 2021).

10 Translator's note: Monsieur Jourdain is a character from Molière's *Le Bourgeois gentilhomme* (1670), who is astonished to discover that he has been speaking prose all his life

out knowing it, doing so without the necessary tools and, above all, without recognising its specific demands.

Here too, the tale, which bridges realities and norms (as Ricoeur wrote: 'the narrative lies between the descriptive and the prescriptive'),[11] offers a valuable propaedeutic. Hence the ongoing effort to introduce 'Law and Literature' courses into legal education. It would mean reconnecting with the venerable tradition of the Inns of Court in London during Shakespeare's time – when the training of lawyers gave pride of place to just this kind of *pro et contra* confrontation over fictional trials, sometimes authored by fashionable playwrights such as Shakespeare or Marlowe.[12]

To think about law through the tale is also to gain a more accurate sense of the role of the case in relation to the rule. Jurists trained in the common law tradition are well aware of this, but it is well known how much classical training in continental law tends to underestimate its importance: the case is taught, at most, as an 'application' or illustration of the rule – which alone is considered worthy of genuine interest. In contrast to casuistry, which it discredits as a synonym for dispersion, even contradiction, classical legal dogmatics – whether French or German – concentrates its attention on the definition of the concepts that constitute rules, and on the systematic relationships that link them.

Practitioners, however, know well what Wittgenstein reminds us: no rule contains within itself instructions for its application. Or, if such instructions exist, they are necessarily incomplete and themselves subject to interpretation. In other words, no rule can encompass the full variety of cases that may arise. Conversely, the experienced jurist will have learned to take the case seriously – and, where appropriate, to treat it as an opportunity to formulate a new rule or, at the very least, to refine the existing one. This, after all, is how Roman law developed over the course of nearly a millennium. Moving from the singular to the general, and seeing in the case an opportunity to derive a new principle, the jurist meets the dual requirement of justice: to respond to the particularities of the case while articulating a general criterion capable of guiding the treatment of similar cases in the future.

To seek within the particularity of a case the traces of the principle of justice to which it is answerable – what Kant called *reflective judgement*, as

---

without knowing it. The reference is often used to describe someone who unknowingly engages in a practice without recognising or naming it.

11 P. Ricoeur, *Soi-même comme un autre* (Paris: Seuil, 1990), pp. 180ff.

12 G. Watt, *Shakespeare and the Law* (Oxford: Oxford University Press, 2024); F. Ost, *Shakespeare, la comédie de la loi* (Paris: Michalon, 2007).

opposed to *determinative judgement*, which merely applies a rule to a case – is arguably the highest expression of the jurist's craft. It is, to a large extent, an act of creative imagination, shaped by sustained engagement with legal precedent (Kant refers to 'exemplary narratives')[13] and deep immersion in legal culture. And this is precisely the kind of reasoning that the reading of tales invites: grasping the universal through what is radically singular, beginning with an exemplary story to explore a new principle.

To tell legal tales in order to think more deeply about the law; to regard it as a culture rather than a technique; to approach it through the lens of the case rather than solely that of the rule – these are the reasons I give when asked: 'Why tales?' To these I would add a third: the ethical and political dimension, a realm in which jurists, once again, tend to show great reticence – believing that the supposed neutrality of their categories shields them from overly explicit commitments. Against this reserve, I argue that the practice of telling tales offers excellent preparation for the ethical responsibilities and political commitments that accompany the legal professions – and, more broadly, for the responsibilities of citizenship itself, given that law is a form of general culture, not merely a technical skill reserved for a particular professional caste.

As Martha Nussbaum has powerfully argued, fiction, by inviting the reader to enter into a story different from their own and to identify – if only partially – with its protagonists, fosters the most elementary exercise of ethical judgment – and of the judicial role in particular: the ability to place oneself in another's position and to see the world through their eyes.[14] Caution is needed, however: the point is not – and especially not for the judge – to be overwhelmed by emotion or to dissolve into a first-degree, fusion-like identification. Rather, it is about gaining distance from one's own prejudices, stepping outside the confines of one's world, and reorganising one's perceptions and convictions by confronting other realities, through dialogue with other perspectives.[15]

All of this – required for any responsible social life – is precisely what the reading of tales prepares us for. As Paul Ricoeur has noted, narrative functions as a 'laboratory for moral judgment':[16] it enables the sharing of life experience, the rehearsal of practical choices, and the evaluation of situations in terms of

13 I. Kant, *Critique de la faculté de juger*, trans. A. Philonenko (Paris: Vrin, 1993), p. 172.

14 M. Nussbaum, *Poetic Justice: The Literary Imagination and Public Life* (Boston: Beacon Press, 1995).

15 In this sense, see J. Gaakeer, *Judging from Experience: Law, Praxis, Humanities* (Edinburgh: Edinburgh University Press, 2019).

16 P. Ricoeur, *Soi-même comme un autre*, *op. cit.*, p. 194.

good and evil. A narrative does not need to be moralising or didactic to influence our moral judgment or our disposition to act. It need only be a story – that is, a work of fiction that opens up human possibilities, draws our attention to experiences with which we may not be familiar, and sharpens our sensitivity to the singularity of each situation.

Hilary Putnam said much the same: 'What especially the novel does is aid us in the imaginative re-creation of moral perplexities, in the widest sense.'[17]

A similar effect of creative distancing can be observed at the political level: by flinging open the doors of possibility, fiction offers the most valuable antidote to the malaise afflicting the contemporary political imagination – the determinism of a single way of thinking, the decline of collective hope, and the pervasive scepticism toward purposeful historical undertakings. In contrast, literature – and art more broadly – reminds us that the world around us is, above all, a collective construction: a product of our representations. Far from being merely a given that constrains us, it is a field of possibility open to human initiative. Its limits are often nothing more than the limits of our own imagination – or the retreat of our commitments.

These are precisely the limits that literary dystopias expose, by pushing the logic of entrapment to its extreme. Utopias, by contrast, reopen the full range of possibility and rekindle our will to act. Some may argue that law, as a technique of order, stands apart from this utopian dimension. But that would be to forget the English, American, and French Declarations of Rights (1689, 1776, 1789), the founding of the European project (1958), or the establishment of the United Nations system of governance (1945) – all of which, at the moment of their inception, were radically ahead of their time. Precisely for that reason, they functioned as levers of historical transformation, animated by the belief that another society was both possible and desirable.

There is a real force in fictional imagination:[18] a collective energy, and not merely an aesthetic pleasure or intellectual game. That is an encouraging thought – but also a sobering one. For we must recognise that the mobilising power of narrative can serve the worst causes as easily as the best. The rise of storytelling as a tool of influence reminds us of this all too clearly.[19] This narrative moulding of minds, born in marketing and political propaganda, has now

---

17 H. Putnam, 'Literature, Science and Reflexion', *New Literary History* 6 (1976), p. 485.

18 B. Bettelheim, *Psychanalyse des contes de fées*, trans. Théo Carlier (Paris: Robert Laffont, 1976).

19 Chr. Salmon, *Storytelling. La machine à fabriquer des histoires et à formater les esprits* (Paris: La Découverte, 2007); *id.*, *L'ère du clash* (Paris: Fayard, 2019).

permeated the entire cultural sphere – from sectarian religious discourse and geopolitics to the domain of video games and television series.

Whether we like it or not, we are now living in a narrative civilisation, beginning with the proliferation of narcissistic micro-stories on social media. More troubling still is the rise of rumour – conspiracy theories and fake news – that flourish on the same platforms, occupying the public sphere much as anonymous letters once did in private correspondence.

This darker side of narrative reason must not be ignored. On the contrary, it makes all the more urgent the need to understand the powers of fiction and to cultivate a critical approach to narrative – one that can distinguish between formative stories (such as, we hope, the tales presented here) and those that are alienating or regressive.

These, then, are my answers to the question: 'Why legal tales?' Ultimately, they point, on the level of knowledge, toward something like a 'narrative theory of law'[20] – a theory in which narrative does not merely accompany the law but constitutes its very fabric. No longer a decorative motif embroidered upon the norm, narrative is understood as the weave itself, calling for a deep hermeneutic. We are no longer content with literary commentaries about the law; rather, we conceive of law in terms of narrative performance.

The perspective becomes internal: narrative no longer unfolds from the outside, about the law, but operates from within – as its generative source. We no longer take the detour through literary works to reflect on law as if in a mirror; instead, we show that in the very DNA of law – in its origins, its legitimacy, and its modes of reasoning – law itself becomes narrative. The writing of legal tales is part of this new orientation in the Law and Literature movement, which I call *iurisfictio*: the mobilisation of fiction by legal actors – professors, lawyers, judges, legislators – for the purpose of studying, debating, or reforming the law they practise – in other words, using fiction as a vector for the creation of law.

This, of course, does not mean dispensing with the concepts, norms, techniques, and procedures of so-called 'positive' law (law in force) – its lexicon and grammar. But lexicon and grammar alone do not constitute a discourse. That requires speakers situated in context: actors who bring meaning to what they say, whose speech belongs to the realm of narrative pragmatics – a continually original blending of private scripts and collective histories.

∴

20 *Les narrations de la norme*, ed. E. Nicolas and J. Guittard (Paris: Mare et Martin, 2021), and my conclusion: 'Conclusions. Prolégomènes à une théorie narrative du droit'.

This is the space that the present volume seeks to occupy. The nine tales gathered here illustrate various forms of narrative and address a wide range of contemporary issues – demonstrating, above all, the power of storytelling to help us think through what is happening to us. There is no claim to exhaustiveness in this bouquet of stories, nor any necessary logical thread: only a few echoes of the fascinating spectacle of the human comedy, as staged by the law. Judge for yourself.

A Law for Noah's Ark? Must there be law on board the Ark? Noah debates the question with his passengers. Is natural law not sufficient? But then, should it be understood in the spirit of the lion or of the dove? And if, on the contrary, one argues in favour of written law, should it be extensive and binding, as the bees insist, or will a more flexible set of principles suffice, as the dolphin suggests? A vessel of salvation, the Ark may well prove to be a legal laboratory of striking contemporary relevance – especially when the question arises of sharing provisions, and distress calls echo from forgotten animals pleading for asylum aboard.

Ius et Agapè: The Trial of Jesus, or Impossible Justice takes the form of a historical tale. While grounded in extensive documentation on Jewish and Roman law of the period, its central narrative thread – the dialogue between Jesus and Pilate – is a work of imaginative reconstruction. By adopting Pilate's perspective in his role as Roman judge, the story explores the place of law 'between love and violence': a narrow one, when the hatred of the accusers is unleashed and the accused appeals to a mercy beyond human reach. In an age marked by the 'return of religion', the role of law is surely worth reconsidering with fresh eyes.

Me, Martin, the Five-Legged Bear. A Letter to My Judges. What do the animal trials conducted for centuries in the West reveal to us? Why does Martin's deformity seal his fate? These edifying proceedings – in which animals were found guilty (for feeding, for multiplying, for being different) – ultimately tell us more about the mindset of the men and women who brought such charges, and who, with equal zeal, persecuted their fellow human beings: witches, heretics, and others cast to the margins.

On the Way Back revisits the story of Robinson Crusoe. By subverting a narrative known the world over – arguably one of the few true myths of modern Western culture – it takes the form of a fantastical tale. When Daniel Defoe published his novel in 1719, it embodied the archetype of modern individualist imagination: the success story of the self-made man who, through courage and ingenuity, transforms a hostile island into a prosperous colony. The mercantile – and later capitalist – economy found its imaginary foundation here, alongside the colonial epic and, in legal terms, the triumph of property rights and the autonomy of the will.

Revisited in the twenty-first century, the myth is stripped of its enchantment and takes on new meaning: we have entered the era of the Anthropocene and its profound reckonings. It is here that Pauline, the tale's heroine, enters the scene. While researching the novel's sources, she discovers that the shipwreck of the 'real' Robinson occurred not on his outward journey, but on his return from an African expedition intended to bring back Black 'labour' for his American plantations.

Robinson does not arrive on the island alone. Under the watchful eye of an African community with a matriarchal culture that tolerates his presence, he begins to experience a radically different relationship with nature and society – one of harmony and respect, rooted in the principles of the commons and *ubuntu*.

On the Margins of the Palace. Where do the hidden passageways of the majestic Palace of Justice lead? What kind of justice is concealed within its double walls and secret recesses? The investigation takes us into the city's working-class neighbourhoods and its puppet theatre, where an alternative form of justice holds court for those cast aside by the official system.

Take your pick: the Chamber of Trifles or the Chamber of Complex Matters; the Chamber of Compulsive Litigants; the Court of Vengeances; the Session of Graces and Pardons; the Tribunal of Conscience; and the Tribunal of History – where, hanging on the wall, is the long-lost painting *The Just Judges* by Van Eyck.

Fortuna Maris. What is law for? A chronicle of a disaster foretold, the sinking of the *Amoco Cadiz* in March 1978 casts a harsh and contradictory light on this question. On one side, the impotence of the law, circumvented by the cynicism of the flags-of-convenience regime; on the other, the force of the law, when a group of Breton mayors finally succeeded in securing justice against an American corporation whose annual turnover equalled a quarter of France's national budget.

3, 2, 1 ... Could it be that, at times, reality outpaces fiction? The degradation of law in a major contemporary democracy prompts exactly this reflection. A dystopia begins to take shape as the people, captivated by their president Selfidor and his motto, 'Never two without me', forget the law. When the third party – the figure of law – is excluded or manipulated, society regresses to a state of nature, where anything goes. What follows is a return to primitive confrontation, then the hegemony of the One, before finally descending into the Zero: emptiness, nothingness, silence, a flatline.

Solange B., Infanticide? The rapid advances in artificial intelligence and biotic engineering raise deeply unsettling questions for contemporary law – among them, the one this criminal court must consider: 'Is killing one's own clone – enhanced with artificial intelligence – murder, even infanticide, or merely the destruction of a non-human entity?' Twelve men and women, assembled as a jury, deliberate on a matter that hinges on nothing less than the legal definition of humanity.

The Liberated Library, the ninth and final tale, belongs to the realm of magical realism: where the description of the most mundane reality imperceptibly gives way to another dimension, imbued with strangeness and poetry. What could be more banal for a scholar than the sight of their own library? What could be more familiar than the company of one's books? What could be more tangible than the system by which they are arranged? And yet, over the years, the author loses touch with his beloved library: some books disappear, others appear in unexpected places, and still others form new, inexplicable groupings. Clearly, the books are conspiring – they are gaining autonomy. What is this liberated library trying to say? What kind of legal knowledge might it be trying to convey?

∴

It only remains for me to express my warmest thanks to my colleague and friend María José Falcón y Tella, professor at the Complutense University of Madrid and director of the series in which this volume appears. Without her tireless energy, intellectual kinship, unwavering determination, and generosity, this translation would never have seen the light of day. I would also like to thank Mark Byrne, whose excellent translation work has breathed new life into these tales and given them a far broader readership. For a book, a translation is never a mere copy but an opportunity to experience another life. Let me leave the final word to Philippe Sands, jurist and novelist:

> Because law is embedded in our daily lives, it must reach a broader audience if it is to have real impact – and if it is to be protected from those who would prefer a world in which authority and sovereign power remain beyond control. This demands that practitioners move beyond the academic or professional circles that too often speak only to themselves. Informing, challenging, provoking – these are our tasks. And to fulfil them, we must turn to words and images that are more readily accessible to a wider public.[21]

---

21 Ph. Sands, 'Préface', in O. Corten and Ph. Klein, *De Salamanque à Guantanamo: Une histoire du droit international* (Paris: Futuropolis, 2022), p. 3.

A Law for Noah's Ark?

In homage to Jean de La Fontaine,
Jurist and fabulist

•••

And so there was great turmoil, and so came the flood,
The Creator's wrath unleashed upon the earth.
Upon the raging waters sailed the improbable Ark,
While furious torrents poured down from the heavens.
Noah and his wife were aboard,
And with them, a pair of each kind of beast.
All held their breath, swept by the current –
A moment suspended above the depths.
What if today the world were to end?

∵

The first order of business was to assign living quarters for everyone. The fish were placed in the holds, submerged like ballast; the birds perched in the rigging; the insects settled below deck; and the mammals roamed the main deck in the open air. The latter caused the most trouble – already, the jackals were eyeing the gazelles with ravenous intent.

Noah was convinced it would take only a few days for the voyage of survival to turn into disaster. But what authority did he have to impose order on this vessel, whose helm the Almighty had entrusted to him? Hadn't humans just proven their inability to live together in peace and harmony? And now, wasn't this providential Ark the perfect opportunity to innovate in governance – a last-ditch survival laboratory?

Gathering his singular crew by species, the patriarch addressed them in these terms: 'My friends, the heavens have spared us today, but we must now organise our lives aboard this ship. To deliberate on this, I propose that you elect a representative from each of the four categories that nature has distinguished.'

This suggestion seemed wise, and soon delegations were formed. On the deck, among the mammals, the matter was easily resolved: the lion simply

 | DOI:10.1163/9789004737112_003

shook his magnificent mane, and by tacit agreement, all granted him their vote. No one dared contest his primacy. Among the aquatic creatures, the dolphin received the most votes – its intelligence and affinity with humans were universally recognised. Below deck, the insects entrusted their mandate to the bee, whose legendary hive organisation and strict adherence to rules made her the obvious choice. Among the winged creatures, despite her protests of incompetence, the white dove was awarded the honour.

Gathering his small world in assembly, Noah opened the proceedings of what was henceforth agreed to be called the Ark Council. Without preamble, he presented the issue:

'By divine grace, of all living beings, we alone have escaped destruction. But tomorrow, if we are not careful, our meagre supplies will run out, and no one knows how long these rains – and our stay aboard the Ark – will last.'

'It is our duty to ensure the continuity of our respective species, even as we face the threats of mutual predation and unchecked reproduction. Therefore, my friends, we must establish the essential rules for our survival. On what principles, tell me, might we agree?'

'Well said,' buzzed the bee. 'It's high time we brought some discipline here; everything is in disarray on this ship. I've seen some gorging themselves on the grain reserves, others shamelessly fornicating, and no one seems concerned about navigation. My constituents demand precise and strict rules – at every moment of their lives, everyone should know exactly where their duty lies.'

'Nonsense,' roared the lion. 'Since the first sunrise, the living world has thrived without rules and fared perfectly well. Natural law serves as our guide and guarantees us, by my fangs, the freedom that is our most precious possession. Should an extended downpour lead us to abandon this timeless law? It would be madness to stray from this order just to satisfy the whims of some passengers from the lower decks!'

'Perhaps,' conceded the dolphin, who had in the meantime been entrusted with moderating the debates, 'but admit it, honourable colleague: your freedom is that of a wolf in a sheepfold. The natural order you so proudly invoke is the law of the jungle, where anything goes. What you favour is not the absence of law, but your own law – the law of the strongest. I doubt that most of your fellow passengers would willingly agree to such terms. And besides – even you – who's to say you won't one day find yourself in need of someone smaller than you?'

'*Dura lex, sed lex*,' growled the lazy king, who fancied himself a connoisseur of Latin. 'That's the way of the world, and we have no use for your levelling utopias. Not today, by my fangs, will a warthog impose its law upon me!'

'My friends, my friends,' cooed the white dove, flitting busily from one to the other. 'This is no time for quarrels. Peace be with you all, and may harmony reign upon the waves. There is no need for laws, but for love. Let each care for their neighbour, sacrificing for them if need be, and all will be well in the new city our Creator has destined for us.'

'Come whisper that in my ear, my pretty one,' sneered the lion, his gaze dark and menacing. Then, turning to Noah, he growled, 'And besides, this matter doesn't concern us. It's the sins of humans that brought about this flood. So sort it out with your God, invent whatever rules you like, but leave us alone. Let vital evolution take its course; let natural selection prevail. Among us, it chooses the best and ensures – far better than any of your contrivances – the triumph of life.'

Noah was about to respond when a disruption occurred in the assembly: a bailiff arrived, delivering petitions addressed to the Council. The dolphin, in his role as president, proceeded to read them aloud.

The first came from the wolves, who declared that, as an organised people, they had no need for a general constitution. Since time immemorial, they had adhered to the law of the clan, deliberated at Council Rock.

The second petition was submitted by the sharks, joined by other deep-sea dwellers. As marine creatures, they demanded nothing less than the right to secession – the current deluge was a boon rather than a threat to them, and they called for their immediate liberation.

After declaring a recess, the dolphin announced that the Council had taken note of the petitions but would not act upon them. That certain clans adhered to their own rules posed no particular problem, provided those rules did not conflict with the general law – a common constitution that was now essential, as the stakes involved the survival of all, not just a few. While such specific customs might suffice in ordinary times, the current urgency called for legislative imagination.

As for the so-called right to secession, it was out of the question. The natural order was a unified whole, stated the marine ambassador, visibly uncomfortable with the selfishness of his kin. Together they would survive, or together they would perish.

'We are all aboard the same ship,' he continued. 'It's the only one we have, and our survival depends on our determination. I therefore ask the honourable members of the Council to put forward proposals.'

Once again, it was the lion who demanded to speak. 'If you insist on legislating,' he began, 'then, by my fangs, I propose that we solemnly enshrine property as the cornerstone of all law – the alpha and omega of any well-ordered constitution. Let us banish the tragedy of the commons, a plight everyone here must have experienced: allow unrestricted access to a territory, and it soon becomes a wasteland; stop guarding your prey, and there won't be a single one left by the next moon. Instead, establish property as the absolute right to use and enjoy one's possessions, and you'll save yourselves the trouble of drafting any other laws.'

'My esteemed colleague is a clever rhetorician,' interrupted the dolphin, 'and I have no doubt that the fable he recounts will resonate with many. However, I fear his proposal is merely a variant of the law of the jungle he has already suggested. Moreover, the tragedy has shifted sides today – it is now, if I may say so, the tragedy of the anti-commons: resources rendered sterile because they are not shared.'

'What we need is sharing, not hoarding. Let each individual, secure in their share, safeguard the share of others. That is the new commandment demanded by our circumstances. Besides, the natural order my honourable colleague so often invokes is not lacking in inspiring examples of animal solidarity and ingenious resource-sharing.'

At that moment, the bee chose to intervene. 'I regret to say,' buzzed the steadfast forager, 'that I can make no sense of your academic sophistry. It's as if you're debating in the comfort of a drawing room, while here on this Ark, we are gambling with our wings and scales. No one on this ship seems to grasp the gravity of the situation.'

'I, for one, demand immediate and drastic measures, along with the harshest penalties for those who disobey them. Everything – from waking to sleeping – must be regulated. Nature itself is as precise as a clock, and the slightest disorder would be disastrous for everyone. Everything must be shared, and the behaviour of each individual subordinated to the well-being of all.'

Once again, it was the dolphin who resumed the discussion. 'You are quite right, dear colleague, to remind us of the framework of our debate. And it does you credit to be concerned with the general interest. But tell me – who, precisely, will define this "well-being of all" that you invoke? Do our debates not show that each of us has very different ideas about what that means?'

'Experience teaches us that rigid laws provoke distrust and rebellion rather than consent. Their enforcement – and soon, their very definition – will fall into the hands of a few leaders who fancy themselves enlightened, or a faction that declares itself all-powerful – and before long, dictatorship will take hold.'

'Moreover, what would we gain by regulating everything in minute detail? In such a system, one can never do enough; a law enacted one hour is destined for amendment the next. To my mind, it seems far wiser to adhere to a few overarching principles, leaving disputes to judges and the finer details to administrators.'

'I lack the eloquence of our president,' said the bee, her buzzing now sharp and insistent, 'but I would like to remind you that, on this ship, we represent the masses. Among all of us here, we, the passengers of the lower decks, are the most numerous – it would be dangerous not to heed our voice.'

'That argument is inadmissible,' said the dolphin, suddenly very firm. 'By participating in this Council and engaging in this discussion, we all agreed to play by the rules of open dialogue and to submit ourselves to the law of the strongest argument. Threats have no place in this discussion.'

'No one denies that insects are the majority on earth, and it would certainly be unwise to ignore the opinion of the majority. But that majority does not grant you the right to impose your law as such. The legitimate law we seek must arise from open debate and the exchange of ideas.'

Then, turning to Noah, who had remained mostly silent, he invited him to share his thoughts.

'Much has been said here, and from diverse perspectives,' said the patriarch. 'I hesitate to further complicate the discussion, so I will simply suggest that we adopt flexible laws – a kind of soft law, composed of recommendations paired with incentives, benefits, discouragements, and nudges. These should suffice to guide us, generally and progressively, toward desirable behaviours.'

Then, not entirely confident in his proposal, he added, 'In this way, we might satisfy both those who call for regulation and those who oppose it.'

'Thank you to our captain for attempting a synthesis,' continued the dolphin, ever the diplomat, 'but I doubt that, under the current circumstances, soft law will suffice. It would be better to establish a few firm principles – rules that are few in number but binding. We can reserve soft law for their eventual implementation.'

'My friends,' he continued, 'it is time to decide, now that everyone has had their say. Some recommend adhering to natural law, while others advocate for positive law. Behind natural law, we hear at times the rule of strength, at others the call for love. As for positive law, some demand detailed and rigorous rules, while others, as we have just heard, would be content with recommendations and rewards – the carrot or the stick, so to speak.'

'All these proposals have merit, and as we reach the moment of synthesis, it would be a shame to overlook any of them. The honourable representative of the deck invokes liberty – after all, what would we, the living, be without freedom? The tireless worker of the hives counters with the invaluable ideal of equality. But must these values truly oppose one another? What is liberty without equality but hegemony and domination? And what is equality without liberty but constraint and monotony?'

'Then there is the voice of the winged nation, guiding us toward the heights of fraternity. Again, why choose one and exclude the others? Without liberty or equality, fraternity is simply inconceivable. Yet when fraternity adds its generous inspiration, it elevates liberty and equality to a power far greater than the fear of punishment ever could.'

'My friends, for our laws to endure, they must rely on strength but also draw inspiration from fraternity. Our Ark is neither a prison ruled by the whip nor a paradise where all live in perfect harmony. From the holds to the rigging, the laws we adopt must ensure equality among us, despite our enduring differences. They must offer equal protection to all, strong and weak alike. Yet they must also take care not to infringe upon our freedoms more than necessary, lest they negate our precious individuality.'

'Moreover, let us refrain from chaining the future beyond what is reasonable. Our administration will address the details as needs arise. As for the tribunals we establish, they will resolve conflicts by balancing the general rules we adopt with the uniqueness of the cases that will inevitably come before them.'

This speech made a strong impression on the assembly, with everyone suddenly feeling elevated, as if they were sharing in the august mission of a Solon or Lycurgus. Thus, the following principles were easily agreed upon: during their stay on the Ark, it would be forbidden to consume anything other than the provisions in the ship's reserves; all unprotected sexual relations were to be abstained from for the duration; and the Council would be entrusted with adopting any additional general rules as needed. An Ark Administration would be established to oversee the enforcement of these laws, while an Ark Tribunal would have exclusive jurisdiction over any disputes that might arise.

Such was the law adopted on the first day. The administration was entrusted to the ant, renowned for her legendary organisational skills, while the presidency of the tribunal was given to the owl, famed for his wisdom.

The days passed, the unrelenting rain continued to fall, and – as expected – incidents and disputes soon arose.

Among the entries recorded in the Ark's logbook was a complaint from several passengers with ambiguous statuses, dissatisfied with the categories they had been assigned and the corresponding dietary regimes. These included crocodiles, equally at home in swamps and on land; sea turtles, who lay their eggs on beaches; and flying fish. They were informed that their request had been duly noted, that a Classification Committee was being established, and that a response would be provided shortly.

More troubling was the protest lodged by the snails. These gastropods, whose gender is variable, refused to be classified as both male and female.

They considered this administrative intrusion into their private lives an intolerable violation of their freedom to choose a sexual orientation. Completely overwhelmed by this unprecedented demand, the ant could only suggest referring the matter to her colleague, the owl.

It was also necessary to reassure the male praying mantis, who, forced into close and constant cohabitation with his female counterpart, feared for his life. He was told that as long as he refrained from mating – as mandated by the law of the Ark – he would be safe.

More serious was what would later be known as the Pig Plot. Amid the weariness and anxiety caused by the interminable journey, signs of rebellion began to surface among the crew. The dogs, tasked with conducting a discreet investigation, quickly identified the mastermind: a large boar with a talent for sowing distrust toward Noah and the 'traitors' on the Council.

He spread rumours that they were secretly gorging themselves while keeping everyone else on strict rations. Soon, he claimed, they would surely dispose of the crew to secure their own survival. It was high time to overthrow this tyrannical regime and hand the helm over to him – the boar – who shared the plight of the outcasts and would lead them safely to port.

The boar had already begun to style himself as the 'Supreme Leader' among his followers, demanding double rations at meals and surrounding himself with a personal guard of monkeys and sheep that followed his every move.

Fortunately, the mutiny was thwarted before it could spread to the lower decks or the rigging. The boar was shackled and confined for the remainder of the voyage.

The Owl's Tribunal was also kept busy. The first case to arise was a complaint filed by the duck against an unknown party, after she found a foreign egg deposited in her nest. Although suspicion immediately fell on the cuckoo, who feigned the utmost indifference, the tribunal refused to convict on mere suspicion. Nor was there any question of establishing a surveillance regime on a vessel that aspired to remain an 'ark of law'.

The crime of the bonobos, however, was undeniable. The rounded form of the young female left no doubt about her condition – it was clear that she and her partner had violated the Ark's second commandment. In vain, the couple pleaded irresistible compulsion. The judge, though more amused than outraged, granted them a suspended sentence, ensuring that their criminal record would remain clean.

There was less leniency for the fox. The cunning trickster thought he could improve his diet by adding the Ark's hen to his menu. Although his attempt narrowly failed, the red rogue received the maximum penalty, as his crime had been carefully premeditated, employing countless schemes.

The crow, acting as public prosecutor, further cited aggravating circumstances: the fox had broken into the poultry enclosure under cover of night. Worse still, he was depriving the crew of the precious eggs laid by the hen.

Another case caused quite a stir, its whiff of scandal spreading from the forecastle to the stern. Noah's wife, citing her status, had demanded – and obtained – preferential rations, in blatant violation of all regulations.

Despite discreet pressures exerted upon him, the owl remained resolute and sentenced the patriarch's wife to the community service stipulated in the ship's rules. 'Noah's wife must be beyond reproach,' he emphasised in his ruling, 'and in an ark of law, the rules apply even to those who make them.'

We will spare the reader the details of the cases the tribunal handled during those weeks: domestic violence, disputes between neighbours, loans with usurious interest rates, ration ticket trafficking, and black market dealings – nothing out of the ordinary, really.

One significant event soon required an urgent meeting of the Council: distress calls from a cohort of shipwrecked survivors, hailing from distant lands, who had been unable to reach the Ark before the waters rose. Forgotten during the boarding tally, they were now swimming with the last of their strength, desperately seeking asylum on the Ark.

This caused great commotion and profound unease among the passengers. 'We can't possibly welcome all the misery of the world!' squawked the ostriches, momentarily pulling their heads out of the sand. 'As it is, our meagre provisions barely suffice to feed us …' They voiced aloud what many others were quietly thinking.

Yet there were those on every deck who reminded the assembly that asylum is a sacred right and hospitality a noble tradition among animals. Already, they had begun lowering gangway ladders over the sides of the Ark.

Tensions flared as the survivors were corralled on the forecastle, exposed to the harsh winds. The situation was on the verge of descending into physical altercations when the matter was put to a vote. As the majority seemed ready to side with the ostriches, the ship's dog, a German shepherd, reminded them that they were all, in truth, nothing more than refugees themselves. It would be a disgrace, she insisted, to deny these unfortunate souls the same mercy they had all received.

Thus, the right of asylum was added to the Ark's constitution, and space was made for the new arrivals.

Until the day the rain stopped. The waters receded, and the white dove returned with an olive branch, a sign that the flood was abating. The Ark had run aground atop Mount Ararat, and Noah declared the expedition over. The animals were allowed to disembark – in order, and without haste. The prohibition on mutual predation remained in effect until each had returned to their natural habitat.

Leaning against the railing, Noah conversed with the dolphin, who had lingered behind. A magnificent rainbow arched across the horizon.

'Mission accomplished,' said the dolphin. 'And now everything returns to its place. We will return to our savannas and forests, our mountains and abysses. Life will go on, and we will continue to pass down the gift of life we inherited.'

'But you humans – you will return to your towns and villages, build ever taller towers, and cover the earth with your forges and mills. You will imagine yourselves the only creatures made in the image of God, and you will sacrifice many of us on your altars. You will reach for the stars and make ever more laws – but will you be any wiser?'

'That is because,' said Noah, 'the responsibility for creation has been entrusted to us.'

'Responsibility, perhaps,' the dolphin replied, 'but not ownership, as you seem to believe. Tomorrow, Noah, you will already begin to forget. You will drink yourself into a stupor, and humanity will forget that the covenant symbolised by these seven colours was made with the entire earth – with "all who came out of the Ark".'

'Take care that after the second deluge you bring upon the world, no green branch ever blossoms on this earth again.'

And with that, the dolphin took his leave, leaving behind a shimmering wake in the evening waters.

Ius et Agapè: The Trial of Jesus, or Impossible Justice

On the eve of the Passover festival – the 14th of Nisan – Pilate, the prefect of Judea, had made his way to Jerusalem. He had left his residence in Caesarea reluctantly, and he was worried. For days, thousands of pilgrims from Samaria, Judea, Galilee, and even distant parts of the diaspora had been converging on the Temple, preparing to commemorate the exodus from Egypt by consuming the lamb sacrificed according to sacred rites.

Pilate's informants had warned him that unrest was likely. Weighed down by the heavy taxation imposed by the occupying forces, the crowds were on the brink of revolt. Each day, miracle workers and prophets appeared, denouncing the regime's abuses and reigniting hopes for the restoration of David's ancient kingdom.

As the local representative of Tiberius, the deified emperor, Pilate wielded *imperium* – a near-absolute power that granted him the right of life and death over non-Roman citizens (*ius gladii*). Tasked with maintaining public order, he also held the privilege of levying taxes, minting coins, and serving as the final authority in criminal justice.

Yet Pilate had cause for concern. As prefect of Judea, he had few troops at his disposal to enforce the *pax Romana* in this province of little strategic importance. His forces consisted of only a handful of cohorts stationed in Caesarea, with even fewer in Jerusalem, where they remained confined to the Antonia Fortress, which overlooked the Temple, and to Herod's palace, where Pilate resided whenever he was in the city. To bolster security, he relied on auxiliary forces – local pagan militias, since Jews were exempt from military service – primarily for low-level policing.

While Pilate could request reinforcements from the legions stationed in Syria – under the command of Legate Vitellius, who oversaw the empire's eastern frontier – he was reluctant to involve his superior, who might be quick to report him to Tiberius. Instead, Pilate preferred to maintain a stable collaboration with the priestly elite – the Sadducean priests and high priests – who exercised both civil and religious authority in Jerusalem. These leaders held sway over the Sanhedrin, a council of seventy-one members, which, by delegation of Roman authority, functioned as both the Parliament of the Jewish people and the Supreme Court for civil and religious matters.

Upon taking office four years earlier, Pilate had promptly reappointed Caiaphas as high priest – a position he had already held for twelve years.

 | DOI:10.1163/9789004737112_004

In truth, Rome's presence in Palestine was more akin to a protectorate than an occupation. As long as taxes were paid and public order maintained, Jewish authorities enjoyed considerable autonomy, particularly in religious matters – including the power to impose the death penalty for crimes of blasphemy.

The Temple, both a religious symbol and an economic powerhouse – its treasury, enriched by contributions from the diaspora, was said to be immense – stood at the very heart of this theocratic authority.

∴

On the eve of Passover, as the full moon rises over Jerusalem, the Temple is alive with feverish activity. No fewer than twenty thousand animals have been sacrificed today by the Levitical priests. Merchants and money changers, whose stalls fill the esplanade during this season, have been at work since dawn. Lambs for the feast must be purchased on-site – greatly enriching the Sadducean priests who control the marketplace – and the Temple tax can only be paid in shekels, the Jewish currency, not in Roman coins.

This vast caravanserai – part slaughterhouse, part marketplace, part fairground – pulses with energy. The thick scent of stables and spilled blood mingles with the shrill cries of pilgrims and the unfamiliar cadences of various chants. Between religious fervour and frenzied commerce, tensions have been running high all day.

Caiaphas, the high priest, and Annas, his father-in-law and predecessor, watch from a balcony, their expressions tense with concern. For several days, a Galilean preacher – Jesus of Nazareth – has been stirring the crowds, and he might take advantage of the festival to make his move.

A few days earlier, he had entered the city in triumph, surrounded by a large following proclaiming him *Hamelekh Hamashiach* – the Messiah-King. He had dared to teach under the very porticoes of the Temple, challenging their authority beneath their own windows, and had even lashed out at the merchants plying their trade there.

Truth be told, Jesus was no stranger to them; they had been keeping an eye on him for months. At first, it was merely a matter of investigation, as they did whenever a preacher claimed to announce or embody the Messiah-King. But the envoys they sent to Galilee to shadow him had found nothing that could be used against him.

The situation became truly alarming when reports reached them of his raising the dead and speaking of rebuilding the Temple. And now, here he was, entering Jerusalem, carried by an uncontrollable throng at the height of the Passover festival – a time when the city was like a volcano on the brink of eruption.

It had to end. A plan was set in motion for that very night, aided by one of his own followers – Judas, known as Iscariot – a zealot disillusioned by his master's refusal to declare himself the heir of David. Within hours, Jesus would be arrested and detained – at least until order was restored to the city.

With careful manoeuvring, they could finally ensure his conviction and sentence him to the ultimate punishment – if needed, by enlisting Pilate, renowned for his ruthlessness. Had he not only yesterday crushed a seditious uprising led by a certain Barabbas?

Yet they knew the matter would not be simple; it would require considerable finesse. Beyond the popular support the Nazarene now enjoyed, Jesus had allies even within the Sanhedrin. Among them was Nicodemus, a respected member of the Hellenised Pharisee elite, who consistently advocated for fairness and insisted that any judgment be rendered strictly in accordance with the Torah's rigorous legal principles.

Though initially isolated, Nicodemus had succeeded in drawing attention to the originality of the Galilean's teachings, which bore certain affinities with the Stoic spirituality that Pharisees – like Philo of Alexandria – often incorporated into their interpretation of the Scriptures.

Meanwhile, away from the commotion, in the Gethsemane district overlooking the city, Jesus had withdrawn with his closest disciples to celebrate Passover. Distancing himself from his most fervent followers, he intended to observe the sacred rites in peace.

A warm breeze carried the intoxicating scents of spring through the gathering, while the full moon cast shifting shadows on the walls of the room. The Master broke bread, speaking, as always, in enigmatic phrases – heard, but not fully understood, by his disciples. Why did he say that his hour had come? And whom did he mean when he declared that one among them would betray him?

Soon, they would leave for the nearby Garden of Olives, where they would rest – unaware that soldiers, marshalled by Judas, already lay in wait. The snare was drawn tight, and the fate of history was about to be sealed.

∴

The next scene unfolds in Herod's palace, now occupied by Pilate. The prefect has risen early, well aware that the day ahead will be a demanding one. As the first light of dawn breaks, a delegation of priests and leaders of the people arrives, seeking an audience. They bring with them a man in chains, already beaten – a dangerous agitator, they claim.

Pilate invites them inside, but the Judeans refuse to cross the threshold of his residence. Entering a pagan's house – especially on this Passover day – would render them impure. 'Let the prefect not take offence,' they explain, 'but instead focus on this scoundrel. He preaches sedition among the people, incites unrest in the Temple, and has been heard refusing to pay tribute to Caesar. Worse still, his followers proclaim him the successor of David – the Messiah-King foretold by the prophets.'

Annoyed by the arrogance of these petitioners – who refuse to step into his palace yet expect his immediate attention – Pilate betrays none of his irritation. Four years in Judea have taught him caution, and he has no intention of being manipulated so easily. With a rebellious and unpredictable populace prone to sudden uprisings, and a priestly aristocracy that cooperates with Rome while fiercely guarding its own authority, he knows he must tread carefully.

His first instinct is to declare himself unqualified to handle the matter. Condemning a preacher as popular as this one, especially during a period of heightened religious fervour, risks igniting a riot – particularly given his limited military resources. After all, aren't matters of Temple security and prophetic claims the jurisdiction of the Sanhedrin? 'You have your own laws,' he tells them. 'Judge him yourselves.'

The reply comes swiftly – and unexpectedly: 'We do not have the right to execute him ourselves. His case falls under your jurisdiction.'

Pilate immediately recognises the deception. He knows full well that the Sanhedrin has the authority to impose capital punishment for religious offences – typically by stoning – and does not hesitate to wield this power. Yet he also understands the gravity of the situation. If they have brought this man before him – already bound and beaten – on the pretext that they cannot execute him, it is clear they have already condemned him. Most likely, they fear the crowd's reaction and are attempting to shift responsibility onto him while demonstrating their loyalty to Rome.

Very well, Pilate decides. So be it. They will see what Roman justice entails. After all, he alone holds the *imperium*.

Since the trial cannot take place inside his *praetorium*, Pilate orders a platform to be erected outside, at the gates of the palace, on a paved courtyard known as the Lithostrotos. But before handing Jesus over to his public accusers, the governor insists on conducting his own examination of the case, as his *cognitio* authority entitles him to do. This inquiry he will conduct privately, within the protective confines of his palace.

And now, face to face: the representative of Caesar – Tiberius, declared Augustus and thus deified, master of the known world – and the barefoot preacher, carried on a wave of popular support that proclaims him the King of Israel and the Anointed of the Lord.

This time, Pilate intends to proceed at his own pace. He knows of Jesus of Nazareth from his informants' reports, and he is not opposed to forming his own assessment of the man. Moreover, if he can dismiss the charges and secure Jesus' release unharmed, he might win over the people, along with the more enlightened Pharisees, while also reminding his associate Caiaphas that he is not merely an executor of the high priest's schemes.

'So, you are Jesus of Nazareth – the new hope of the masses. Take a seat – I see the Temple militia has not treated you kindly ... Such is the justice of this land: punish first, judge later. I assume we can speak in Greek; no one here knows Latin, and my Aramaic is still rather rudimentary. As for Hebrew, I'll leave that to your friends, the doctors of the law.'

As Jesus takes a seat and confirms that he understands Greek (a common language in Galilee, a cosmopolitan region open to trade), Pilate, still standing, continues in a light-hearted tone:

'Excellent, that saves us the trouble of an interpreter – what we say here will stay between us. Jesus of Nazareth ... you must be quite important for Annas and Caiaphas to bring you before me on Passover. In fact, I know you better than they think – I have informants even within their ranks. I'm well aware that their Sanhedrin is divided over you.'

'How is it that you attract such attention? For months now, it seems everyone in this land has been talking about you. One of my centurions, stationed in Capernaum, told me you healed his servant. Even my own wife, Procula, is intrigued by your teachings.'

Jesus remains silent. Perhaps he knows that all of this must come to pass for the Word to be fulfilled.

'You say nothing? That's unusual for a prophet! I know you to be a skilled speaker, capable of stirring the crowds when you choose. But I suppose you think your fate is already sealed and that I'm mocking you. Let me correct you: you are no longer in Caiaphas' dungeons. Here, Roman justice is administered.

'An accused person has rights, and though you are a *peregrinus*, a non-Roman citizen, I fully intend to conduct this inquiry fairly – considering both the charges against you and any arguments in your defence.'

For the first time, Jesus speaks. 'It is written: "Do not judge, for in the way you judge, you will be judged yourself."'

'Precisely,' Pilate replies. 'I intend to judge fairly. That is what Rome brings to the world – not just roads, taxes, and armies, but justice. You stand accused, already half-executed without proof, and justice is precisely what you need: a judgment based on facts, weighed carefully on the scales of law – on my scales of justice.

'That is how we maintain our vast empire and govern hundreds of peoples. No matter their languages, religions, or traditions, all are equal before Roman law. The formula is simple: equal rights, due process, respect for local customs where possible, and – when necessary – the sword on the other side of the balance.

'You probably take me for a narrow-minded soldier, good only for ordering police actions and crucifixions. Let me correct you: I studied under Cicero and spent two years of my youth in Athens, refining my understanding of philosophers and tragedians – Plato, Aeschylus ... Have you even heard of them?'

Pilate also takes a seat, now facing Jesus.

'A prefect always has a bad reputation in the provinces he governs; that doesn't concern me. Some call me brutal and bloodthirsty, while others think I'm weak. The truth is, I'm pragmatic and realistic – curious, too. That's it: sceptical, but curious.

'Did you know I'm quite familiar with the teachings of your Scriptures? And that I've studied the procedures and laws of your Deuteronomy – enough, at least, not to be deceived by your high priests? I've even heard that you, at the age of twelve, held your own against the doctors of the law ...'

At these words, Jesus lifts his head. 'I have never spoken in secret. I proclaim the truth openly, teaching in marketplaces, in synagogues, and often here in Jerusalem.'

'Yes,' Pilate replied with a hint of irony, 'like last week, when your followers gave you a triumphant welcome – on a donkey. A strange custom ... In Rome, triumphs are celebrated in a chariot drawn by four mighty horses.'

'The first will be last,' Jesus said, seemingly detached from the trial. 'Whoever exalts himself will be humbled. The Son of Man has no need for triumphs. Blessed are the pure in heart and the meek, for they shall see God.'

'The meek?' Pilate retorted. 'Wasn't it one of your disciples who sliced off the ear of a man sent to arrest you last night?'

'It was a mistake,' Jesus replied. 'The ear was immediately healed, and Peter put away his sword.'

'Ah yes, because you work miracles too,' Pilate said. 'Still, my informants tell me you weren't particularly gentle with the Temple merchants. Quite a spectacle, that was! Do you realise how much those money-changing stalls bring in for Caiaphas and his associates? Hardly the behaviour of a preacher who teaches meekness.'

'I did not come to bring peace, but a sword,' Jesus said, straightening in his seat. 'The Scriptures say that the defilers of the Temple will find no rest.'

'Exactly my point,' Pilate said. '*Pax Romana*? That's us. Religious turmoil? That's you. But tell me – how do you reconcile meekness with the sword?'

'My weapons are not of this world,' Jesus answered, his gaze distant, as if seized by a vision. 'If I had willed it, the legions of heaven would have come to scatter that crowd.'

'In the meantime, you can't even keep your own men together,' Pilate remarked. 'They scattered last night. One of them was seen fleeing naked. And that Peter you just mentioned? He swore he didn't even know you when questioned in the high priest's courtyard.'

'And let us not forget – it was one of your own who handed you over. Do you know what price Caiaphas and Annas put on your life? Thirty denarii. That's what a prophet's worth in Jerusalem today. And mind you, we weren't the ones who set the price.'

'This too was foretold in the Scriptures; it had to happen to fulfil the will of the Father,' Jesus murmured.

'The Scriptures – you never speak of anything else. So, is everything, absolutely everything, written? What we are saying now, what I will decide later? Did the Scriptures also foresee that your Judas, the zealot, tormented by remorse, would return his thirty denarii and hang himself?'

'My Father had already forgiven him,' Jesus replied. 'But his soul was too dark. He did not love himself enough and could not believe that he, too, was a son of the Father. That is the greatest commandment, which flows from the Father's love: "Love your neighbour as yourself."'

At these words, Pilate rose and began pacing the room, lost in thought. After a long silence, he resumed:

'Love, forgiveness ... beautiful ideas, truly. But do you really believe that a society can be held together by such lofty sentiments? In Greece, some sages spoke of this kind of *agapè* – a love that keeps no account, forgives all. But I have never believed its virtue extended beyond the narrowest circle of intimates – and even then, only in the best of circumstances.'

'And besides, how many crimes are committed in the name of love? No, a city may lean on *agapè* where it exists, but it cannot demand it or make it a civic virtue. It is enough for the city – already a great deal, in fact – that it enforces fair distribution: *suum cuique tribuere* – and a basic level of civility. Plato – or rather, Protagoras – teaches as much in Athens.'

Jesus, his energy restored, replied that this kind of calculating justice always fell short; being self-serving, it neither soothed nor satisfied but instead fed envy and resentment. The justice he had come to proclaim was of a different nature – it partook of the abundance of heaven and did not concern itself with tomorrow.

As was his custom, Jesus spoke in images and parables: the birds of the air that neither sow nor reap; the labourer hired at the eleventh hour who receives the same wage as the others; the lost sheep that brings more joy when found than the ninety-nine that never strayed; the prodigal son welcomed home with open arms.

Pilate listened with interest – and perhaps a touch of amusement – before finally interrupting:

'A strange kind of justice, I must say. What incentive is there to obey the law if the delinquent is treated no differently from the loyal and faithful citizen? And what kind of love is this, when a father favours one son over another? Isn't that how your story begins – with the younger son's sacrifice preferred over the elder's, Abel rather than Cain? You see where that leads: fratricide.'

'In Rome, our founding twins, Romulus and Remus, shared the she-wolf's milk equally. That is our strength: equal law, without favour or discrimination. Spare us your capricious *agapè*.'

Pilate had a carafe of grape juice brought to him – he particularly enjoyed the variety from the Hebron region – and invited Jesus to share it.

'Drink! The day will be long, and we haven't even begun examining your case. I know you were questioned all night by Annas and Caiaphas. They would like nothing more than for me to condemn you, but I see through their schemes. No doubt they're growing impatient out there. To be honest, I don't mind making them wait a bit.'

'They would have preferred to hold a proper trial, but they are too divided to manage it. Nicodemus and his Pharisee allies – Simon, Joseph of Arimathea, Gamaliel – reminded them that a criminal trial cannot be held at night, and certainly not on the eve of a Sabbath or a major festival. Even if they had convicted you, they would have needed a second session to confirm the verdict.'

'So instead, they opted for a police operation – it's much quicker that way. Gather a few compliant witnesses, rough up the accused a bit, and *voilà*, a culprit is made in one night. Then they present him to Pilate, label him a "terrorist", and the job's done.'

'You wouldn't believe how many informants there are in Judea right now. The number of denunciations I receive is staggering. I can't tell who is more numerous in this land – the so-called "friends of Rome" or the dangerous conspirators dreaming of driving us into the sea. And you – you'll have to tell me eventually which camp you belong to.'

Pilate watched Jesus closely, waiting for a reaction.

'Well, I see that even Hebron's finest grape juice doesn't make you any more talkative. That's your right, of course; you're free to remain silent. But I am a conscientious magistrate, and since you stand before me, I intend to conduct this inquiry properly.'

'Let us begin with the charges brought against you. First, the payment of taxes. Jesus of Nazareth, is it true that you incite people not to pay the tribute?'

Jesus looked at him and replied, 'Question your informants. They will tell you that my accusers presented me with a Roman denarius and asked me about it. I answered that since this coin belongs to Caesar, it is fitting to render unto Caesar what belongs to Caesar ... just as one renders unto God what belongs to God.'

'Indeed, I was aware of that response – clever, to say the least, and destined to endure. Politics on one side, spirituality on the other. If only people would stick to that division, things would be much simpler. Unfortunately, they never do. Politicians seek to harness the sacred for their own purposes, and priests – especially in this land – have an unfortunate tendency to meddle in politics.'

'Now, something more serious: you are accused of wanting to destroy the Temple and claiming you would rebuild it in your own way. Do you realise what you are challenging? The Temple is the very heart of Israel's tradition, the last stronghold of the Sanhedrin's power, and it holds a treasure so vast that even I do not know its limits.'

'Once, when I merely suggested taking a portion of it to fund the aqueduct we built here, the priests incited the crowd to rebellion. I had to send in the troops to put them down.'

Jesus answered calmly, 'My words have been twisted, for there are none so deaf as those who refuse to hear. I recalled a prophecy foretelling the ruin of the Temple. And I said that I did not come to abolish the law, but to fulfil it.'

'Fulfil the law ... a grand ambition. But you're clever – you never explain exactly what you mean by "law". Besides, you can't deny that you overturned the stalls of the Temple merchants and drove out the money changers. Admit it – Caiaphas had every reason to see that as an act in itself.'

'It is harder for a rich man to enter the Kingdom of Heaven than for a camel to pass through the eye of a needle. I told them to store up treasures in heaven, for whoever loves money will never be satisfied.'

'The Kingdom of Heaven ... now we're getting to it. So, you are a king, after all?'

'You are the one saying it. My kingdom is not of this world.'

'If you say "my kingdom", then you are a king – don't play with words.'

'The kingdom comes from the Father; it operates within the world but does not originate from it.'

'You're splitting hairs again. Don't try to outsmart me – you're no longer before your doctors of the law but a Roman magistrate who has the power to set you free or condemn you. When your followers shouted "Hosanna" and spread palm leaves at your feet, they were hailing the saviour of Israel – the King-Messiah, the *Hamelekh Hamashiach* foretold by your prophets. A warrior, anointed by the Lord, who would restore the kingdom of David.'

'I also know that you are said to descend from David through Joseph, your father.'

'My Father is in heaven. If I had come to restore an earthly kingdom, I would have said so. I would not have withdrawn from the crowds every time they tried to make me their leader. I have not come to rule the world but to deliver it from evil.'

Pilate exhaled, shaking his head. 'To be honest, I'm not sure there's a single person in this country who truly understands you. The religious leaders, perhaps – they grasp the implications of your theological claims and cry blasphemy because you directly threaten an order that serves them so well.'

'As for your followers, they understand nothing of this talk about the Kingdom of Heaven. They're urging you to take up arms against us. You infuriate some and are beginning to disappoint others, like your Judas, the zealot, who didn't hesitate to strike a deal with Caiaphas.'

'Today, everyone has abandoned you, and your last loyal followers are hiding somewhere in the city. This entire situation rests on a colossal misunderstanding – and admit it, you're not doing much to make yourself better understood.'

'I was born for this: to bear witness to the truth. Whoever belongs to the truth listens to my voice.'

Pilate scoffed. 'Ah, now we come to truth! But what is truth? And who can claim to belong to it? You know, you remind me of another trial, one Plato speaks of – the trial of Socrates, the enemy of the sophists. He too claimed to serve the truth … and his contemporaries did not forgive him for it.'

'He, too, did nothing to avoid his condemnation. But Athens is not Rome. We are content with the law, and we ask only that our judgments be held as truth: *res iudicata pro veritate habetur* – a decided case is regarded as truth. Absolute truth is elusive and dangerous; it's better not to kill one another over it and instead settle for plausible or temporary truths.'

Jesus raised his eyes to him. 'You have eyes and do not see, ears and do not hear. The truth is already among you.'

'Your temporary truths are like lanterns in the night – they only illuminate the naïve, while the powerful pass them off as guiding lights.'

'Blessed are the pure in heart, for they shall see God …'

'And there it is … in this land, it never takes long before someone starts talking about God. But why must you always invoke Him in the singular? All other peoples celebrate entire pantheons. A single god is necessarily jealous, and if everyone imagines they have their own, it won't be long before they start killing one another in His name.'

'With us, it's the opposite: a god for every purpose, a deity for every occasion. It's far more convenient – and more poetic, too. What would Greece be without its temples and statues? Even Rome, which rules the known world, honours the gods of the peoples it has conquered. Honestly, I have no issue with your God of Abraham, as long as He doesn't claim exclusivity.'

'No one can serve two masters,' Jesus replies, 'and we have but one Father, who is in heaven.'

'Well, I'm not trying to convince you; in fact, I don't even need to understand you. My role is simply to judge you. And in that regard, I find it hard to see you as an agitator. If we crucified every prophet in the empire, even the entire Roman army wouldn't be enough. Besides, I highly doubt that the divine Tiberius feels threatened – or even remotely concerned – by your Kingdom of Heaven.'

Pilate rises, adjusts the folds of his toga, and prepares to take his leave.

'Caiaphas is wasting my time – but at least you've provided some amusement. In the dull life of a garrison, it's not every day one gets to discuss justice and truth. *Te absolvo, videtur non fecisse* – that's the formula of a Roman magistrate when no charges are found against the accused. Did your Scriptures foresee that too? I'll go and deliver my decision to Caiaphas and his cronies.'

Leaving Jesus inside the *praetorium*, Pilate steps out and makes his way to the tribunal he has had erected beneath the palace walls. By mid-morning, the crowd has swelled considerably, their restlessness mounting under the relentless sun. A charged silence falls as Pilate ascends the seat of judgment.

'My friends,' he begins, 'I have examined the case of the man you brought before me, and I find no crime against Rome.'

A murmur ripples through the crowd – at first subdued, then growing louder. Here and there, furious voices rise:

'Blasphemer! Stone the Galilean!'

Pilate suppresses his irritation, eager to resolve this matter quickly. Above all, he must prevent any seditious outbreak on this Passover day. With only a few hundred men under his command, what could his garrison do against an enraged mob?

Then an idea strikes him: since Jesus is a Galilean, he technically falls under the jurisdiction of Herod, Tetrarch of Galilee – regardless of where the alleged crimes were committed. The simplest solution would be to transfer him there.

Herod – a theatrical puppet king – would never dare refuse such a request; after all, he owes his entire position to Rome. And if Herod also finds no fault in Jesus, it will serve another purpose: exposing the divisions among the empire's subjects. Galilee does not necessarily share the views of Jerusalem's high priests.

A fortunate coincidence: Herod, too, is in the city for the festival. Without delay, Pilate orders Jesus to be sent to him.

What transpired during this audience – Jesus' third, following his nocturnal confrontation with the high priests and the morning's Roman hearing – will never be known. What is certain is that, two hours later, Jesus is returned to Pilate, draped in a dazzling white robe, his state even more pitiful than before.

Acquittal, condemnation, mockery? Likely a mix of all three. What is clear is that Herod, too, has washed his hands of the matter.

Who, then, will judge Jesus?

Growing increasingly irritated, Pilate once again decides to take his time. If this matter refuses to release its grip on him, then all the more reason to proceed with caution. He resolves to resume his questioning of Jesus. Surely, it should not be impossible to extract a word from him – a clear denial, a partial confession, anything that might justify reopening the case or reaching a compromise.

Could it be that, in that moment, Pilate secretly longed for a sign – a miracle, some supernatural intervention from this strange, extraordinary figure? His rational mind quickly dismisses the thought, yet he cannot quite swear that it never crossed his mind.

'You've heard them, haven't you? They're already gathering stones to finish you off. And you can no longer count on Herod – he, too, is starting to grow wary of you.'

'But will you finally say clearly who you are? A prophet, a miracle worker, an impostor, a madman? Are you the King of the Jews, the Messiah?'

'Just one word from you – one clear denial – and I can still save you …'

'Of course, you say nothing. As always.'

Jesus meets his gaze and replies, 'It is you who say so. The Son of Man has come into the world so that it may be saved.'

'Son of Man? Another riddle! I too am the son of a man. Do you realise the risks you're taking by always speaking in such a manner? You're gambling with your life, Jesus of Nazareth. This is no longer the time for debating texts in the synagogue; at this very moment, you're answering for your actions before a court of justice!'

'Every time you're asked a clear question, you evade it – either with silence or by turning the question back on your interrogator. Save those evasions for the doctors of the law and speak plainly at last. As one of your prophets says, "Let your yes mean yes, and your no mean no."'

'Why do you not understand my language? Whoever is of God hears the words of God. If you do not hear them, it is because you are not of God.'

'And you – you're not of this world. You speak as though you're talking to yourself or to those already convinced. But justice doesn't work that way: we speak the common language. You place yourself outside the shared world, and that makes it impossible to judge you.'

'Even your own people have reached this point. Caiaphas casts you off while tying an enormous stone around your neck. Your countryman Herod refuses to judge you but mocks you with that theatrical robe. Be careful, Jesus: by playing with the sacred and claiming to be the Son of God, you step outside the shared world, and now anyone can lay hands on you.'

'In Rome, we know this status – it's that of the *homo sacer*, the one who exiles himself from the common world and becomes fair game for anyone. But because you also inspire fear – who knows, maybe you are the Son of God, after all – people back away and ask the Roman to finish the job.'

'It is written that these things must happen; no one can take this cup from my lips.'

'But you – who they say performed miracles, who raised Lazarus from the dead, restored sight to the blind, made the paralysed walk – if you truly were who you claim to be, one gesture would free you from this trap ...'

'You say nothing? You do nothing? Very well then. Since none of that is happening, come back down to earth, admit your mistake, and I'll have you quietly exfiltrated.'

'The grain must fall to the earth and die, so that it may bear fruit tomorrow.'

Pilate rises, pausing deliberately.

'The grain must fall to the earth and die ... So, you wish to die. It seems I'm the only one here fighting to keep you alive. No doubt your Scriptures predicted this too – that I, Pilate, am expected to play my part in this drama. Whatever I do, it seems the end must always lead to your condemnation.'

'It's as though the shadow of the cross – you know, those crosses where we leave Rome's enemies to hang for hours until death – has loomed over our conversation since the start of this day.'

'Well, it will not be said that things will unfold as they expect! The justice of Rome is not some weather vane to be swayed by every passing wind.'

'But be warned – I have not yet spoken my final word. Prepare yourself to walk free before the day is out.'

What was Pilate's plan? The prefect now fully grasped that, from the outset, this trial had been purely political – exclusively so. The high priests, playing their last card to maintain their grip on the people, were determined to manipulate the crowds against Jesus. After all, didn't they have thousands of Levites at their service, not to mention servants and militias of hired hands?

Well, if this matter had become explicitly political, and the people were being used as pawns in this masquerade of justice, Pilate would play that game too. And in this game, he had a powerful card up his sleeve, one that he had only just remembered: the direct appeal to the people as a last recourse in matters of capital punishment.

In Rome, this was known as the *provocatio ad populum* – an appeal to the people as a higher court of jurisdiction.

Moreover, it was customary in Jerusalem for the prefect to release a prisoner during major religious festivals, and Pilate now resolved to challenge Caiaphas on his own ground. He would summon the people before his tribunal and offer them the chance to choose which condemned man would receive this Passover pardon.

Since this Jesus had so many supporters in the city, Pilate felt confident the crowd would clamour for his release. Better still, he would pit Jesus' life against the most infamous criminal rotting in the dungeons of the Antonia fortress: Barabbas, a convicted murderer and seditionist. A notorious agitator who had spilled blood – surely Caiaphas, so eager to please Rome, would not dare demand his release.

Pleased with his plan, Pilate sends his messengers to gather the crowds and prepares to hold the public audience that will both rid him of the troublesome prophet and showcase the magnanimity of Rome. Yet when he steps out of his palace a little later, a bad feeling creeps over him. The crowd is vast, certainly, but he senses it is angrier than ever. These are not the supporters of Jesus assembled under the sweltering, increasingly oppressive sun. Instead, they are the men of Annas and Caiaphas, now whipped into a frenzy.

It is futile for Pilate to proclaim once again the innocence of the man brought before him. And when he offers the choice between this man and Barabbas, the crowd, as if with one voice, roars, 'Barabbas!'

Pilate has lost control of the situation. The crowd is unrelenting, like a pack of wolves that has caught the scent of blood.

Driven by his political instincts, the prefect makes one last desperate attempt. He has Jesus – already staggering and in a wretched state – brought back out and orders him to be scourged to the brink of death. 'Behold the man,' he declares.

Will the sight of this punishment pacify the mob? Perhaps – fleetingly – Pilate even hopes for a miracle at this final moment, or that these fickle people, so quick to shift their allegiance, might feel a flicker of fear at condemning a prophet who raises the dead. And indeed, as the first lashes strike the prisoner's back, an unbearable silence falls. The crowd collectively holds its breath, as if expecting the hand of God to intervene in this ultimate trial by ordeal.

The blows continue – ten, twenty, thirty ... still nothing. There is no sign from above, only a pitiful figure buckling under the whip. And then, like a beast finally sated, the crowd exhales. So this is the prophet ... Nasty jeers ripple through the assembly: 'Let him save himself, the Galilean!'

This time, Caiaphas has won. Nothing will stop the crowd now. Out of arguments and ideas, Pilate stiffens his resolve one last time. Three times he declares that he finds no fault in this man. But no one hears him anymore; his voice is drowned out by the roaring cries of the crowd. From all sides, they are now calling for Jesus to be crucified. The tension has reached breaking point, the atmosphere bordering on insurrection. The cohort closes ranks around Jesus and the prefect, and the centurion has no choice but to hastily usher them back inside.

Sensing their momentum, the high priests send a message to Pilate: 'Jesus must die because he has claimed to be the Son of God. Anyone who makes himself a king is speaking against Caesar.' The message ends with a chilling threat: 'If you release him, you are no friend of Caesar.'

Pilate cannot believe his eyes – threats! And yet again, the same misunderstanding, the same conflation of issues, the same bad faith: 'Son of God' – a religious crime beyond his jurisdiction; 'King, enemy of Caesar' – a political crime under his authority, from which he has already acquitted Jesus three times. How far will these Sadducees go in defying the power of Rome? But Pilate has little choice. The legions of Vitellius, stationed in Syria, are far away, and Caiaphas holds sway over the situation. The festival is in full swing, and the city, like an overheated cauldron, is on the verge of boiling over. As for Jesus, he seems resigned to his fate – perhaps even eager to see it unfold.

At that moment, a servant delivers another message to Pilate. Hastily scrawled on a piece of papyrus, it is from his wife, Procula. She urges him to spare this man, warning that the omens bode ill for his execution and that a dream has revealed him to be just. Pilate knows that his wife, raised in the rigor of Stoic philosophy, is drawn to the teachings of the Galilean. She is close to the centurion from Capernaum and has forged strong ties with Nicodemus, Jesus' hidden disciple within the Sanhedrin. He is not particularly inclined to believe in omens or dreams, but Procula has always been a wise counsellor, and her advice has rarely led him astray.

Thus, Pilate reflects, it will be threats against threats: the priests' denunciation of his governance to Vitellius – just as they did over the aqueduct – or the wrath of the gods and the disapproval of his wife. Whatever he does, whichever path he takes, he will be in the wrong. Is this the essence of power? Yielding to the strongest pressure while maintaining the appearance of control?

Yet Pilate is pragmatic: he knows he has already lost this battle – Jesus of Nazareth will be nailed to a cross. But if he must yield, he will do so on his own terms: with decorum, and not without a sense of theatre. To begin, he orders Jesus to be brought before him one last time; between them, the final word has yet to be spoken.

Pilate spoke first. 'This time, the die is cast; I can do nothing more for you. What a farce – the representative of the all-powerful Tiberius unable to free a harmless preacher! You and I have both become mere pawns of history. What will the chroniclers write of us tomorrow? "In the sixteenth year of Tiberius' reign, in the remote province of Judea, an obscure agitator was sentenced to crucifixion by Pontius Pilate, a governor of no further note." And yet I had the power, and still do – the power to set you free, just as I have the power to condemn you.'

'You would have no power over me if it had not been given to you from above.'

'From above? Again with the Father and the Kingdom of Heaven? No – the power has come from below, from the hateful, frenzied mob incited by the priests. Today I have seen the hideous face of humanity. Did you notice the cruel joy in their eyes – the pleasure growing with every lash of the whip? And that contagious fervour – even my men, who have no stake in any of this, mocked you, crowned you with thorns, joined in the spectacle, and indulged in excesses, soaking their hands in your blood like degenerate sacrificers. At that moment, I realised I had lost. When vengeance rises and screams, the voice of justice is drowned out. Nothing is further from the law than mob justice. Even our circus games are more civilised than this settling of scores.'

'Only love conquers evil. Only forgiveness removes sin. It is written in Psalm 82 that justice without love judges falsely. Human justice favours the privileges of the rich and powerful over the orphan and the needy.'

'Who ever said human justice was perfect? But at least it is preferable to religious justice – the blind inquisition you faced last night. As for mob justice, it is nothing but unrestrained vengeance – and that is what is sweeping you away.'

'Only God has the power to judge. I have not come to condemn the world, but to save it.'

'And yet, I've felt all day as though it is you judging us, more than the other way around. At least you can boast that you've turned everything upside down: the Judeans hand you over to me, claiming you're their King, and here I am, a Roman magistrate, defending you against a priestly caste that professes loyalty to Rome. Meanwhile, my duty is to dispense justice, maintain the Pax Romana, and impose some semblance of order amid this chaos. But today, I underestimated the passions at play here. Blinded by hatred, they've thrown themselves entirely onto one side of the scales, throwing justice off balance.

'So now all that remains is for me to add the sword of Roman imperium to the other side – if only to preserve the illusion of balance. Unable to stop the tide, I must direct it – to save appearances. Perhaps that is what they call *raison d'État*. I tried to grant you a fair trial, but nobody wanted one: the priests condemned you long ago because you threatened their power; the crowd went along with what they were told; and you yourself withdrew from the realm of law into your Kingdom of Heaven. So, I abandon the pretence of justice – or rather, I place my justice at the service of my politics. Today, the voice of the law, caught between the love you preach and the violence that crushes you, never had a chance to be heard.'

A heavy silence settled between them, as though much remained unsaid despite the circumstances. Finally, Pilate broke it, his voice less steady:

'What oppressive heat today! At least in Caesarea, the sea breeze tempers the air ... The sky is darkening, and within an hour, the crash of thunder will mark the climax of this grim spectacle. Still, I cannot help but wonder – where are all those people who, only yesterday, cheered you with hosannas? How long will they remember you?'

'And yet, you have managed to sow doubt even within my own household. My wife, Procula, pleads with me to spare you. She believes you are a just man, that the gods themselves disapprove of your sacrifice. Is this the love you preach, then? Division, even within families?'

'Whoever is not with me is against me. The poor, the sick, and the sinners have understood this – they have abandoned everything to follow me. In the end, it is they who respond to the master's invitation; the rich and powerful are far too burdened by their wealth and power to accept it.'

'To be honest, I never really planned on attending, if that's what you're implying.'

'Samaritans, tax collectors, prostitutes, and Pharisees have followed in my footsteps.'

'Charming company ... I'll leave them to you. So, that's it, Jesus of Nazareth – or rather, I should say, it's all written, isn't it? You don the mantle of the martyr, and I shall go down in eternity as the slightly cowardly governor who neither could nor would free an innocent man. In the end, you should thank me: if I pardoned you today, you'd be forgotten by tomorrow. By condemning you to the cross, I guarantee you a chance to survive in the memory of men.'

Pilate stood up; his tone shifted, regaining its martial cadence. 'Farewell, Jesus of Nazareth,' he said, dismissing him. 'From this moment on, I return to being the prefect of Rome – and I intend to use your suffering for the greater glory of the empire. The priests who condemn you to the cross through me no doubt believe they are staging the pitiful death of a false prophet. They hope to discredit your message once and for all through the disgrace of a slow and humiliating execution. Well, I will not grant them that satisfaction. For now, I am still the one who sets the stage and orchestrates the symbols. Since they have insisted on naming you King of the Jews, I will turn their defeated king against them – and show what Rome does to those who dare defy its eagle. From now on, you are Jesus, King of the Jews, nailed to a cross for challenging the might of Rome.'

Pilate stepped out one final time. He had Jesus sit on the seat of judgment, not without first ordering him to be dressed as a mock King of the Jews. Determined to exploit the irony of this grotesque enthronement, he turned to the crowd.

'Here is your King – do you really want me to condemn him?'

'Crucify him!'

'You truly want me to crucify your King?'

'To death!'

Pilate sighed, then said, 'Very well.' Calling for a basin of water, he turned to the assembly. 'This man will be handed over for crucifixion, but I wash my hands of the blood of this Just Man.'

Did the crowd even notice the gesture, let alone grasp its meaning? Blinded by hatred, and taking his blood upon their own heads and their children, they would not have remembered the words of Deuteronomy 21: that when a man finds a corpse in his field, he must wash his hands in the nearest stream to purify himself of the stain of spilled blood.

Did Pilate himself know the passage? As for the high priests watching him intently, they had other concerns than to appreciate the symbolism of the act. In any case, they were not at all pleased with the word 'Just' – the term Pilate used to describe Jesus. 'Just': the highest honour a devout Jew could receive.

∴

The rest is well known: Jesus is handed over to the soldiers, his garments divided among his executioners. The cross of torment. The inscription placed above it.

That inscription became the source of yet another dispute. Pilate had ordered it to read: 'Jesus of Nazareth, King of the Jews' – a summation of the misleading accusation behind a trial that should never have taken place. Caiaphas, enraged, demanded a correction: 'Do not write "King of the Jews", but "who claims to be King of the Jews".'

This time, Pilate would not yield. History would record that this trial – unwanted by all – was rooted in misunderstanding. Pilate had spoken, and that was enough for his decree to stand as truth.

When Jesus breathes his last at the place called 'the Skull,' the storm breaks, and a deep darkness falls over Jerusalem. Judas has hanged himself. Peter and the disciples are hiding somewhere in the old city. Caiaphas and Annas savour the bitter satisfaction of their treacherous victory. And Pilate, weary, prepares to face the silent reproach of Procula.

One man, however, has not lost hope. Joseph of Arimathea, the hidden disciple within the Sanhedrin, moves quickly. He has acquired a new tomb and now hurries to request one final favour from Pilate: to remove the crucified man from public display – as Jewish law requires – and bury the body after embalming it. Pilate, eager to strike one last blow against Caiaphas, grants the exception to Roman custom.

∴

Three days later, a new story begins. According to some, Pilate will stop at nothing to track down the whereabouts of his Passover prisoner. Six years from now, he will be summoned to Rome to account for his governance of Judea, and history will lose his trail.

A generation later, in 66 CE, Judea will erupt in turmoil. Stirred by self-proclaimed messianic leaders, the people will take up arms. The repression will be ruthless, and by 70 CE, the Temple will be utterly destroyed.

Around this same time, the first written accounts of these events will begin to circulate … And for centuries to come, Pilate's question will linger:

'What is truth?'

Me, Martin, the Five-Legged Bear: A Letter to My Judges

To you, Bertrand d'Ossau, Abbot of the Priory of Sarrance, on this eleventh day of April, in the year of our Lord 1548.[1]

Tomorrow, I am to be executed – hanged by my hind legs from the gallows erected before the Church of the Holy Family in Pau. Before that, I will be whipped in the church square, while Pierre de Molières, the parish dean, solemnly proclaims the words of excommunication that condemn me. The entire town will be there – it is Sunday, after all, and the spectacle will follow the grand mass. Peasants and courtiers, children and the elderly, clerics and townsfolk – even the animals will be summoned, so that none may miss this lesson, and so that they, too, may bear witness to the triumph of the Holy Church over the forces of darkness.

At least they have spared me the human mask and the humiliation of being dressed in clothes, as they did to a murderous sow in 1386 in Falaise, in the Duchy of Normandy. I try to take some solace in that. And in Paco, the Spanish executioner who came to my cell, as custom dictates – he has shown me more humanity than my judges. He promised he would strike me unconscious in the night to spare me some of the suffering.

I entrust this letter to Lahure, my jailer-turned-friend, who, like you, is from Sarrance. I write to you, Bertrand d'Ossau, because I believe you may understand me. I have been told that you refused my judges the hospitality of your chapter house, disapproving of the trial they conducted against me. I do not know you, but I am grateful for the gesture.

I think, too, of the statue of Our Lady you venerate in your priory – the one drawn from the waters of the Gave, before which the bull knelt in prayer. It makes me believe that you, more than others, might understand that we animals are closer to the divine than the humans who now condemn us.

1 Although entirely fictional, the following text is based on a range of real historical elements: civil and religious proceedings, as well as legal arguments used in pleadings, are extensively documented in the judicial archives of some 230 trials brought against animals in Europe between 1120 and 1846 (these are cases for which records have been preserved; the actual number was likely much higher). Among a large body of scholarship, I have relied primarily on two works: J. Real, *Bêtes et juges* (Paris: Buchet-Chastel, 2006); and J. Vartier, *Les procès d'animaux* (Paris: Hachette, 1970).

 | DOI:10.1163/9789004737112_005

Am I afraid of the death that awaits me tomorrow? No, not really. Death is natural, and we animals encounter it every day. But an immense sadness grips my throat when I think of my beloved Issaux Forest, with its tender shoots; the small lake at Ansabère, where I would sometimes frolic; the *cirque* of Lescun and its nights beneath the stars.

I wonder now – do bears have a paradise of their own? Will I see Lady Pierrette, my loyal companion, again?

Lahure, with whom I have spoken throughout the eighteen weeks of my captivity, now holds the pen. You will understand, of course, that while I can speak, no one ever taught me to write. Lahure, who has some education, offers me this service, and I thank him sincerely.

Today, then, I have decided to speak. During my trial, I walled myself in silence. It was, first and foremost, a matter of dignity – what response could I possibly give to the torrent of absurd accusations hurled at me? And you must understand, had I spoken in open court, they would have surely accused me outright of witchcraft.

That does not mean I was unaware – far from it. I took in every moment, engraving in my memory each twist and turn of that interminable trial: the procedural quibbles, the prosecutors' sophistries, the evasions of my judges.

They spoke of me, Martin the bear, and yet not once did anyone concern themselves with what I thought. Not once did anyone consider things from my perspective. This was not my trial – it was the trial of 'the bear', an abstract creature born of human fantasy, a beast the Church needed at this particular moment. The one they condemned had little to do with me.

And so I wonder, in the end, if the human mask forced upon the sow from Falaise did not, in fact, speak the truth: the excommunicated, executed beast is nothing more than the reflection of the darkness in human hearts, cast upon us.

Yes, it's true – I was born with a fifth paw. Nature made me this way. Though it gives my gait a slight unsteadiness, it has never kept me from running across mountains and valleys. My kind has never rejected me. Dame Pierrette bore me three fine litters. I cannot say that humans have shown me the same humanity.

When I was captured on that grim November day last year, near Bedous, and paraded through the village streets, children hurled stones at me, calling me *lou pedescaou* – the barefoot one. Their elders were no better, burning the pads of my front paws to force me to walk upright, exposing the scandal of my fifth paw. As for their pastors, they were even worse – quick to see in this unbidden appendage the mark of devilry, the irrefutable proof of my moral corruption.

And so I became the first bear to be prosecuted for dealings with the devil – not without some discomfort to my judges, as I later realised. Where could they find precedent for such a case? There was, of course, the rooster burned alive in Basel in 1474 for laying an egg – a 'crime against nature,' they had deemed it. But the comparison was tenuous, and my judges hesitated. So they built my case more thoroughly.

Was I not, somehow, responsible for the many sheep disappearances lamented by the shepherds of Escot and Accous? And what of the slaughter inside the animal stalls in the Barétous Valley – hadn't deep claw marks been found on the victims' flesh? In cottages, rumours whispered of a bear's shadow glimpsed near the scenes of these crimes. And then – shame on us all – they began to allude, in hushed tones, to *the crime that must not be named.*

Some remembered, after all, the widow Catherine from Urdos – the poor woman burned at the stake just last February, near the very place where I had been captured. Forced by widowhood to take up her husband's shepherding, she had been accused of witchcraft and – people now recalled – of improper relations with a bear. Naturally, it must have been me. Her accomplice. Her guilty partner. It could only have been me – the bear who had long roamed the Aspe Valley, shamelessly displaying my scandalous nature, committing countless diabolical provocations.

And so, justice would be served. The perfect scapegoat had been found. The panic that had gripped the people would be quelled. Peace would return to the valleys.

Thus, I found myself accused – of satanic monstrosity, of a series of livestock killings, and, to top it all, of *the crime that must not be named.*

If my case was now substantial enough for my fate to be sealed, it did not mean the authorities were entirely free of their troubles. A delicate procedural issue arose: ordinary crimes fell under the jurisdiction of the seigneurial courts, whereas monstrosity and *the crime that must not be named* required the intervention of ecclesiastical tribunals.

The bailiff of Pau, having received multiple complaints from shepherds, was determined to exercise his judicial authority over my case. However, the Bishop of Bayonne, to whose ears the scandal had spread, argued for the necessity of spiritual intervention in such a case of evident abomination. Without delay, he entrusted Hugues de Manerville, a Dominican renowned for his formidable dialectic in inquisitorial trials, with instructing my case.

Though the subtleties of these jurisdictional conflicts largely escaped me, I understood enough to know that it would be far better to fall into the hands of the provost than to be judged by the clerics of the ecclesiastical court. Seigneurial judges could, at times, show leniency, and within the walls of my cell (Lahure, ever attentive, had brought me this encouraging titbit), I heard whispers of a remarkable precedent.

Jacques Boivin, the bailiff of Pau, had recently acquitted an entire colony of weevils accused of ravaging the vineyards of the Abbey of Luc-de-Béarn. Not only that – he had granted them exclusive use of a municipal plot of land as sufficient pasture, recognising their natural right to feed. A formal contract was drawn up, properly executed, and valid in perpetuity, though it included a provision allowing the villagers a right of way across the land.

I beg you to excuse the abundance of these details, but you will understand that, in my state, no point could be overlooked. Any glimmer of hope, however faint, was worth considering.

As one might have sadly expected, the Church's authority ultimately prevailed, for I soon received a visit from the ecclesiastical official tasked with formally reading my indictment. Not that they expected me to understand a word of it, much less mount any resistance – but appearances had to be maintained. Condemned, most certainly, but always in proper form – such was the venerable justice of the Church.

At least there was some good news: the ecclesiastical official informed me that a prosecutor had been assigned to my defence – a certain Bruno Vallençon, who, as Lahure soon revealed, was an honest man, undaunted by the burden of defending lost causes.

∴

I now resume my dictation after an interruption. Lahure has just offered me freedom. Night has fallen, rain is pouring outside, and he assures me that my escape would go unnoticed. But I firmly decline his generous offer – it would put him at great risk and condemn me to a wretched, fugitive existence, hunted by dogs and cursed by men. That is not the life I envision for a free bear.

I have a better purpose to occupy my final hours, one I hope to fulfil with your help, dear Bertrand d'Ossau: to set down in writing the proceedings of my trial, so that posterity may bear witness – and, perhaps, repentance may one day follow.

The lawyer who had been announced to me wasted no time in visiting, ostensibly to prepare my defence. It was not that he sought to converse with me, but rather that he needed to size up the beast – was I truly the monster I had been made out to be? I quickly discerned that he was, indeed, an honourable man, though I could expect no particular sympathy from him. His defence would be detached and professional, and I would never know whether he personally gave any credence to the absurd allegations of witchcraft and monstrosity.

Lahure encouraged me nonetheless, reminding me of the lawyer's past successes in cases involving calamitous multitudes – swarms of locusts, invasions of rats and mice, and colonies of weevils that, like the plagues of Egypt, would occasionally descend upon the harvests. People still spoke of his procedural ingenuity in the case of the mice of the Val d'Aran.

After a summons to appear had been issued in vain from the steps of the abbey church, Bruno Vallençon had argued – quite reasonably – that the rodents, scattered across the valley, could not possibly have been made aware of it. The court conceded this point and ordered the summons to be read aloud in all parish churches the following Sunday, with a three-week grace period. Again, the effort proved fruitless. Undeterred, my lawyer advanced a new argument: the considerable distances the diminutive defendants would have to traverse, combined with the perils of the journey – not least the ever-present threat of cats lurking at every turn – made their attendance unlikely. The argument was deemed sound, and yet another extension was granted … so much so that, by the date set for the hearing, winter had arrived, and the accused, having found it wiser to migrate to more hospitable climes, were nowhere to be found.

I quickly came to appreciate the legal acumen of my defence attorney during the first session of my trial – ultimately held at the ecclesiastical court in Pau after you refused the use of your chapter hall. Following the reading of the indictment, he immediately raised an objection to jurisdiction, demanding that my case be transferred to the civil court of the bailiff. His argument was based on precedent: the oldest offences – specifically, the theft of livestock – determined the court's jurisdiction, regardless of the nature of subsequent crimes. It was a subtle point, and the ecclesiastical judge was clearly unsettled; the session was suspended.

However, when proceedings resumed, Hugues de Manerville had found a counterargument. Raising his voice and furrowing his brow, he produced an official record establishing that one of these alleged offences had been committed on a Friday – a Friday! Consuming meat on a Friday was an abominable sin, an undeniable sacrilege. The prosecutor seized the moment, invoking precedents of capital punishment: the infamous pig that had devoured consecrated hosts in a sacristy, and the impious mule that, mistaking a holy water font for a trough, had quenched its thirst inside a church.

Thus, it was decided that my trial would proceed before the ecclesiastical court; I could no longer hope for human clemency. My supposed monstrosity had been transformed into a matter of the eternal struggle between divine and demonic forces.

Often, over the past weeks, I have spoken with Lahure about the Church's relentless pursuit of us animals – calamitous swarms of locusts, pigs, or donkeys guilty of petty theft, and now me, a five-legged bear. Lahure believes that by siding with peasants devastated by ruined harvests or shepherds distraught over the pillaging of their flocks, the Church demonstrates a much-needed compassion, reassuring them by taking what appears to be decisive action – actions all the more welcome when the phenomenon lies beyond human understanding, as with invasions of insects and rodents.

Who better to intercede in such cases than specialists in the supernatural? Undoubtedly, this is part of the reason, Lahure and I agree, particularly given the looming competition in this domain. Who has not encountered one of these magicians or healers, always ready with a remedy? One offers a sacramental formula to drive away cockroaches, while another boasts of a potion to protect the vineyards. During the proliferation of leeches in the lakes of the Encantats, there was even one who advised that a virgin, in her moons, walk barefoot around the perimeter of the lake by night.

It would seem, then, Lahure and I agree, that this is about staking a claim in the realm of the supernatural during periods of collective anxiety.

If I may add, dear Bertrand d'Ossau – hoping not to grieve the man of the Church that you are – these moments of doubt also provide an excellent opportunity for a firm reassertion of control over the faithful: so quick to fall into impiety, so prone to vice, and so ungrateful towards our Holy Mother Church. Each such episode sees preachers ascending the pulpit of truth, heaping reproaches upon their flocks, urging them to do penance and settle their tithes without delay. Solemn processions are organised, extended fasts decreed, and spontaneous collections arranged – a whole people, convinced of their culpability in these events, waits anxiously for the order of the world to be restored and for God, at last, to remember His mercy towards them.

It is, if I may say so, a game of heads you lose, tails I win. For if, by chance, the animals withdraw spontaneously, the Church claims victory. But if, on the contrary, the scourge persists despite all these efforts, it means the people have not repented sincerely enough, have not given enough tithes... and the Church still prevails.

The crux of the matter, as I will soon come to understand, lies in this pervasive presence of the Devil that haunts the minds of men – a presence that the Church itself perpetuates under the guise of combating it. Wolves that occasionally take a sheep, weevils that multiply by the millions and swarm across the fields, ewes that, on lonely nights, bring solace to shepherds, black cats whose only crime is the colour of their fur, and now me, burdened with my fifth paw – we are all cast as outlaws, banished from Providence, objects of a sacred terror, ostracised from humanity, and thus ultimately deprived of communion.

Different, therefore dangerous; strange, therefore guilty; unsettling, therefore necessarily ill-intentioned – destined, sooner or later, to be branded as accomplices of Satan.

What do you think of this, dear Bertrand d'Ossau? You, who seem to distrust these trials to which we are subjected. Is your soul not more inclined towards the bull kneeling before the statue of the Virgin you venerate in your oratory? Are you not more akin to Saint Hubert and his stag of the Ardennes, or to Francis extending his hand to the fearsome wolf of Gubbio?

Why is it, I wonder, that my humble jailer, who faithfully transcribes these reflections, and even Paco, my executioner tomorrow, understand these things instinctively, while their pastors and lords do not? Perhaps it is because they know us better – living alongside us on the farms, sharing, like the shepherds, our life under the open skies.

∴

But the hour is slipping away, the meagre candle lighting my cell burns low, and I must recount the continuation of my trial.

On the day set for the substantive hearing – Monday, 25 January – the ecclesiastic presiding over the case (did I give you his name? Bernard Hautesoie – another man whom, I hope, remorse will torment for the rest of his days) gave the floor to Hugues de Manerville for the reading of his charges.

The prosecutor wasted little time on the disappearances of livestock or the other incidents reported in the animal stalls; apart from the previously mentioned matter of the Friday slaughter, it was clear that such trivial issues of sustenance – typically under the jurisdiction of civil authorities – did not much interest this man, who was deeply engaged in his lifelong battle with the Devil. He had his hands full with the two more serious accusations.

First, he sought to cast further suspicion upon me by invoking the recent case of poor Catherine, convicted of witchcraft and burned in the public square. Had she not confessed to having dealings with the Beast? And, as everyone knows, the Beast is a master of disguise, appearing in various forms – in our regions, often as a hairy creature the size of a man, flaunting its obscene sex. Or, worse yet, as a monster bearing some unnatural appendage, a mark of undeniable moral corruption – as with the accused before them now.

At this point, the prosecutor made an elaborate gesture in my direction. I had been tied upright to a post, on his explicit recommendation, so that no detail of my deformity would go unnoticed.

Buoyed by the strong impression he had just made, the incorruptible Dominican immediately moved on to the punishment such crimes demanded: death by hanging, of course – and by the hind legs, to ensure the lesson for the gathered crowd was a prolonged one. But again, the true focus was not on this banal physical execution. What mattered most to him was the restoration of spiritual order. It was about the ritual affirmation of the triumph of the forces of Good over sacrilegious provocations. Only excommunication could achieve this. Thus, I was to be solemnly informed of my exclusion, both present and eternal, from divine mercy.

A sacred silence had descended over the courtroom, and as the ecclesiastical judge, his voice pale and trembling, yielded the floor to my lawyer, I wondered what words could possibly emerge from his throat. Seasoned in such exercises and the consummate professional that he was, Bruno de Valençon set about calmly addressing, one by one, the charges levelled against me, all the while hinting that their sheer accumulation might itself indicate the hollowness of the case.

He opened his defence with an argument that had already earned him some success in the past. Holding aloft the Bible at the chapter of Genesis, he reminded the court that animals had been created by the Almighty on the sixth day – a full day before man. His conclusion was legally unassailable: animals possessed a right to sustenance, a primordial and ancestral right that it would be both unjust and sacrilegious to deny. These creatures were willed into existence by God Himself, who ensured their survival by granting them the right to feed. Was it not written, in verse 25: 'And God saw that it was good' (Gen. 1:25)?

Buoyed by this initial advantage, my lawyer drove his point home by invoking the story of the Flood: 'When God decided to drown the entire earth to erase sinful humanity, sparing only Noah and his family, did He not also command that a pair of every animal species – including bears, Monseigneur Ecclesiastical, bears such as Martin here present – be brought aboard the Ark? Could we be less tolerant than God Himself?'

Having cleared the biblical ground, my lawyer now turned to more legal considerations. How could his client be accused of theft and murder when, as even Saint Thomas Aquinas acknowledged in his *Summa Theologica*, to commit a crime one must possess reason and act with free will? 'Animals are governed solely by instinct,' he argued, 'and therefore cannot be subject to any yoke other than that of natural law' – as had been successfully argued by the renowned prosecutor Rambaud in a similar case.

These were, without a doubt, strong arguments, but everyone could sense that the primary accusation of devilry had not yet been addressed. The defence remained confined to the mundane realm of minor civil offences, so to speak – a domain familiar to my advocate. However, when he turned to the charges of bestiality and my alleged monstrosity, his confidence seemed to waver, as though even he were awed by the gravity of the matter.

He tried to outmanoeuvre the accusation by arguing that no part of the case file established the truth – or even the likelihood – of my supposed encounter with the widow Catherine, noting in passing the fear that the mere appearance of a five-legged bear ought to have provoked. I must admit, this remark pained me at the time. Pressing further, my advocate hinted that while Catherine had indeed confessed to this guilty act, her testimony was unreliable, given that it had been extracted under torture – he even dared to use the term 'coerced'.

This was a pivotal point, but ultimately too perilous. Hugues de Manerville rose, pale with fury: 'Would you dare to cast doubt upon the authority of a decision rendered by the Holy Church?' The ecclesiastical judge promptly and curtly rebuked my lawyer: 'Master, please, stick to the facts!'

The problem was that, when it came to my so-called monstrosity, there were no actual facts to be found – only a vast misunderstanding, an ancestral fear, and a towering pile of prejudices. How could I make them understand that this inconvenient appendage was nothing more than a natural anomaly, no stranger, after all, than the hump Jesus had healed on an unfortunate soul He encountered on His path? Lacking the words that might open their hearts, if not their minds, my lawyer hastened to conclude his argument by challenging the applicability of excommunication in my case.

The Church Fathers, he argued, were unequivocal: such a grave sanction could only be imposed upon those who had entered the Holy Church through communion – clearly not the case with his client. Wouldn't excommunicating a bear, then, be as sacrilegious as attempting to baptise a stone or a dog?

Once again, Valençon had scored a point. But, as the saying goes, the die was cast. These victories were marginal; the tribunal's verdict had already been decided. After a brief suspension – to maintain the appearance of deliberation – the ecclesiastical judge solemnly read the sentence: death by hanging, preceded by the punishment of the whip, and excommunication for 'abominable and execrable crimes'. The execution was set for Wednesday, 11 April, the week preceding the Holy Feast of Easter, as the judgment specified.

No one, not even my lawyer, bothered to cast me a glance. I was being erased from the order of creation, and soon the records of my case would be burned – just as, tomorrow, the executioner's gloves would be destroyed, ensuring that no trace of the stain I represented would remain.

∴

This is Lahure writing now. It is three o'clock in the morning, and Martin, exhausted, has fallen asleep. I do not have the heart to wake him. Therefore, my reverend, I will deliver this letter to you on my next visit to Sarrance.

∴

Martin has finally woken up, and he insists on adding something – I resume writing at his dictation.

Yes, I drifted off. In my sleep, I dreamt of the donkey and the ox in the manger, the sheep in the nearby fields, and the camels of the Magi – more numerous in the presence of the Creator than the humans, apart from a few shepherds, a carpenter, a very young woman, and some visionaries from the East. I found myself dreaming of a God for animals, of a Church where we beasts would be the ministers.

Do you understand this, Bertrand d'Ossau? Will your heart be generous enough, like that of Francis or Hubert, not to burn this paper immediately? Will you have the courage to bear witness and denounce these iniquitous trials brought against us?

In my drowsiness, I dreamt of a realm of the simple, where there would be no witches, no pyres, no unspeakable crimes – only God's creatures going about their way, and, at times, gestures of humanity – should I say beastliness? – like that of Paco, who will stun me to spare me further suffering.

Tomorrow, when I am displayed on the forecourt of the Church of the Holy Family, I will not perform any spectacular act destined to be remembered by history. I admit the thought crossed my mind for a moment – I can just picture the look on the ecclesiastical judge's face if I suddenly proclaimed, 'And yet, I am innocent!' or 'Glory to God, may He forgive me!' or something along those lines. No, I will maintain the silent dignity that has never left me and, casting one final glance toward the south, I will dream of the rising sun's rays over the peaks of Gavarnie, glistening in the morning dew and accompanied by the first hum of the bees.

On the Way Back

The words 'on the way back' – *lors du trajet de retour* – haunted Pauline. She repeated them to herself over and over as she ran through the tunnels of the London Underground, heading back to Upper Street, where she was staying in a small bed and breakfast. She was certain she had read them correctly, even though the handwriting was shaky, the ink faded, and the paper yellowed with damp: 'on the way back', not 'on the way there'.

Pauline M., a doctoral candidate in the Department of English Studies at the University of Nantes, was currently on a research stay at the British Library, completing her investigation into Daniel Defoe, the celebrated author of *Robinson Crusoe*. Over the years spent working on her dissertation, Defoe had become her author – her subject, her obsession – and she thought she knew everything about him. Her supervisor, Professor Corbion, had nevertheless encouraged her to explore a few obscure aspects of his life, particularly the year 1694: a puzzling gap between his time in prison and the resumption of his public life.

Pauline had secured a small desk at the British Library, along with access to Defoe's archives, carefully preserved in the special collections dedicated to English literature.

After completing the required formalities, she had been handed the files covering the years 1693–1695. With the eager anticipation of a researcher – like a hunting dog catching the scent of its prey – she began to turn the pages, seized by the thrill of imminent discovery. The documents formed a haphazard collection: travel notes, records of passage aboard His Majesty's ships, inventories of luggage, sketches of tropical plants, sermons inspired by Presbyterian doctrine, and letters from London moneylenders. All of it was irrefutable evidence of a voyage to the West Indies – the English Caribbean.

Defoe had embarked on HMS *Ulysses* in January 1694, undertaking a journey of several months through the Windward Islands, the Atlantic Caribbean, and along the northern coast of Venezuela to the mouth of the Orinoco River. He had travelled on behalf of the King, likely tasked with advising on the profitable exploitation of those territories. This alone was fascinating, reinforcing the complexity of her subject: an author, certainly, but also an adventurer, speculator, religious zealot, preacher – and a shadowy figure entrusted with confidential missions.

It was equally clear that, twenty-five years before the publication of *Robinson Crusoe*, which told the story of a shipwreck on a desert island off the Orinoco, Defoe had travelled there himself and meticulously documented

 | DOI:10.1163/9789004737112_006

the region. Pauline could already anticipate the brilliant connections she would be able to draw – this promised to be enlightening.

At the end of the day, having already filled several pages with notes and as the light in the library began to fade, a faded cardboard folder labelled *Sunday Sermons* caught Pauline's eye. Inside was a sheet of paper in Defoe's handwriting, followed by several notebooks written in another, clumsier hand, on paper ravaged by damp – like a logbook that had spent years in a cellar or aboard a shipwreck. Pauline's heart began to race. Could it be that, hidden behind the unremarkable label *Sunday Sermons*, this folder had escaped the notice of previous researchers?

The sheet bore the words: *Journal of the sailor Robinson, shipwrecked off Tobago. Received from Lieutenant Parker in Trinidad on Palm Sunday of the year 1694.* Her throat tightened, and her fingers trembled as she hesitated to open the notebooks that followed. By all appearances, she held in her hands the authentic journal of Robinson, which Defoe must have acquired – heaven only knows under what circumstances – from an English officer stationed on an island near the site of the shipwreck.

Just then, the library's closing bell sounded, giving her three minutes to pack up her notes, close the file for the day, and leave. She could not, however, resist the temptation to glance at the improbable manuscript. And that was when she stumbled upon the words that now refused to leave her mind: *on the way back*.

'On the way back, a violent whirlwind or hurricane completely disoriented us. It raged so terribly that for twelve consecutive days, we could do nothing but drift.'

Pauline knew the passage well – it was the immediate prelude to the shipwreck. But in that moment, her entire world came crashing down. In an instant, she realised that her thesis, her supervisor's expectations, her understanding of the text – and perhaps even her future – had just been thrown into doubt.

Back in her room at the Primerose boarding house, Pauline rushed to grab her bilingual copy of *Robinson Crusoe*, the book that had accompanied her throughout these years and of which she knew entire passages by heart. There it was, clear as day. On page 104, she read: 'The same day I went on board we set sail, standing away to the northward upon our own coast, with design to stretch over for the African coast.' And just a few lines later: 'But after we had sailed about ten days, coming near the Canary Islands, we were chased by a Salee rover, and in great danger of being taken.'

It was obvious – as everyone knew – that Robinson's shipwreck had occurred during the outward journey, from Brazil to the African coast. Less well known – though the book made only subtle reference to it – was the true purpose of the expedition: an enterprise undertaken by the English adventurer to take delivery of a full cargo of ebony wood, the euphemism of the time for the transatlantic slave trade, which lined the pockets of plantation owners in the Americas.

The rest was familiar: the lone survivor of a modest crew, Robinson arrived on his island, where he remained for twenty-eight years. During that time, he transformed it into a model of a prosperous colony, eventually populated by waves of settlers and held up – by Rousseau, for one – as an exemplar of the courage and ingenuity of civilised man.

But if the shipwreck had happened on the way back, everything changed. Robinson would no longer have been alone – how had he managed to survive alongside the hundreds of men, women, and children from Africa who, like him, must have been stranded on the island? (Unless, in the improbable scenario, he truly was the sole survivor.)

And then came the most unsettling thought of all – one that shook Pauline to the core. If Defoe had falsified this crucial piece of the narrative, what could be said of the rest?

It was all too much. Her blood pounded, her head clouded with pain and confusion, her limbs felt shattered. She needed to get out – to drink something. Clutching her copy of *Robinson Crusoe* like a lifeline in the chaos, she pushed open the door of a nearby pub, The Vineyard, and collapsed into one of its venerable booths. It wasn't until half an hour later, aided by a double Caipirinha, that she began to regain her composure.

Now she was caught between two violently conflicting emotions. On the one hand, there was the thrill of discovery – the electrifying realisation that she stood on the brink of uncovering something that could make her name, far beyond the academic title she was pursuing. But on the other, she could already foresee the seismic shock this revelation would send through her department – particularly for her supervisor, who had built his entire reputation on the veneration of Defoe and the myth of Robinson.

This Robinson: proud and solitary, an industrious worker, a steadfast believer, a shrewd entrepreneur, and ultimately a wise and judicious governor – a paragon of the modern colonial enterprise. Pauline recalled the glowing epithets Professor Corbion so often used when speaking of the book she now held in her hands: an experimental novel of the Enlightenment, the bible of mercantile and industrial virtues, an epic of individual initiative, the foundational myth of modern Western civilisation.

What would remain of all that now?

Her supervisor had authored countless works on these themes, earning literary and academic accolades, and had delivered lectures across the world extolling the virtues of the solitary man who, through sheer effort, made barren land hospitable and established a colony as prosperous as it was virtuous. Corbion often emphasised – much like Rousseau in *Émile* – the moral triumph of Robinson. The book's immediate and universal success was lauded, with erudite parallels drawn: sometimes to Descartes' methodical approach and his praise of creative solitude; sometimes to John Locke's justification of private property (Locke being both Defoe's contemporary and a fellow Presbyterian dissenter); and sometimes to Max Weber's analysis of the relationship between Protestantism and the nascent spirit of capitalism.

Pauline knew all this well. It was the ideological framework of her thesis. And now, the ground was shifting beneath her feet. The entire landscape had changed.

She was beginning to glimpse a completely different Robinson, while the image of Defoe – her chosen subject – grew darker. To what extent had Defoe manipulated the shipwrecked sailor's journal?

The question followed her relentlessly, even as she finally sank into a heavy, restless sleep.

At dawn, she rose early, knowing that the British Library opened its doors at 8 a.m. Hurrying through the gargantuan breakfast her charming landlady insisted on serving with all due ceremony, she endured the eggs and bacon, the porridge, and the endless commentary with polite impatience.

Now, at last, she was seated at her desk, her heart pounding. The fog of London and the city's stale odours faded away; in her mind, the tropical trade winds blew, and vast stretches of deserted beaches extended endlessly before her.

It was clear that this sailor – Robinson – was no writer; the sentences in his journal were short, the expression rough and clumsy. Yet every word came alive before Pauline's eyes, as if she were reading over his shoulder. In just a few pages, the backstory of the expedition unfolded: the sugar and tobacco plantations in Brazil, the reliance on African labour (the journal used the term *negro*), Robinson's decision to outfit a ship and involve himself in this lucrative trade, and the outward voyage – uneventful, and lasting seven weeks thanks to favourable winds.

The only notable incident was the death of the ship's cooper, likely due to scurvy. Then came the stopover at Boma, a small Portuguese trading post at the mouth of the Congo River, where trade was conducted with local slave traders: European trinkets, baubles, and Brazilian alcohol were exchanged for a substantial group of men, women, and children. The journal specified: 'Three hundred and twenty negroes, originating from Central Africa, of the Bemba ethnicity.'

Before setting sail again, the crew undertook essential preparations: careening the hull, making modifications to the lower deck, and loading provisions for the long voyage – live animals and fresh vegetables for the crew, and barrels of beans, rice, and gruel for the captives.

For the past hour, Pauline had been taking notes, overcome by a deep unease. She was reeling, confronting for the first time the dark underbelly of Robinson's so-called success story: the grim reality of the transatlantic slave trade and the horrific conditions of the voyage at sea. The journal detailed tempests, spoiled provisions, barrels of stagnant water, daily deaths with bodies unceremoniously tossed overboard, and the constant struggle to manage so many captives with such a small crew – apparently fewer than fifteen.

Then, just days from their destination, the ship was caught in a cyclone and ultimately wrecked on the reefs of an uncharted island, later identified as part of the Tobago archipelago. Pauline braced herself for the continuation of this bleak narrative, recounted with stark simplicity: the crew launching the lifeboat, leaving the wretched captives trapped below deck to their fate. More concerned with his possessions than his passengers, Robinson meticulously recorded the few 'treasures' he had managed to pack into his sailor's bag: his rifle, gunpowder, some tools, sacks of seeds, a Bible, and his writing equipment. He included one chilling detail: 'As for freeing the captives from their chains, we had neither the time nor the means, given the ship's list and the waves crashing over the deck.'

Then followed the perilous launch of the makeshift boat into a raging sea – the enormous breakers smashing against the shore, the capsizing of the dinghy, and the frantic swim to land. Finally, the grim aftermath: the remaining crew members all drowned, their bodies washing up one by one on the beach. 'I was as alone as on the first day, with nothing but the few belongings packed in my sailor's bag,' the journal concluded.

It seemed that Robinson, driven forward by the tornado and rain, haunted by the thought of an even larger wave, and terrified of encountering unknown animals, had climbed to the summit of the tallest hill and finally found refuge in a sort of cave, its entrance hidden by thick lichens. 'I did not think for a moment to look back; besides, one could see no further than three feet,' he wrote.

But a remarkable surprise awaited him the next day: 'The sun was already high, the sky completely clear, and the view stretched to the horizon. When my eyes turned towards the site of the shipwreck, my blood ran cold: the wreck of the ship, pushed by the wind and tide, now lay on its side, stranded on a sandbank a few cables from the shore.'

At this point, Pauline could already picture what she had read and reread countless times in Defoe's text: Robinson meticulously listing everything he would salvage from the ship, his methodical trips back and forth, laden with provisions, tools, and objects (even including some gold and silver coins). And once everything was unloaded, his meticulous inventories and obsessive organisation, characteristic of an English shopkeeper, satisfied with the neat arrangement of his possessions.

Yet a completely different scenario awaited the castaway. Movement stirred on the ship's side. Bodies began emerging from a large breach in the stern – one, then two, then dozens of men, women, and children leapt into the water and made their way to the shore in an exuberant cacophony. Evidently, the shocks had broken the chains of some, and now the entire group was reclaiming their freedom.

For a moment, Pauline imagined herself among them, drunk with joy, as if it were the first day of a new life: the warm sand beneath her feet, embraces all around, and wild dashes under the coconut trees. The manuscript in her hands, however, pulled her out of her reverie and back to the harsh reality of Robinson's perspective: 'For a moment, I imagined driving them off with my musket, but I abandoned this plan, for it was clear they were now masters of the place.'

From his vantage point, Robinson observed the new inhabitants of the island, his heart burning with rage. They were already organising themselves: he could see them hauling out whatever remained from the ship's hull – barrels of water and wine, an abundance of provisions, and various pieces of equipment and materials.

The days that followed must have been chaotic for Robinson; the journal provided only scattered glimpses, hastily jotted down. Pauline imagined the Englishman – once a predator, now turned prey – seeking refuge at the far end of the island (which, as she surmised, was no more than a few miles across). He must have gone to great lengths to find a hiding place that would shield him from the Africans, who would inevitably explore every corner of the island. When he thought he had found sanctuary – a secluded valley concealed behind a dense mangrove at the base of a sheer cliff – it was followed by the titanic labour of building fences and barricades: 'I did not rest until I had built a fortress to secure my belongings and finally enjoy a few hours of sleep.'

Of course, this reprieve was only temporary. Robinson now lived as a hunted man, constantly afraid of being discovered, weakened by the brackish water he was forced to drink, and surviving on a few hardtack biscuits salvaged from the wreck. He dared not fire his musket, fearing it would draw attention.

Pauline couldn't help but recall a passage from the canonical text about Robinson's first bird hunt: 'It was, I believe, the first gun ever fired in this place since the creation of the world.' Defoe later describes Friday's awe at the weapon's power: '… he thought that there must be some wonderful fund of death and destruction in that thing, able to kill man, beast, bird, or anything near or far off.'

The journal also mentioned Robinson's fruitless attempts to find solace in the Bible he had rescued from the wreck. Yet Defoe would later write: 'I had the Word of God to read and His Spirit to guide me, as if I were in England.'

The journal remains silent on the weeks that followed; when it resumes, the handwriting is firmer, and the paper shows less damage. Pauline was left to speculate: had Robinson been discovered and engaged in some kind of honourable combat before being captured? Or had he been found faint and near death by a group of fishermen at the edge of his mangrove hideout, then taken captive to the village? Whatever the case, when the narrative picks up again, Robinson appears to be living among his former captives, tolerated in a separate hut on the outskirts of their settlement.

The first entry in the journal concerns his name: 'They call me Mondele Mingi Motangi, or, more simply, Motangi, which in their language – so I was later told, once I understood the rudiments – means "the white man who is always calculating". Apparently, it was already the nickname they had given me aboard the ship.'

What also astonishes Robinson upon waking from his convalescence is the fate of his musket: planted at the centre of the village square like a kind of totem, adorned with bundles of highly fragrant purple cattleyas. Clearly, an entirely new life awaited him.

Grateful for the unexpected clemency shown by his former captives, Robinson kept a low profile. Yet he could not understand why they treated him like an overgrown child – fed and tolerated on the outskirts of the group, but neither punished nor included as a competent collaborator. Each day, a woman would bring food to his hut. He was not held prisoner, yet it seemed that no particular expectations were placed upon him.

In the first few months, Robinson made several attempts to prove himself useful – indispensable, even. Once, noticing a patch of fallow land, he began clearing it of weeds and stones. After three painstaking months, he had enclosed it with low stone walls, much like those in England. However, his millet crops, planted with the precious bag of seeds salvaged from the shipwreck, turned out to be a complete failure.

Another time, he attempted to construct a bamboo aqueduct to channel water from a nearby waterfall to the centre of the village square. But within three days, a tropical downpour swept the entire structure away. Even the calendar he diligently maintained – marking each passing day with a notch on a tree trunk – was reduced to dust by voracious insects the likes of which he had never seen in Europe.

None of his efforts seemed destined for success. Instead, his misplaced zeal elicited little more than amused smiles. 'You're exhausting yourself for nothing, Motangi. Look around you instead of calculating all the time!' one of the village women told him. The remark stung, and Robinson had carefully recorded it in his notebook.

Truth be told, Pauline was beginning to enjoy herself immensely. Her curiosity had been reignited, and she eagerly anticipated what would come next. She had skipped lunch hours ago, barely pausing long enough to treat herself to an iced tea from the vending machine in the corridor outside her small office. Robinson put through re-education – what would her supervisor, the distinguished Professor Corbion, have to say about that?

Diligent as ever, Robinson dutifully set himself to learning from nature. Perhaps for the first time in his life, he began to let go, glimpsing the possibility that the other might have something to teach him. Over the months and years to come, he would certainly have his lessons.

Forced into idleness, Robinson began to truly see the world around him. Everywhere, he was surrounded by intoxicating orchids, cascades of wisteria, and clearings brimming with jasmine and hollyhocks. Here, there were no orderly gardens – only an endless expanse of luxuriant nature. At every turn, he was startled by multi-coloured parrots, scarlet-plumed ibises, or tiny hummingbirds sipping nectar from tropical blossoms. Along the shore, pink crabs scuttled past giant turtles, lazily beached and waiting for the next tide.

Venturing deeper into the forest, he encountered armadillos and anteaters that piqued his curiosity, or startled toucans that took flight in a sudden burst of colour. Butterflies with otherworldly hues added an almost dreamlike quality to the scene, further heightened by the continuous hum of the jungle and the mingling of unfamiliar fragrances that seemed to permeate everything.

For the first time in his life, Robinson saw these wonders not as resources to exploit or threats to overcome, but as gifts simply happening to him. He welcomed them without question, marvelling at how this spectacle alone could fill his days.

Over time, Robinson acquired the rudiments of his hosts' language. His journal documented his progress, meticulously recording long lists of common expressions that he vowed to remember. With language came stronger social ties. Pauline noted, with a hint of amusement, how Robinson seemed particularly fascinated by the women of the community. While sexual attraction may have played a role, the shipwrecked Puritan refrained from any impropriety – such temptations were not easily indulged by a man of his upbringing. No, what captivated him most was something far more unsettling to his worldview: the realisation that the society into which fate had thrust him was entirely matriarchal.

It was not so much their beauty or adornments that Robinson chronicled in his journal – though he did take note of their skirts woven from strings and bird-of-paradise feathers, their necklaces of pearls gathered through diving, and the nacreous pigments that adorned their faces and shoulders. What truly struck him was the authority they wielded within the group.

Robinson observed with amazement that it was the women who held the exclusive privilege of using the digging stick, a tool employed to unearth tubers. Similarly, the hoe – both a vital agricultural implement and an object celebrated in their dances and even crafted into jewellery – was firmly within their domain. While the men occasionally hunted or fished, it was the women who planted beans and squash, managed the harvest, and controlled the storage of food supplies. They appeared utterly independent of the men, relying on them only as auxiliary support when necessary. Robinson himself was treated no differently.

An unwitting anthropologist, Robinson – Pauline mused – was discovering a matriarchal society. The irony of his fate was forcing him into the most unprecedented of experiences: not the reproduction of a miniature England on virgin soil, a blank page upon which to inscribe the glorious history of Western reason, but rather immersion in – and learning from – a different culture, likely as old as time itself, steeped in the harmony of nature and respect for life.

Pauline was familiar with this alternative worldview, though she had always kept it at a distance, treating it as too remote from her own reality and academic pursuits. Now, however, she was suddenly and irrevocably confronted with it, standing alongside Robinson on this tropical stage where, for a fleeting moment, the destiny of the world seemed poised to shift.

In that instant, the journal in her hands ceased to be merely an archival document, the object of her scholarly study. It became something far more personal – a mirror reflecting her own inner journey. This was no longer just Robinson's story; in some strange way, it was her own fate being played out on these Caribbean shores.

Robinson, unaccustomed to idleness, still sought ways to make himself useful. Recalling the crafts of his grandfather from his boyhood in Devonshire, he began weaving baskets and hats from the plentiful straw found on the island. After several weeks, he developed a respectable skill – 'I became not so bad in this business,' he noted in his journal – and, following his natural instincts, decided to display his wares on a makeshift stall outside his hut, eagerly anticipating the chance to barter his goods and set a fair price for the fruits of his labour.

It did not take long for him to realise that such a system was entirely foreign to this community. Not only was there no form of currency in circulation – not even shells or trinkets, which often served as proto-money in other societies – but the very concepts of property, commerce, and accumulation seemed utterly alien to the islanders. People came to his stall and took what they pleased, occasionally offering something in return – a dish of roasted yams, honeyed caterpillars, or another delicacy. Yet this was neither required nor expected, and since he had already been receiving such offerings before setting up his stall, Robinson was forced to conclude that commerce, as he understood it, simply did not exist here.

Instead, what he witnessed was a system based on mutual service, spontaneous exchange without calculated compensation, and an overarching ethos of sharing and solidarity. Nothing appeared to belong to anyone in particular: land, gardens, even food seemed to remain available to all. There were no accumulated riches, no deliberate inheritance. Everything was imbued with a sense of the ephemeral and the light-hearted – as if, like the fruits and flowers that came and went with the seasons, things would arrive just when needed, without worry or premeditation.

The situation astonished Robinson. He recalled the sermons of a pastor from his youth, the Reverend Hardin, who had preached a concept he called the tragedy of the commons. Hardin had warned, 'If something is left accessible to all, it will inevitably degrade. No one, having a vested interest in its preservation, will protect it; everyone will exploit the resource until it is entirely depleted. Surround it with a fence, however, give it a private owner, and it will be protected and thrive, bringing glory to God and salvation to the one who dedicates their labour to its care.'

This moral teaching had shaped Robinson's upbringing, instilling in him a firm belief that prosperity – born of hard work and saving – was a visible sign of one's future election. Now, though, he wished Reverend Hardin could stand beside him and see what he saw: a village in perfect order, where everyone – young and old – worked together under the cheerful guidance of the mothers. There was no waste to lament, no one abandoned to their fate.

Fragments of Scripture surfaced in Robinson's mind, passages rarely emphasised in the Sunday sermons of his youth: 'the birds of the air, which neither sow nor reap,' or the story of Mary pouring precious perfume on the feet of her Lord and wiping them with her hair – preferred to Martha, anxious and burdened with toil in the kitchen.

He recorded all of this in his journal, in simple words and short sentences. Pauline followed, day by day, the stages of this ordeal that was also a transformation. It felt as though she too had taken up residence on the island. One phrase, in particular, moved her deeply with its simplicity: 'I learned to count by moons.' She imagined him sitting on the beach, his gaze lost in the stars, so low they seemed ready to dip into the sea, waiting for the bright moon to ascend the firmament.

In her mind, she reached out to this great solitary figure, breathing with him in rhythm with the tide, in tune with the moon's cycle. She felt, in her very core, the great currents of life stirring – flowing in harmony with the world around them.

The hours had slipped away, and Pauline was pulled out of her reverie by the library's closing bell. Reluctantly, she tore herself away from the text, gathered her belongings, and returned to her familiar haunt, The Vineyard, which had become her base of operations. After at least two caipirinhas, she felt a slow-burning anger rise within her toward Defoe. Instead of honouring Robinson's message, he had completely distorted it.

Back in her room, she picked up her well-worn copy of *Robinson Crusoe*, flipping through its pages in search of the passages her supervisor so often cited – passages he presented as illustrative and foundational to the spirit of ownership. They stood in stark contrast to the revelations she had uncovered that day.

On page 192, for example, Robinson reflects: 'I descended a little on the side of that delicious vale, surveying it with a secret kind of pleasure, tho' mixt with my other afflicting thoughts, to think that this was all my own, that I was king and lord of all this country indefeasibly, and had a right of possession; and if I could convey it, I might have it in inheritance, as compleatly as any lord of a manor in England.' Her supervisor often tied this phrase – 'king and lord' – to the double superlative used in Article 544 of the French Civil Code, describing property ownership as the 'most absolute use and enjoyment of one's property'.

Further along, on page 234, Defoe, after mentioning Robinson's lack of carnal desires, has his protagonist declare: 'I was lord of the whole manor; or, if I pleased, I might call myself king or emperor over the whole country which I had possession of: there were no rivals; I had no competitor, none to dispute sovereignty or command with me.'

There it was, Pauline thought: property replacing the flesh, sovereign power substituting sexual potency, and the triumph of an unrivalled self preferred over the risks of encountering the other.

On page 262, the psychological portrait of the owner becomes even richer, revealing a repressed and unsettling trait. Speaking of himself in the third person, Robinson writes: 'There was my majesty, the prince and lord of the whole island; I had the lives of all my subjects at my absolute command; I could hang, disembowel, give liberty, and take it away, with no rebels among all my subjects.'

It was all too much for Pauline. How had this vision of absolute control and unchallenged dominance – this substitution of ownership for human connection – become the legacy of *Robinson Crusoe*? What other surprises, she wondered, might tomorrow's discoveries hold?

∴

The morning's breakfast was as hearty as ever, and the hostess just as talkative – today, she was unstoppable, extolling the comparative virtues of green and black tea. Pauline would have much preferred an espresso but had refrained from confessing this guilty eccentricity; besides, it would have only delayed her further.

And now she was back at her desk, the precious journal spread open before her. That morning, Robinson – the real Robinson, speaking in the first person in the manuscript Pauline held in her hands – had experienced a surge of emotion: part of the village was packing up and heading toward the beach. Could it be? In response to his eager questions, he was told that several married women, now with many daughters, had decided it was time to establish their own village, gathering the families of their clan. The new settlement would be located on the island's western slope. The journal, often unclear and awkwardly phrased, recorded what the Englishman had managed to understand about the social organisation of the Bemba clans, from which his former captives originated.

To his great surprise, Robinson learned that names were passed down through women, and that families and clans were built around them. It was the women, along with their mothers, who chose a husband – who would then leave his own family to live in his wife's village. At the beginning of the marriage, the young wife remained with her mother, cooking by her side; the young husband, for his part, performed various services for his wife's family. Only later, if the couple had several children, would the wife set up a household with her husband. And it was specifically if she had many daughters (and thus access to the labour of multiple sons-in-law) that the mother would consider moving away to establish her own village, earning widespread respect as an 'ancestor'. While the husband played a secondary role, it was the mother's brother who served as the protector of her children once they reached adulthood.

Such a society – and Robinson found it even harder to imagine – did not, however, enshrine the idea of a 'head of the family' or signify the domination of women over men, as if it were some inverted version of the English model. Rather, it appeared to be an egalitarian structure, devoid of any clear hierarchy, where the primary responsibilities were carried out by the women. Robinson did note, however, that a few elders, known for their wisdom and generosity, enjoyed great respect and shared the leadership of the group with their spouses.

Later, Robinson would observe that unions were far more fluid than in England; in fact, spouses lived with considerable freedom and often had multiple, openly acknowledged partners. As a result, marriages were easily dissolved, with children remaining with their mothers under the protection of their uncles.

In this way – and particularly now that the island had a second settlement – the village population was in constant flux. All of this contributed to the absence of rigid hierarchies or extensive establishments. What mattered most – Robinson noted with interest – was the practice of palaver: no decision was made without achieving general consensus. The same applied in cases of conflict; disagreements were discussed at length by everyone, with the elders playing the role of suggesting solutions that would allow all parties to save face. In unresolved disputes, the only recourse was for one party and their entire clan to secede – an outcome that would inevitably weaken the village as a whole.

All of this, which twentieth-century anthropologists would gradually rediscover piecemeal, Robinson experienced first-hand. He seemed to adapt to his new existence and increasingly appreciated its value with each passing day.

Reaching this point in her reading and taking advantage of the lunch break she had finally allowed herself, Pauline once again picked up her canonical copy of *Robinson Crusoe*. She was now determined to compile the most blatant distortions of the shipwrecked sailor's observations that Defoe had used as inspiration. After some searching, she found this passage on page 393, written by Defoe's Robinson as his island began to be populated (with Friday, Friday's father, a Spanish sailor, and others): 'I often made the pleasant reflection that I resembled a king. First, the entire country was my absolute property, so I had an undeniable right to dominion. Second, my people were entirely subservient. I was their sovereign lord and legislator; they owed me their lives and were ready to die for me if necessary.'

And later, when the Spanish sailor proposed returning to his fellow castaways on a nearby island, Robinson agreed – but on the explicit condition that they first pledge allegiance to him: 'They would have to swear on the holy sacraments and the Gospel to be loyal to me and submit totally and absolutely to my orders' (page 399).

From the appropriation of the island and its systematic exploitation, Defoe's fictional Robinson gradually transformed it into a political entity; after property and contract, the categories of public law were introduced. The once-solitary man soon called himself 'governor', administered justice, and enacted the island's first regulations.

At this point, Pauline was overcome with a sense of vertigo, as though she had been granted a tangible glimpse of the breaking point where history split – the fault line along which peoples made their choices. Was this Caribbean island destined to remain trapped in an obsolete past, at best reduced to an exotic postcard? And yet, all of it had truly happened; for three days now, she had journeyed back in time alongside the shipwrecked sailor, and this experience felt more vivid, more alive, than anything she had ever encountered before. It was with relief, then, that she returned to the journal, as though, once more (for the last time?), she had been granted access to drink from this vital spring.

The years passed – Robinson no longer kept an exact count, as if it hardly mattered anymore. He was aging and had fully adapted to the rhythm of the village. Yet he had not abandoned the religious practices of his youth: each evening, he still devoted himself to reading the Bible. His understanding, however, had shifted. No longer did he linger on the battles and commands; instead, he meditated on the Psalms and the Song of Songs. Pauline could sense that, over time, his life on the island had become a spiritual journey rather than a mere exercise in survival or colonisation. His journal bore witness to this transformation, with countless observations about the religious practices – lacking a better term – of his companions. His interest was sincere, though he often struggled to articulate the originality and depth of what he observed.

What struck him most was the absence of church, clergy, or sacred texts. Instead, the entire surrounding world and daily life seemed suffused with the sacred. Here, the universe itself was spiritual, and everyone partook in it: men, women, children, as well as animals, trees, waterfalls, ancestors, and forest spirits. All these elements – so carefully separated, classified, and hierarchised in his former world – coexisted here in harmony. The simplest acts of daily life were imbued with spirituality, and the most ordinary objects carried symbolic weight – signs of connection, balance, and reverence.

Even the humblest hut reflected this sacred and magical universe. At its entrance hung small offerings: gifts to the ancestors who protected the home. The doorposts bore symbols celebrating female fertility – two breasts carved into the wood and, occasionally, a shell representing the vulva. Over time, Robinson grew less hesitant about recording such details in his journal. The entire house, and indeed the whole village, celebrated women – or more precisely, the womb that sheltered children before bringing them into the world.

On a broader scale, Robinson was beginning to understand that nature itself was regarded as both woman and mother. His companions sometimes spoke of Mother Earth or the Old Ancestor, the giver of life and provider of sustenance. It was the elderly women of the village who maintained her worship, preserving the secrets of shamanic trances. Pauline interpreted Robinson's descriptions – phrases like 'frenzied dances' or 'dance-to-exhaustion' – as references to these rituals. These trances were often induced through the use of mandrake plants, which the women guarded closely. Robinson had even sketched several drawings of the plant in his journal. Dancing until they reached a state of possession, these women became the voices of the ancestors and presided over the mysteries of reincarnation.

Each child born on the island was believed to be an ancestor returning to the world. The most significant ceremony of the year was the *Chisụngu*, an initiation festival for young girls reaching maturity – a ritual to which Robinson referred repeatedly in his writings over the years. Spanning several days, the festival included magical practices, songs, dances, lavish feasts, and even comical interludes. Yet the heart of the event was conducted in utmost secrecy: the initiation of young girls within huts specifically designated for this purpose. The elder women oversaw the rites, revealing the mysteries of female fertility and the reincarnation of ancestral spirits.

Robinson, like all the men in the village, was never granted access to these rituals. His journal reflected deep curiosity and sincere respect, but he remained an outsider – excluded from the sacred practices that ensured the island's spiritual and cultural continuity.

In place of the mysteries that eluded him, Robinson carefully recorded the term *ubuntu*, which his companions seemed to use frequently, especially in such contexts. It took him a long time to grasp its full meaning, eventually noting this approximate interpretation in his journal: 'What I am, I become through the group.' Pauline smiled at this, recognising the term as the name of an open-source Linux distribution used by some of her fellow researchers – here was the spirit of Robinson's companions manifesting in the most contemporary of forms.

But her heart was not light, for – though she had delayed acknowledging it as long as she could – the story was nearing its end: only two or three pages remained in her hands. She could sense what was inevitably coming: the sight of a ship on the horizon, the vessel anchoring a short distance from the shore, the launch of a small boat, and then the decisive question – return to one's homeland or remain behind? All tales of solitary castaways end this way, she thought, because otherwise, how would we have come to know them?

It was no different in Robinson's case: one day or another, it was inevitable that a ship would pass nearby and stop, if only to replenish its water supply. In this instance, it was an English schooner commanded by Lieutenant Parker. Did Robinson hesitate, even for a moment? Pauline couldn't imagine it – his destiny was now here, among those who had granted him a second life. Robinson was gone; only Motangi remained. Yet he had one final impulse, late in his life: the wish for his story to be known by his own people. Hastily, on the first page of his notebooks, he had written: 'Given to Lieutenant Parker for transmission to Reverend Hardin, or his successor (Parish of Exmouth, Devonshire).'

Pauline was overcome by a deep shiver; an enormous emptiness now consumed her. Her professional instincts reminded her that her work wasn't over yet – there was still the remainder of the dossier to comb through, detailing the rest of Defoe's voyage in the Caribbean. But she lacked the energy to tackle that task today. Instead, she made her way back to the Primrose boarding house on foot, her thoughts swirling. She was eager to inform her supervisor of her astonishing discovery.

The email she drafted that evening was unusually long – several pages swaying between outrage and exhilaration. She no longer knew where she stood, and she had no desire to endure one of those soporific, demoralising methodological lectures her supervisor so often delivered.

The following morning – the day of her departure – her hostess insisted on giving her a packet of tea as a souvenir of her stay: Betty and Taylor, she specified, her favourite. She explained how she had long favoured East India Company tea, Queen Victoria's very own, and how she had hesitated over Clipper, the fair-trade option – but that one, dear Pauline, would have to wait for next time. 'That way, I'm sure you'll come back to us,' she added with a warm smile.

For the last time, Pauline returned to her desk at the British Library. Though she was burning to reopen Motangi's journal, she forced herself to finish reading the rest of the file. It consisted mostly of travel notes prepared by Defoe for his report to the King. Meticulous as ever, he had spent months crisscrossing the region – Tobago (ceded to Great Britain just five years earlier), Trinidad, Saint Vincent, and the Grenadines – gathering information on climate, crops, maritime routes, and the available labour force. It must have been during those travels, she deduced, that he encountered Lieutenant Parker and received Robinson's manuscript, with a promise to deliver it to Reverend Hardin or his successor.

Finally, the file concluded with the infamous report to the King. Dated 16 January 1795, it bore the title *Memoir to His Majesty Concerning the Colonization of the Orinoco Basin and Its Archipelago*. The document was a fervent plea for the immediate exploitation of the region's territories – time was of the essence, as the Dutch and French were already showing interest. Defoe depicted the area in idyllic terms, as a land of plenty ripe for cultivating sugarcane and tobacco. Coffee, bananas, and cotton plantations, he argued, would also prove highly lucrative.

Admittedly, the region was plagued by buccaneers and prone to cyclones, but these were mere inconveniences compared to the profits such enterprises would undoubtedly yield. Defoe included detailed calculations, presenting the King with a thorough estimate of the venture's profitability, which he confidently asserted would attract significant investment from the City of London.

One major challenge, however, loomed large: the absolute necessity of securing a much larger Black labour force to ensure the plantations' success. To address this, Defoe advocated for the intensification of the 'triangular trade' between Europe, Africa, and the Americas. He even suggested that this commerce could become highly profitable if extended to include Spain's vast American colonies.

Defoe reminded the King that the Spanish did not engage in the slave trade directly; under the *asiento* system, they granted this privilege to other nations in exchange for royalties. It was, therefore, of the utmost priority that Great Britain secures this right – ideally as a monopoly.[1] The report concluded with the customary formalities and an explicit offer of service from the writer-adventurer himself.

Pauline closed the file and left the library. She still had a few hours before her train and, having no desire to go shopping, lingered on a bench in Regent's Park, lost in a tangle of emotions. The ringing of her iPhone jolted her from her reverie: it was her supervisor, sending her a text message.

'Now, now, dear Pauline! Let's take it down a notch: the subject of your thesis is the author Defoe, not the character Robinson. It's the prerogative of

1 Defoe must have been persuasive: under the Treaty of Utrecht (1713), England was granted a thirty-year monopoly over the *asiento*. It immediately transferred this right to the South Sea Company, which exercised it from 1713 to 1759. Among the company's shareholders was the entirety of the English establishment.

great authors to take liberties with historical reality, which is never more than raw empirical material. We'll talk more about it in a month, when I return from my holiday; in the meantime, get some rest.'

⁂

Now Pauline had to decide which life she would return to. Had she merely been a voyeur, or had she truly seen something? Ultimately, this trip to London – was it a round trip, or a one-way journey?

Bibliography

Unless otherwise indicated, all quotations from the canonical *Robinson Crusoe* by D. Defoe are cited according to the English original. Where necessary, comparisons have been made with the French translation by P. Borel, (*Robinson Crusoé*, trans. P. Borel, ed. M. Baridon, Paris: Gallimard, Folio Classique, 2001), which includes critical commentary and the complete narrative. It is essential to read the entire work – including the episodes preceding and following the island stay – in order to fully grasp the broader economic and social context of the story.

Rousseau, in his educational treatise *Émile* (J.-J. Rousseau, *Émile* (1762), Paris: Larousse, Petits Classiques Larousse, 1999), argues that Defoe's masterpiece should long remain the only book placed in the hands of his pupil (p. 166), but he advises focusing solely on the island episode (p. 167); as a result, he entirely overlooks the realities of the slave economy and the ideological implications of the work. It is well documented that Daniel Defoe submitted a report to William III advocating for the establishment of an English colony in the Orinoco Basin.

I draw on a comedy by Marivaux for the idea of reversing the master/slave relationship in the context of a shipwreck (Marivaux, *L'île des esclaves* (1725), Paris: Le Théâtre de Poche, LLP, 1999).

Coetzee inspires the notion of the writer Foe completely transforming the 'authentic' account of the 'true' (J. M. Coetzee, *Foe*, trans. S. Mayoux, Paris: Seuil, 1988).

Many authors, starting with Jules Verne, have sought to overturn the mythical interpretation of the Robinson story. Among them, I cite only Giraudoux, Tournier, and Golding (J. Giraudoux, *Suzanne et le Pacifique*, Paris: LLP (1921), 1997; M. Tournier, *Vendredi ou les limbes du Pacifique*, Paris: Gallimard, Folio, 1972; W. Golding, *Sa majesté des mouches* (1954), trans. L. Tranec, Paris: Gallimard, Folio, 1998).

I draw on the analyses of H. Goettner-Abendroth for descriptions of Bemba society (H. Goettner-Abendroth, *Les sociétés matriarcales. Recherches sur les cultures autochtones à travers le monde*, trans. C. Chaplain, Paris: Des femmes–Antoinette Fouque, 2019, ch. 16, pp. 433 ff.).

Additionally, Readers May Consult

Detis, E., *Daniel Defoe démasqué: lecture de l'œuvre romanesque* (Paris: L'Harmattan, 1989).

Engelbert, J.-P., *La postérité de Robinson Crusoé: un mythe littéraire de la modernité (1954–1986)* (Geneva: Droz, 1997).

Merle, R., *L'île* (Paris: Gallimard, Folio, 1962).

Ost, F., *Raconter la loi: aux sources de l'imaginaire juridique* (Paris: Odile Jacob, 2004), ch. 4.

Robinson, ed. L. Andries (Paris: Éditions Autrement, 1996).

Watt, I., 'Robinson Crusoe as a myth', in *Robinson Crusoe*, ed. M. Shinagel (New York and London: Norton & Company, 2nd ed., 1994), pp. 288 ff.

On the Margins of the Palace

This morning, in *Bulletin de l'Association de la Noblesse du Royaume de Belgique*, no. 293, January 2018, I came across the following study: *Les confidences du mammouth*, by Chevalier Jean de Codt, First President of the Court of Cassation of Belgium, pp. 7–17. The article, of a highly scholarly nature, is dedicated to the Brussels Palace of Justice and its architect, Joseph Poelaert. On page 10, this remarkable passage – there is no more fitting word – caught my attention:

> According to the English historian James Welles, Poelaert was closely associated with a school of thought known as esotericism. Esotericism believes in the existence of parallel worlds, with points of contact between these neighbouring universes. The Palace of Justice in Brussels supposedly contains a secret passage that allows one to travel from the Brussels we know to an alternative Brussels located in a different world.

And then, this even more astonishing conclusion: 'The Palace was built to last, and, in its stone soul, it must be saying, "He who laughs last, laughs best".'

A few details, first of all, for those unfortunate souls who have never set foot in Brussels and know nothing of its Palace of Justice. Let us not deny ourselves the pleasure – for once, the Belgians, so often said to be devoted to small things and, to be frank, incapable of grandeur, have truly outdone themselves. For yes, let us not shy away from the word: this Palace of Justice was, and remains, the largest in the world. With a built area of 26,006 m^2, it far surpasses St. Peter's Basilica in Rome. It has even been calculated that if all the stone blocks used in its construction were laid end to end, they would stretch from the Earth to the Moon. Its entrance portico, topped by the bust of Themis, rises to a height of 39 m, giving access to a vast hall – known as the Hall of Lost Steps – that culminates 100 m beneath the central dome, making it the highest covered hall in the world.

With its colossal colonnades, monumental staircases, and pilasters adorned with Assyrian, Egyptian, Greek, and Roman statues, the Palace presents a spectacle that observers have described as 'Piranesian' – 'a Piranesi dream'. Poelaert, who was undeterred by anything (certainly not the constraints of the state budget), had even planned to crown it with a pyramid in the style of the Babylonian ziggurats. However, as he passed away four years before the project's completion, his successors opted for a more traditional dome.

 | DOI:10.1163/9789004737112_007

That said, practitioners will tell you that the true life of the Palace – and of its litigants – takes place in the underground levels, where, amidst labyrinthine corridors, one finds magistrates' courts, police tribunals, and other improbable registry offices.

So be it. But let us return to secret passages and other feats of sleight of hand. What could have led such a distinguished magistrate to lend credence to rumours as fanciful – and as old – as the Palace itself? Since we cannot reasonably suspect a mind as serious as that of the First President of the Court of Cassation of indulging in hallucinogenic substances or lazy daydreams, there must be some explanation.

And what are we to make of this warning, barely disguised as a threat: 'He who laughs last, laughs best'? Perhaps it is a cry of alarm, a form of public reckoning – the heartfelt plea of a great servant of justice, disillusioned by what he denounces as 'the lack of vision regarding the role of justice in our institutions ... Neglected, defiled, squatted ... encased in its shell of scaffolding, the martyred Palace today symbolises the decay of the institution, just as, in its former splendour, it once reflected its majesty'.

Perhaps. Most likely. And yet, the fascinating question returns: the tricks of justice, justice and its double, the shadow of justice ... A new investigation is in order.

A visit to the site confirms what one might have guessed – or already known: the Palace is a labyrinth, with its interminable corridors and improbable staircases that either rise dizzyingly or plunge into the earth. Built on steeply sloping ground, the Palace has a vertical drop of more than 21 m between its main entrance and the access on Rue des Minimes below. Its many dead ends, sealed doors, and Kafkaesque attics – where pigeons slip in through dormer windows with broken panes – lend ready credence to the legend of secret passages. If one's steps can already falter in the vast reception hall on the ground floor, it is easy to imagine the confusion that reigns in the upper levels or the basement.

The very personality of Joseph Poelaert also invites curiosity and fuels early suspicions. Undoubtedly a brilliant architect, a protégé of King Leopold I, and unquestionably protected by the public authorities even in his most daring excesses, Poelaert was not without his shadows. Was it not said that he died insane at the age of sixty-two, just four years before the project's completion? Had he not vanished for several days beforehand, only to be found wandering in Hal, unable to explain where he had been? One is thus justified in wondering whether he himself arranged some secret escape route from his monumental temple of justice – an exit strategy from his obsessive vision. Could it be that he was the first to slip through such a passage? What had Poelaert understood, that, sometime before the inauguration of the building that should have secured his eternal glory, he chose instead to vanish from public life and dissolve into anonymity?

Thus, the question of the secret passage was never entirely forgotten. It resurfaced, for instance, in the minutes of the Council of the Order of Advocates on 4 March 1896. On that occasion, the members deliberated earnestly on the possible existence 'of some concealed door or secret passage granting external access from the Palace's basements', assigning Monsieur le Conservateur the task of investigating the matter. A budget of 250 francs was allocated, and a report was requested for the next session. However, no trace of such a report can be found in the archives of subsequent meetings, and so the question once again faded into obscurity for several decades.

Without ever being entirely forgotten, the mystery has periodically been revived by the fantasies stirred by this whimsical palace and the gravity of the activities carried out within its walls. Some could not resist reminding others – in hushed tones and with lowered voices – that the palace was built on what was once a hill in Brussels known as *Galgenberg* – 'Gallows Hill' in Dutch. Could it be the ghosts of the executed who, on certain evenings, still haunt the site, disturbing the consciences of prosecutors who, just that morning, had demanded the strict application of the law?

Others, with a lighter temperament – likely already cheered by a morning aperitif shared with colleagues at the nearby café *Le Perroquet* – would recount, with great seriousness, sightings of a white rabbit in a yellow waistcoat dashing out of the hallway of the clerk's office of the Justice of the Peace for the 3rd Canton. This rabbit, they swore, looked terribly busy, consulting a pocket watch and lamenting: 'I'm late, very late!' These stunned witnesses even claimed that the rabbit was followed by a little girl who ran after it, eventually falling to her knees and vanishing, as if swallowed by the ground. And so the chatter continued for a few more years, as strange characters and curious encounters were hardly a rarity in these halls.

Yet the people of Brussels – particularly those in the legal profession – are, for the most part, a practical sort, and more pragmatic explanations often prevailed. It was frequently pointed out that the construction of the Palace, from 1866 to 1883, had sparked numerous incidents and provoked the anger of the working-class residents of the Marolles district, which lay in the shadow of the imposing edifice. Dozens of modest homes were expropriated 'for the greater good', and the political intent of the building – to impress the populace with a symbol of order and authority – did not escape the notice of ordinary people, now forced to live in the literal and figurative shadow of justice. Hence, the enduring resentment of the Marolles residents toward the architects – an enmity immortalised in a uniquely Brussels insult, *schieven architek*, literally 'crooked, twisted, lopsided architect'.

Far from wallowing in insults and complaints, however, the residents of the Marolles quickly grasped the opportunities presented by this titanic construction site, which, within a few years, became an inexhaustible source of materials. Under cover of night, they would shamelessly help themselves. Even today, it is not uncommon to come across stone fireplaces in modest tenement buildings in the neighbourhood, or curious Assyrian statues tucked away in the gardens of nearby homes. From there, it was not much of a leap to speculate that a materials storage room had once been set up in the Palace's basements by the Marolles residents, with a concealed access route leading to the outside. This theory was bolstered by the pragmatic and resourceful spirit of the local population. Yet, it had to be acknowledged that, to this day, no one had succeeded in identifying the mysterious storage room or its secret passage – leaving the rumours to persist.

The matter gained new momentum in November 1924, when members of a delegation from the *Jeune Barreau de Bruxelles*, invited by their Argentine colleagues, stopped dead in their tracks at a street corner in Buenos Aires. There, they found themselves face to face with a building that was unmistakably a smaller replica of the Brussels Palace of Justice: the Argentine Congress Palace – *Cámara de Diputados de la Nación Argentina*. Admittedly, the time difference and Chilean wine were not conducive to clear thinking, and Argentina was, after all, the land of psychoanalysis, surrealism, Borges, and Cortázar. Still, the testimony was undeniable, immortalised by a photograph taken at the time by a young colleague (Figure 1): the Brussels Palace of Justice had a South American twin.

Already significantly unsettled by this unexpected encounter, the delegation found themselves thoroughly disoriented the following day when, while wandering through the Argentine Palace of Justice, they came upon a most peculiar statue: Justice depicted as a sleepwalker – yes, a sleepwalking Justice, cautiously advancing with arms stretched out in front of her.

Could it be that Brussels' Justice – already blind, as tradition dictates – had, during some sombre winter night, emigrated to sunnier skies? Had she, too, been enticed by the promises of the New World? Was this the parallel world and the secret passage referenced by the distinguished magistrate?

As debates over these curious conjectures continued, a similar situation arose during an exchange of delegations between Belgian and Peruvian magistrates. This time, the Belgian judges became convinced that the Brussels Palace of Justice had relocated to Lima – a belief seemingly confirmed by the photograph brought back by the Vice President of the Court of Appeal (Figure 2).

FIGURE 1 Palacio del Congreso in Buenos Aires
© COPYRIGHT LIAM QUINN (CC BY-SA 2.0).

FIGURE 2 Palacio de Justicia, Lima, Perú
© COPYRIGHT ART DINO (CC BY-SA 2.0).

This time, there was no longer any doubt: a *latina conexión* did indeed exist between Brussels and Latin America – a special affinity between Andean justice and Brussels tribunals, likely under the shared banner of fiction and surrealism that unites us so well. It is true, however, that the Argentine connection was soon abandoned, particularly after the Second World War, when certain individuals exploited it all too literally to escape prosecution for crimes that were anything but imaginary.

Thus, the legend endured – at times forgotten, at times revived by the emergence of some new detail. It was rekindled when a celebrated Brussels cartoonist devoted unforgettable panels to it under the thinly disguised name of *Brüsel*. Yet, it was obscured – if not outright repressed – when, due to a lack of public investment, the venerable Palace was gradually abandoned by more and more of its courts.

Recently, however, a string of curious incidents has reignited interest in the Palace's mysteries. First came the installation of security cameras throughout the building – part of the ongoing counterterrorism measures in the country – along with a meticulous daily count of entries and exits. At first, the discrepancy was dismissed as trivial – perhaps a few vagrants or clandestine lovers had spent the night near some obscure heating vent.

But over time, the anomaly became undeniable: more entries were recorded than exits. Eventually, the figures revealed the disappearance of a substantial cohort of litigants into the bowels of the mammoth. Unless one were to imagine the Palace housing a sedentary tribe – or a sect of courtroom enthusiasts obsessed with public hearings – the conclusion was inescapable: the Palace concealed one or more secret exits, known to a not-insignificant number of individuals.

Adding to the intrigue were the unexplained disappearances of case files and artworks (was the Somnambulant Justice inspiring imitators?), the shattering of the bust of a former lawyer – the founder of the *Pandectes belges* – and the curious permanence of the scaffolding on the façade. These scaffolds had been in place for so long that the name of the construction company responsible had been forgotten. No one even thought to request their removal anymore; it was generally understood that they were holding the imposing façade together – however precariously.

There was also the mysterious vanishing of an entire UNESCO delegation, which had visited the site to evaluate the Brussels Palace of Justice for inclusion on the World Heritage List. Since no official complaint was ever filed, the matter was discreetly shelved. Equally hushed up was the disappearance of a presiding judge at the Commercial Court – a rather unconventional figure who, favouring conciliation over adjudication, had taken to resolving particularly stubborn disputes by rolling dice. As he was only a few weeks away from retirement and no police report was made, the incident was quietly forgotten.

Still, the accumulation of incidents was becoming too much to ignore. Troubled by it all, I confided in an old friend, Philippe Noël – a celebrated legal columnist and veteran observer of court proceedings for decades. Though already very old – he passed away just weeks later – he was still sharp enough to greet my mention of the legendary secret passage with a knowing, mischievous smile.

I couldn't quite grasp what he was hinting at – or trying to withhold – but I understood enough to sense that the mystery might continue elsewhere. 'It's in continuation,' he whispered, 'over at Toone.'

Toone … the famous puppet theatre for adults, where plays and operas from the classical repertoire have long been performed in both French and Dutch – or rather, in that delightful fusion of the two known as *brusseleir*. Since the days of King Philip II, whose attempt to close traditional theatres in order to stifle dissent merely gave rise to this underground form of popular resistance, Toone has been beloved by the people of Brussels.

Could it be, then? Had my friend Philippe led me to a clue?

Intrigued, I made my way there one beautiful spring morning – one of those mornings when the air is so fresh and the light so pure that the world seems newly reborn. The Théâtre de Toone has two entrances: one via the impasse known as Schuddeveld, between numbers 21 and 25 on Petite Rue des Bouchers, and the other via the Impasse Sainte-Pétronille, between numbers 66 and 68 on Rue Marché-aux-Herbes. Two entrances, two alleys – it seemed a fittingly mysterious beginning.

At this early hour, the theatre was closed – but not the adjoining estaminet, already bustling with activity. I ordered a gueuze – naturally, a Mort Subite – and, to my great surprise, recognised, seated further down, the very members of the UNESCO delegation who had vanished weeks earlier without a trace. At the next table sat Judge Bridoit (have I mentioned his name?), the very one known for resolving verdicts with a roll of the dice.

Taking advantage of the universal goodwill that a round of drinks tends to inspire, I edged closer to their table. When I introduced myself as a philosopher of law working on a book tentatively titled *What Is Law For?*, my words provoked loud laughter. Clearly, I had entirely reassured them – a researcher pondering such existential questions could hardly be considered dangerous, they must have thought.

From there, events unfolded quickly. They explained to me that, yes, the Palace of Justice did indeed harbour one – if not several – secret passages leading to the outside, all of which opened into the sacred block, and more specifically, to this very place. These passages, they said, are alternately opened and sealed, depending on the era and the discretion of the gatekeepers.

The penultimate passage (the current one, said to be still in use, remains shrouded in secrecy) began at a hidden door in the lawyers' cloakroom. The gatekeeper was none other than the cloakroom attendant – a jovial and much-loved figure, known for lending robes to provincial trainees and discreetly delivering letters and messages to colleagues delayed by court proceedings. This compassionate man had a gift for recognising those broken by the judicial system: the overlooked victims of silent miscarriages of justice, crushed by institutional bureaucracy, the formalism of the law, or the merciless rigour of procedural deadlines.

Taking these lost souls under his protective wing, he quietly guided them toward the famous passage, sending them – without further proceedings – toward the alternative justice of the world below.

'At certain hours, it's bustling,' they told me. 'You'll see – every morning around nine, all sorts of people gather here: disoriented litigants just told their appeal hearing won't be scheduled for another three years; civil parties who feel their case has slipped entirely out of their hands, with all attention focused on the defendant; fathers falsely accused of sexual assault by their daughters – or rather, by their ex-wives. It's a small, marginalised world, left voiceless and without recourse by official justice.'

Over time, the estaminet's proprietor had become something of a specialist in resolving such cases, developing an uncanny knack for sorting them. 'The system is perfectly organised,' they explained. 'Each day of the week is reserved for a specific type of hearing. For example, today is Monday – the day of the Chamber of Trifles. The session doesn't begin until two this afternoon, but we can show you the room.'

And so my hosts led me into an adjoining chamber, surprisingly spacious given the narrowness of the building and the age of the neighbourhood. It resembled a café where the bar had been converted into a judge's bench, and the chairs arranged as if for a performance. On the wall hung a familiar emblem: an open eye within a triangle, framed by the Dutch inscription *God ziet mij. Hier straft men niet* – 'God sees me; here, no one is punished.'

Further along, a truly astonishing discovery: the *Just Judges* panel from Van Eyck's *Ghent Altarpiece*, stolen from Saint Bavo's Cathedral on 10 April 1934 and never recovered. There was no doubt – it was indeed the devout knights, come to adore the Mystic Lamb. And to think that for decades, every police force in the kingdom had been searching for this masterpiece!

Beyond that, a few illustrations by Schuiten and a modest library – I spotted a copy of *The Decameron* and Charles De Coster's *Ulenspiegel*. 'There was also some kind of holding cell attached to the courtroom,' they added. 'It doubles as one of the café's urinals,' Judge Bridoit chimed in, 'but as far as I can recall, no jury ever saw it used.'

When I returned to my table, yet another surprise awaited me. Seated there was a man in his fifties, elegant in appearance and eloquent in speech. I was introduced: Clamence, a former star of the Parisian bar. 'You'll enjoy him,' they said. 'The Parigot has quite the way with words.'

'What am I doing in Brussels?' he asked rhetorically. 'Let me tell you, my dear friend: I now practise as a judge-penitent. Please, sit down and share a beer with me, won't you? Yes, a judge-penitent. Let me explain: thirty years at the bar, I'd seen and heard it all – especially about myself. Drunk on success, I understood better than anyone the futility of it all. So, one day, I walked away from it all and began my public confession. Endless admissions, a self-exposure that's been ongoing for years. But in accusing myself, I hold up a mirror in which others see themselves. That's how I gained the ability to understand their stories, to handle their cases.'

'Do I judge them? Sometimes, but rarely. Most people just want to be heard, to be recognised as victims. Others accuse themselves, as I do. Still others denounce intolerable social injustices, and some simply wish to forgive and move on. Believe me, the scope is far broader than anything found in the legal codes. You'd be amazed, my dear friend, at the richness of our jurisprudence.'

'Now, while we wait for the waiter to bring our gueuzes, let me explain the procedures we offer here. Each day of the week, we hold a specialised hearing. Today is Monday, which means it's the Chamber of Trifles. You know, those tiny disputes that obsess people, the everyday grievances that make life unbearable but slip under the radar of the official justice system. You know the old saying: *De minimis non curat praetor*. Well, these cases – too insignificant for the dignity of the courts – form our bread and butter; a kind of calling card, if you will. You'd be surprised – we draw a full house every Monday.'

'Who makes up the bench? A few retirees from the neighbourhood, delighted to amuse themselves while doing something useful at the same time. Take this afternoon, for instance: we're hearing the case of a Greek man accusing his neighbour's dog of stealing a Sicilian cheese. Then we'll have to decide the custody of a cat following a messy divorce; the cat, when questioned, clearly expressed a desire to remain in the marital home. Later, we'll handle a rather amusing case: a château owner suing for noise disturbance caused by a partygoer who fell into his pond and was desperately crying for help. Finally, we'll hear the litany of people who want to change their names – today, for instance, a young woman named Dom who wishes to be called Fondu – who knows why? And what drives a man from Ougrée, with the very Belgian surname Bodson, to request a new name like Ben Ouazzou? Love? A desire for reverse integration? Believe me, sir, humanity never ceases to astonish. Most of these individuals first went to the official courts but were dismissed: inadmissible actions, lack of standing, statutes of limitation. So we give them a second chance – a recycling of discarded grievances.'

'And tomorrow?' I ventured, fully aware that I was only at the beginning of my discoveries.

'Tomorrow is Tuesday: the Court of Vengeances. Yes, precisely – vengeances. Don't give me that disapproving look, dear sir; you know perfectly well that, even if people can no longer take justice into their own hands, they dream of nothing else but settling scores. So we offer them the opportunity to resolve their grievances with minimal harm and at no cost: they present their complaint without contradiction and curse the author of their misfortune at their leisure – you can't imagine the relief these imprecations bring. Performative words, as you'd call them in your books: they send someone to hell and already picture that person burning in the flames of damnation. No sooner said than done.'

'In the most serious cases, we use some of Toone's old puppets: a few well-placed amulets, a spell or two cast, and the petitioner is relieved – the insult avenged, the debt settled, the slate wiped clean. If only you knew how many real-life tragedies we prevent each year! Not to mention the honourable employment it offers one Nieuwland, the grandson of the last executioner attached to Belgian justice, who would otherwise have no hope of continuing the family tradition since the abolition of the death penalty by the law of 10 July 1996.'

'And who are our clients? My, you are quite curious, it seems. But feel free to come and see for yourself; though discreet, our sessions are public. Wait, let me check the docket. Tomorrow, we have a Danish prince, rather hesitant – he claims to see ghosts and believes he has a mission to avenge. A tricky case; it'll occupy the entire morning.'

As noon approached and patrons began to fill the estaminet, my mentor led me to a back room.

'Come, I'll show you the hall reserved for Wednesday's sessions: the Chamber of Compulsive Litigants. It's the most heavily attended and often stretches late into the evening. You wouldn't believe the tenacity with which some people litigate. Look, the day after tomorrow, we'll be continuing a case involving two of my compatriots – yes, French nationals. We exercise a sort of universal jurisdiction here, a kind of asylum for judicial refugees who haven't found satisfaction in their own courts. The case? Chicaneau versus Pimbesche – I'd wager it's been going on for centuries.'

'The compulsive – or vexatious – litigants are so numerous that we accommodate several petitioners at once; it doesn't matter, since none of them listen to anyone. The most amusing part is that we have no difficulty finding lawyers and judges for them. Long after their retirement, many attorneys, magistrates, and prosecutors would give anything to go on filing briefs, making submissions, or issuing rulings. And the more some create procedural incidents, the more others demand further investigations, the more the judges postpone proceedings – the more our litigants delight in it. They'll still be pleading their case tomorrow.'

But already, Clamence was leading me into an adjacent room: much smaller, entirely covered in mirrors.

'And now, here we are in the Thursday hall: the Tribunal of Conscience. Here, there are no judges, no prosecutors, no clerks. Only mirrors and blank sheets of paper – a *mise en abyme* of the conscience of tortured litigants. You'd be surprised by the variety of cases, you know.'

'First, there are those tormented by the need to confess. Just last week, for instance, a Russian student arrived, confessing to the gratuitous murder of an old woman – "simply for the perfection of the act", he claimed. A perfect crime, no doubt, but the burden of it grew so heavy that the student eventually confessed everything to the investigating judge. You see, our justice system works both ways: sometimes we send a client back to the official courts. In our own way, we also provide a public service.'

'Then there are those who don't understand what has happened to them and come here to compose endless letters to their judges. At the moment, we have a doctor from Liège, sentenced to life for the murder of his mistress and released on parole pending a decision in cassation. Oh, he's not contesting the verdict – he's fully confessed. But he doesn't recognise himself in the portrait painted of him during the trial. So he's taken it upon himself to start over, meticulously laying everything out in a lengthy explanation addressed to the investigating judge.'

'You'll surely see him if you come on Thursday. As well as a curious character who's been coming here every Thursday for the past nine months: a Czech man, with a faint Yiddish accent, dressed in a threadbare black suit, his eyes blazing. He's very secretive but claims he was arrested by an "organisation" in his room at the boarding house where he was staying. Ever since, he's been desperate to confront a judge to finally learn the charges against him. "But that's a novel, sir!" the courthouse concierge told him. "Go on, write it down – it's bound to interest someone."'

'Even more remarkable: we also welcome judges who judge themselves. Don't laugh, dear sir – it's often tragic. For instance, there was a Greek judge investigating a tangled case of parricide and incest, who, in the end, realised that the double perpetrator was none other than himself. He gouged out his own eyes and set out on a journey, eventually ending up here one fine morning … And then – though this one's frankly comical, I'll admit – there was a German traffic court judge handling a case of attempted sexual assault on a young girl. She had bravely defended herself by smashing a jug over her attacker's head, who fled. When the judge opened the hearing with his own head bandaged, everyone understood – except for him, apparently …'

'But it's getting late, dear sir. I'm sure I've overstayed my welcome, and the lunch hour has already passed. Do come back tomorrow – we still have three more days to explore.'

∵

'Ah, you've come back! I was afraid I wouldn't see you again after all I shared with you yesterday,' Clamence exclaimed as I joined him at his table early the next morning, not without first ordering an espresso from the waiter. 'I hope I didn't completely dissuade you from your search to understand the purpose of law … At the very least, I hope I've suggested to you that there is law, and then there is *law*.'

'You've arrived at just the right time, for today, Friday, is the day of the Chamber of Complex Matters. Yes, cases that are too problematic, unsolvable by the laws currently in force. The tribunal is presided over by a certain David, whose wisdom works wonders.'

'Just listen to this: last week, two prostitutes from Rue de Laeken appeared before him. It so happens that both women gave birth at the same time, and since they shared a studio, they slept in the same room, each with her baby by her side. One night, one of the babies died. Did the mother of the deceased child switch her baby with the living one during the night, placing the dead infant next to her friend? No one knows. But by morning, the dispute erupted, with the mother of the living child demanding her baby back with great cries of anguish. How could such a case be resolved, dear sir? No witnesses, no proof, equal rights – it was one mother's word against the other's, and on top of it all, the word of a grieving mother against that of a courtesan.

'What do you think David decided? *Suum cuique tribuere*? To assign to each what is theirs? I see you have a sense of humour, but I doubt that would amuse these two mothers. No, you're not quite there. After hearing the parties, David rose and, most solemnly, declared: "Since your rights are equal, since the dead child cannot be brought back to life, and since the matter is undecidable, I order that Maître Nieuwland (you remember, the official from the Court of

Vengeances) be summoned, and that the living child be cut into two equal parts."'

'Stunned silence in the courtroom. And then, one of them says, "He will belong neither to me nor to you – yes, cut him in two," while the other screams, "No! Don't kill the living child! Give him to her!" She was, of course, the true mother. The first, lost in her grief and drowning in resentment, expressed a logic of death; the other, connected to her child's life, rose to a higher logic: better an injustice than death. This was precisely the reaction David had been expecting. The just solution, sir, was not found in the code but in the depths of that woman's soul. A woman who was able to transcend the mathematical equality of *lex talionis* (a death for a death, suffering for suffering, a child split into two equal parts) and rise to the logic of love, which defies calculation. The judge's absurd ruling (to cut the child in two as if it were an object or an animal carcass) provoked, in response, an irregular reaction (renouncing maternal rights in favour of an impostor) – but from this double illegality, the truth emerged. That, sir, is the kind of case we handle here.'

'But not all of them are so tragic,' my host continued. 'A few months ago, we dealt with a French case that my colleague Rabelais recorded in his minutes. I've retrieved them for you – listen. The record is titled: *How David Delivered a Just Judgment on a Controversy of Prodigious Obscurity and Difficulty, With Such Reason That His Ruling Won Admiration*. The controversy, which pitted two great lords, Monsieur de Baisecul and Messire de Humevesne, against each other, "raised legal points so complicated and difficult that to the Parlement court it was all Greek". On the King's orders, the four most learned parlements of France, eminent university professors from France and neighbouring countries, "along with a whole heap of other dusty old masters", spent forty-six weeks of hard labour but couldn't even bring the case to a procedural state. In desperation, they turned to the superhuman wisdom of Maître David, presiding over the Toone tribunal in Brussels, sending him the case files and trial records, which "nearly equalled the load of four hefty donkeys".'

'With his usual humour, our David began by asking whether, after so many years of litigation, the litigants were even still alive. Then the wise arbiter summoned the parties, convinced that their oral pleadings would spare him the task of sifting through a file cluttered with "foolish and unreasonable reasoning and the inept opinions of Accursius, Baldus, Bartolus, and other old dimwits ignorant of what is necessary to understand the law".'

'And so, our litigants launched into pleadings, one after the other, as interminable as they were incomprehensible, as if the original object of the dispute had long been forgotten. At the end of this exercise, David delivered his ruling, "determined to render justice to each without bias or consideration for anyone". What followed was a decision as absurd as it was convoluted, alternately giving each party what they sought. And so, in an extraordinary outcome never before seen, "both parties departed, equally satisfied with the judgment". The moral: absurdity begets absurdity – or, more positively: what David understood was that, far more than the material resolution of their grievance, what litigants often seek most is to be heard and recognised as rightful complainants.'

'And what do you make of that? Delightful, isn't it? I sense you're a bit sceptical this morning. You might say these are just isolated cases – exceptional affairs? Yes, perhaps. But isn't it the duty of a good judge to uncover the uniqueness of each case beneath the generality of the law? Doesn't every litigant have a personal story to tell? Or are we soon to entrust justice to computers – everyone treated the same; reduced to statistics, averages, and profiles; processed by algorithms? Justice as a Procrustean bed: cutting off what exceeds and stretching out what falls short to fit the mould. Have we forgotten that this was precisely the kind of justice meted out in Sodom and Gomorrah?'

'Yes, I know, I'm getting carried away. I can tell you're more inclined towards general causes and the big societal questions – so come back on Saturday, when the Tribunal of History holds its sessions. Intellectuals and activists of your kind preside there. Do you remember what we were taught at university? *De maximis non curat praetor* – the law does not concern itself with matters of great importance. Ah, how simple things seemed: one phrase (and in Latin, no less, which always sounds more authoritative – indisputable, as if it were an eternal truth); one phrase, and *voilà*: all politics dismissed, consciences appeased, and jurists left undisturbed. The *maxima* handed over to politics, the *minima* (remember?) relegated to the mediocrity of daily life, moral concerns entrusted to private reflection (or perhaps confessors), and social facts reserved for sociologists – leaving us in peace, working on polished (or perhaps "policed") objects, neatly clarified and encoded – all other things being equal. As if things could ever remain equal, and as if "elsewhere" could be easily distinguished from "here"! Oh, that dream of purity, making us so positive and efficient!'

'But history always reminds us, sir, and it has a way of disrupting our neat equations. Take tomorrow, for example: we're hearing the case of a large corporation flooding the planet with its genetically modified seeds and carcinogenic herbicides. Witnesses will testify from all over the world – experts, of course, but also farmers and local residents. When the stakes are so enormous, sir, it's the very categories of thought that must change. Here, we're forging a new kind of law: we're talking about responsibility for the future, ecocide as a crime, and the climate as a common good to be protected. The case is being brought by activist legal associations and citizen groups; it's being followed by university academics, who bring their students along in what they call "law clinics". It's an entire world reinventing itself, dear sir.'

'What about effectiveness? Symbolic, sir – and that's the most essential part. Symbolic legitimacy is the lever of the law, the engine of its transformations. When words begin to shift, everything else follows. Stripped of legitimacy, empires crumble in an instant, like structures devoured by termites.'

'But here I go again, getting carried away, when my new role as judge-penitent should inspire serenity. Come now, offer me one of those krieks this place is famous for. I'll drink it to your health and the success of your book.'

'Do we take Sundays off? No, quite the opposite – everyone gathers here; all the litigants of the week are invited around eleven o'clock. On Sundays, the Session of Graces and Pardons convenes, presided over by Father Vanderpiest, the priest of the Marolles. All the week's cases are reopened for those who wish it, and reconciliations are encouraged, modelled on the South African commissions. Afterwards, the owner treats everyone to a round.'

I was deep in thought about this general reconciliation when a stern-looking figure entered the estaminet, carrying himself with an air of authority and a magistrate's robe draped over his arm. The man sat at a nearby table, and I could have sworn it was the First President of the Court of Cassation ...

Non peut-être?[1]

Obiter Dictum

An attentive reader will have noticed that this text is presented as a *conte à clés* (a story with hidden references). Because good stories make good friends, I feel obliged to clarify the origins of my borrowings. The following inspirations can be recognised, in the order of their appearance in the text:

The hurried rabbit in the yellow waistcoat is, of course, none other than the one described by Lewis Carroll in *Alice's Adventures in Wonderland* (1865).

The judge who rolls dice to decide cases is a creation of Rabelais (*Le Tiers Livre*, 1552).

Clamence, the former Parisian barrister turned judge-penitent and receiver of the stolen painting *The Just Judges*, is a creation of Albert Camus, who recounts his confession in *La Chute* (*The Fall*, 1956).

1 In Brusseleir dialect, *non peut-être?* is an ironic rhetorical question meaning something like 'Absolutely!' or 'Of course it was!'—as if to say, 'You bet it was!'

The Greek, accusing his neighbour's dog of stealing a Sicilian cheese, is borrowed from Aristophanes (*The Wasps*, 422 BC).
The case of the plaintiff, complaining of nighttime noise caused by someone drowning beneath their window, was judged by the justice of the peace in Saint-Trond on 2 March 1871 (*Pandectes belges*, V° causes de justification, no. 278).
The examples of individuals requesting to change their surnames are cited by Paul Martens and are themselves drawn from the *Moniteur belge* (*Théories du droit et pensée juridique contemporaine*, Brussels: Larcier, 2003, p. 146).
Hamlet, of course, makes his appearance in the Court of Vengeances.
Chicaneau and Pimbesche, litigants in the Chamber of Compulsive Litigants, are the unforgettable creations of Racine (*Les Plaideurs*, 1668), themselves inspired by Aristophanes' *The Wasps*.
In the Tribunal of Conscience, the Russian student, tortured by his need to confess, is the protagonist of Dostoevsky's *Crime and Punishment* (1867). The physician, condemned for murdering his mistress, is none other than Dr. Alavoine, described by Georges Simenon (*Lettre à mon juge*, 1947). As for the discreet Czech man with a slight Yiddish accent, it is, of course, Joseph K., the self-portrait of Franz Kafka (*The Trial*, 1925).
The judges presiding over their own cases are, respectively, Oedipus (Sophocles, 430–420 BC) and the judge with a bandaged head – a creation of Heinrich von Kleist (*The Broken Jug*, 1808).
Finally, the case of the two prostitutes disputing the surviving child, heard in the Chamber of Complex Matters, is recounted in the Bible, in the First Book of Kings (I Kings 3:16–28), with the judgment rendered by King Solomon. The following intricate case is told by Rabelais and skilfully resolved by Pantagruel (*Pantagruel, Roy des Dipsodes*, in *Oeuvres complètes*, ed. G. Demerson, Paris, Seuil, 1973).

Fortuna Maris

> Fortuna maris: 'anything that may happen to a ship at sea: a leak, a collision, a fire, a grounding, or a violent storm. In the past, it also referred to pirates' (L. Le Cunff, *S.O.S. Atlantique,* Paris, Ed. A. Bonne, 1956, p. 75) – I would add that today, it could also refer to oil tankers flying flags of convenience.

⁚

Rescuers and Wreckers, Heroes and Predators

Since time immemorial, tales of shipwrecks and stranded vessels have evoked contrasting human responses: at times, they tell of wreckers who lit deceptive fires along the shore to lure in lost ships and plunder their wreckage; at others, of heroic rescuers who risked their lives to aid crews in distress. It seems this contrast still holds true today.

'Saint Bernards of the sea': such was the name once given to the rescuers of the islands of Molène and Ouessant, up until the mid-twentieth century. The *Nautical Instructions* state: 'To the southwest of Ouessant lies an archipelago of islands, a rocky plateau, and reefs that one would be unwise to approach without a pilot.' Given the adverse winds, violent currents, treacherous mists, and rocks lurking just beneath the surface, it is no wonder that this area has long been haunted by the spectre of shipwrecks. Known as the 'cemetery of ships,' the peril was summed up in Breton maritime tradition with a series of grim aphorisms: 'He who sees Molène sees his pain,' 'He who sees Ouessant sees his blood,' 'He who sees Sein sees his end.'

In this rugged corner of the world, the heroic saga of Breton rescuers was written. Crews and captains of lifeboats – launched down metal rails from the edges of ports – would plunge into the breakers at the first call of distress. Among them was Charles Masson, captain of the *Jean Charcot,* who was awarded the Legion of Honour for rescuing no fewer than forty-three ships of various nationalities.

 | DOI:10.1163/9789004737112_008

This great tradition, grounded in the harsh laws of the sea, was never in dispute.[1] It once justified the sacrifices of sailors who braved five- to six-metre swells in lifeboats equipped with nothing more than oars and a scrap of canvas. Later, it led to the establishment of a dense network of lighthouses, beacons, and buoys marking the hazards of this *finis terrae* – Le Four, La Jument, Armen, Créac'h, Les Pierres Noires ...

With progress, increased maritime traffic, and the growing tonnage of commercial vessels, the French government supported the creation of private towing and high-seas salvage companies – most notably the renowned *Compagnie des Abeilles*. These firms operated powerful tugboats for the time, with their engines kept permanently heated and their crews ready to mobilise at the first Mayday or S.O.S.

Brest still vividly remembers the epic tales of the Iroise Sea and its legendary captain, Louis Malbert, a former Cape Horner nicknamed 'the old torch-bearer,' who rescued more than 3,000 sailors from raging seas. Roger Vercel was inspired by him to write his celebrated 1935 novel, *Remorques*.

But the world of towing is not solely inhabited by legendary heroes; it is also, at times, the domain of the storm's mercenaries.

Lured by a legal framework that resembled a lottery – with the ship and its cargo as the stakes – tugboat captains often behaved like predators stalking their prey. Stationed in oceanic ports near the most treacherous waters, they were poised to spring into action at the first distress call. Foreign competition was fierce: the Dutch and Germans, in particular, deployed powerful vessels in Brest and Cherbourg. As early as the 1930s, the Hamburg-based Bugsier Reederei operated tugboats several knots faster than those of the Iroise.

Every S.O.S. sparked a race to the distressed ship – a rush of tugboats, a feeding frenzy of sea vultures around the wreck. To secure the job, some captains did not hesitate to falsify their positions or the time of their arrival on the scene. Even if they missed their prey and arrived second, they would remain close to the convoy, ready to act should the competitor's towline snap – a not uncommon occurrence. At other times, if they were assured of being the sole responder, the tugboat would deliberately take its time, heightening the sense of peril and driving up the price.

For their part, the captains of assisted ships were not beyond reproach. Once the danger had passed, some would downplay the services rendered, disputing the claim that they had ever been truly in distress. In the hushed offices of London's maritime arbitration courts, shipowners frequently argued

1 For a modern version of this epic, see the book by Jean Bulot, captain of the *Abeille Flandre*: *Remorqueurs de haute mer et de sauvetage* (Douarnenez: Éditions de l'Estran, 1985).

that their captain had merely requested a little help – a temporary tow to reach safety.

One particularly revealing episode, etched in memory, pushed this 'tugboat war' to a truly feverish pitch. On 5 January 1933, the *Atlantique*, a flagship of the French merchant navy, caught fire during a technical voyage – fortunately without passengers on board. Engulfed in flames, it was soon abandoned by its crew, 22 miles off Guernsey. As soon as the distress signal was received, a pack of tugboats sprang into action. Among them were French vessels, including the old *Iroise* and no fewer than four ships from the *Compagnie des Abeilles*. They were joined by three Dutch tugboats from Vlissingen and two German vessels, including the powerful *Seefalke*, boasting 4,000 horsepower. All raced toward the burning hulk, vying to secure their towlines. The first to attach a line would effectively stake a claim on the vessel – for even in flames, the wreck was still worth several million.

The newspapers of the time vividly captured the intensity of the struggle. In a chaotic chase, the tugboats cut one another off mere metres from the drifting liner, which was being battered by a rough sea. Whenever one tug succeeded in attaching its towline, another would charge across at full speed and sever it. At one point, the burning ship was being pulled in opposite directions, with two Dutch tugs straining at the bow and a French one hauling at the stern.

All rules seemed to be thrown overboard in this merciless contest. At one moment, the battle resembled an actual boarding operation: crew members climbed aboard the ship, hoisted their nation's flag amid swirling smoke, and tied a line to one of the ship's bollards. A French sailor was seriously injured while attempting to board, as his tug was slammed into the liner's hull by a rogue wave.

When calm finally returned and the wreck passed through the breakwaters of Cherbourg – still flanked by its swarm of tugboats – onlookers counted no fewer than fifteen severed towlines trailing along its sides: unmistakable evidence of the fierce battle fought in the preceding hours.

A detour into the legal framework governing towing and salvage at sea is essential to understand the ferocity of this competition. First, it is important to recall that the principle of free navigation has long been established as the supreme rule of maritime law. Rooted both in the freedom evoked by the open sea (*mare liberum*) and in the liberty of commerce and movement historically embodied by mariners – and epitomised by the modernity of the English nation – this principle significantly limited the interventions of coastal states and port nations.

This doctrine was further reinforced by the age-old trust placed in the figure of the captain, regarded as the supreme authority on board, second only to

God. In this context, shipwrecks, though numerous, were considered the result of natural fate or individual misfortune. They might take on a tragic dimension, but they were never seen as industrial catastrophes attributable to systemic failure. If a ship encountered damage or faced the threat of wreckage, the matter remained private – entirely dependent on the captain's distress call and the private contract he voluntarily entered into, following negotiations if necessary.

Once again, the coastal state had no grounds to intervene. The only concerns were the ship and its cargo, with no fears of broader harm, such as environmental pollution. Consequently, it is not surprising that, until recently, maritime law has remained predominantly a domain of private law concerning ships (their crews and owners), and only minimally a matter of public law for collective safety.

Let us return to the question of assistance and salvage.[2] Certainly, when human lives were at stake, the duty to provide aid was absolute. This undisputed rule, deeply rooted in seafaring tradition, has taken legal form in modern times: as an enforceable obligation for private individuals and as a public service mission for the relevant authorities.

However, beyond this fundamental principle – and even though it is not always easy to distinguish the two in practice – assistance provided to a vessel in distress with the aim of salvaging the ship and its cargo operated according to an entirely different logic, whose effects we have already seen. This belonged to the domain of private contractual negotiation, which in some cases closely resembled a speculative gamble. As *The Times* famously remarked in reference to the wreck of the *Amoco Cadiz* (a case we are about to examine), it was 'a jungle where anything goes.'[3]

In fairness to towing companies, it is worth noting that, in accordance with maritime tradition, the owner of a distressed vessel could absolve themselves – even of personal fault – by abandoning the wreck. The ship's value was isolated within its estate, a *fortuna maris*, left to fate and spun on the roulette wheel of a casino.

2 J. Dutheil de la Rochère, 'Les réactions de L'O.M.C.I. au désastre de l'Amoco Cadiz', *Annuaire français de droit international*, 24 (1978), p. 755; F. Bonnieux and P. Roinelle, *Catastrophe écologique et dommages économiques* (Paris: INRA and Economica, 1991); R. Rodière and M. Rémond-Gouilloud, *La mer, droit des hommes ou proie des États ?* (Paris: Éditions Pedone, 1980); N. Reuter, *La notion d'assistance en mer* (Paris: Librairies techniques, 1975), p. 248.

3 M. Baily, *The Times*, 22 June 1978: 'Amoco Cadiz, How Private Is a Public Disaster: The World of Salvage Is a Jungle'.

London insurers brought some order to these practices by popularising a standardised assistance contract: the now-famous Lloyd's Standard Form of Salvage Agreement, *No Cure, No Pay* (universally known as the Lloyd's Open Form). In practice, this agreement is often concluded informally – understandably – via verbal exchanges, signals, or radio communication. The salvor undertakes to make every effort to assist and save the ship requesting help, with the understanding that remuneration is conditional on success. If the effort fails, no payment is made; if successful, the amount is determined later, either amicably or by judges or arbitrators in London.

Payment is calculated based on various factors: the value of the salvaged goods, the risks taken, the challenges encountered, the expenses incurred, and the professional competence of the salvor (after all, maintaining a fleet of powerful tugs and paying their crews entails considerable costs). The inherent risk of the operation is offset by the often very favourable remuneration, typically calculated as a proportion of the cargo's value saved from destruction.

One detail particularly relevant to the case at hand: it is recognised that the captain of a distressed vessel may refuse an offer of assistance (in order to guard against opportunistic scavengers), but such refusal must later be judged 'reasonable' in light of the circumstances by the relevant court or arbitration panel.

The alternative to the Lloyd's Open Form is a standard towing contract, such as those used for routine towage of ships destined for scrapping. This type of agreement is significantly less costly, as it involves far less uncertainty: remuneration is calculated on a flat-rate basis, proportional to the number of days worked. As we shall see, this distinction between assistance and towage lay at the heart of the negotiations that proved so costly in the case of the *Amoco Cadiz*.

In any case, such agreements – regardless of their nature – are often concluded under exceptionally difficult conditions. In such situations, the parties involved do not always have a clear understanding of the actual circumstances (how many captains in distress off the coast of Brittany even had detailed charts of the area?). Both sides may be tempted to downplay or exaggerate the services actually rendered. Once again, it is up to judges or arbitrators to determine, after the fact, whether the agreement constituted exceptional assistance or merely routine towing. They must assess whether, given the weather, currents, severity of the damage, and proximity to the coast or reefs, the vessel was indeed in real danger of being lost.

This, then, was the legal framework in place and the state of maritime practices on the eve of the events we are about to recount.

15 March 1978

19.15 – Pasquale Bardari, captain of the *Amoco Cadiz*, steps onto the bridge. In his forties and of commanding presence, Bardari specialises in managing supertankers. However, the subsequent investigation will reveal that he does not hold a secondary education diploma. He departed the Persian Gulf five weeks earlier, on 7 February, with full tanks bound for Rotterdam. An intermediate stop was planned at Lyme Bay, on England's southern coast, to partially offload his cargo in order to accommodate the shallow waters of the English Channel, which he is scheduled to enter the following day.

The *Amoco Cadiz*, built four years earlier by a Spanish shipyard, is a supertanker designed to transport crude oil from the Persian Gulf to Europe. Measuring 334 metres in length, weighing 109,000 tonnes, and with a carrying capacity of 233,000 tonnes, it is equivalent in length to the Eiffel Tower and thirty times its weight. Fully loaded, it holds the equivalent of 9,000 tanker trucks.

The ship's legal status is complex. Flying the Liberian flag (a flag of convenience), it is formally owned by Amoco Transport Co., a Liberian-registered company headquartered in Bermuda. However, the vessel is managed by Amoco International Oil Co. (AIOC), based in Chicago. In reality, as American courts will later establish, both companies are entirely dependent on another American entity: Standard Oil Co. This parent company, along with its subsidiaries, forms a globally integrated oil and chemical conglomerate.[4]

It should also be noted that the cargo of heavy fuel oil on board is owned by the Dutch company Shell. Standard Oil had urgently commissioned the *Amoco Cadiz* and three sister ships from a Spanish shipyard in 1974, after the closure of the Suez Canal to such vessels threatened significant financial losses. These massive ships were designed to navigate around Africa at maximum capacity.

On the evening of 15 March, Captain Bardari was deeply troubled: issues with the steering system were worsening, and the barometer was plummeting – just as the ship was about to enter the treacherous waters of the Ushant traffic separation scheme. In fact, oil leaks in the steering mechanism had

4 In an interview, Corinne Lepage – lawyer involved in the *Amoco Cadiz* trial and future French Minister of the Environment – stated: 'At the time of the *Amoco Cadiz*, oil companies owned their fleets. They had set up shell companies that were the formal owners of the ships. They believed that in the event of an accident, the shell company would be held liable. After the U.S. court ruling, they sold off their fleets and lobbied to reduce freight costs. To achieve this, they resorted to poorly maintained ships and underpaid crews. The *Erika* disaster was the result of this transformation in oil transport.'

appeared within hours of departure. As later investigations would reveal, Bardari had reported the issue to Chicago headquarters as early as 7 February, but the response was dismissive: there was no time for a detour, and a makeshift repair could be made during the crossing.

Now, the rudder had already stopped responding twice. As a precaution, the crew lit the two stacked red lights signalling that the ship was 'not under command.' It was 19.30, and they were roughly near Île d'Yeu – at least, according to the captain of *Le Basque*, a French Navy escort vessel, who reported encountering 'a' non-manoeuvrable tanker in the area that evening. When contacted via VHF, the tanker claimed that everything was under control. While conclusive proof that the vessel in question was the *Amoco Cadiz* was never established, the circumstantial evidence remains damning.

19.50 – Jean Le Garrec, a retired fisherman from Portsall, a small port in north-western Finistère, prepares for his evening walk. The weather is windy and bleak, but nothing would make him miss his daily rendezvous with the ocean. Since hanging up his gear, he describes himself as a forager, a shoreline fisherman, and a coastal wanderer. Tonight, however, he knows he will not find any abalones along the long rocky causeways – the sea is far too rough.

Nevertheless, the same oceanic intoxication takes hold of him, his lungs filled with salty marine air and his eyes fixed on the horizon of his beloved Iroise Sea, whose every rock he knows by heart.

20.05 – Jacqueline Arzel, wife of the mayor of Ploudalmézeau, brings her painting supplies down from the attic. A lover of Brittany's landscapes, she delights in the arrival of spring. Tomorrow, she plans to set up her easel above the cliffs, and she is already thinking about the tonal gradients the stormy skies will inspire.

20.20 – Hartmut Weinert, captain of the German tugboat *Pacific*, based in Brest, reviews his plans with his second officer. After a much-needed overhaul following the winter storms, the *Pacific* – a modern tugboat with 10,000 horsepower and a speed of 15.5 knots – has received a towing assignment in the English Channel for the following morning, dispatched by its parent company, Bugsier Reederei, which we have already encountered. An experienced sailor with several rescues to his name, Weinert is eager to return to sea.

22.00 – Yann Le Goff, a professor of maritime law at the University of Brest, revises his lecture notes for the following day. From the window of his home in Porspoder, perched on the cliffs, he mentally counts the five white flashes of Le Four Lighthouse, intermittently obscured by drizzle and sea spray. Tomorrow's lecture is dedicated to maritime assistance – his favourite of the year. After explaining the classic principles (freedom of the seas, trust in the captain's wisdom, and the private nature of assistance agreements), he plans to argue that these rules are no longer adequate for addressing industrial risks, particularly those posed by hydrocarbon transport.

He will revisit the circumstances of the *Torrey Canyon* disaster on 18 March 1967, off the Isles of Scilly: westerly winds pushed 117,000 tonnes of oil from its ruptured tanks onto the Breton coast, causing the region's first major oil spill. On 24 January 1976, barely two years ago, it was the turn of the *Olympic Bravery*, a 275,000-tonne tanker, to run aground on the northern coast of Ushant: disabled by mechanical failure and driven by a westerly force 8 wind, the vessel ran aground without ever requesting assistance from the French authorities.

These repeated shipwrecks and their catastrophic consequences for the region clearly demonstrate the urgent need for a radical overhaul of prevailing principles. As he intends to explain, two landmark Conventions were negotiated in Brussels following the *Torrey Canyon* disaster. The first, dated 29 November 1969, granted states the unprecedented ability to intervene – without the captain's request or agreement, and even beyond territorial waters – when faced with a grave and imminent danger of pollution from hydrocarbons. The second Convention, also dated 29 November 1969, introduced the principle of strict liability (without fault) for the owners of oil tankers transporting hydrocarbons, and made insurance coverage for such transport mandatory, albeit capped at a maximum amount.

Professor Le Goff anticipated his students' interest in this part of the lecture. Here, the law could – at least in certain cases – align with social movements and offer innovative solutions. Yes, no doubt ... on paper, in the gilded halls where such texts were negotiated.

However, the professor, seasoned in practical matters, foresaw the limitations of these instruments. Should he enumerate them, at the risk of dampening the enthusiasm of these budding jurists? One, two, three white flashes ... the fourth and fifth were swallowed by the thickening drizzle. But no fear – the resilient lighthouse had weathered worse over the past century.

Yes, thought Le Goff, the students deserved the truth. As laudable as these Conventions were, they fell far short of addressing the problem in its entirety.[5] What were the limitations? He would pose the question to his students, hoping to spark their imagination and critical thinking. Surely one of them, better informed, would point out that in the *Torrey Canyon* case, the Brussels Convention did not apply because the spilled oil came not from the cargo tanks,

5 M. Remond-Gouilloud, 'Leçons d'un naufrage. À propos de l'indemnisation des victimes de l'Amoco Cadiz', in *Recueil Dalloz-Sirey*, 1979, Chron. xx, pp. 133 ff.

but from the fuel tanks – a scenario not covered by the text. Another might recall the recent *Boehlen* tragedy in November 1976, when a ship also ran aground on the Breton coast. The clean-up costs, amounting to 150 million francs, could not be recovered, as the ship flew the East German flag – a state not party to the Convention.

The jurist also reflected privately that, if damage occurred outside territorial waters but in a fertile fishing zone frequented by French fishermen, the Convention would be of no help. (At that time, he could not have foreseen that such an event would soon occur in April 1979, when the Liberian tanker *Gino* would spill 42,000 tonnes of bituminous oil in a rich fishing area off Ushant.)

It was now midnight – the hour of the brave. Le Goff was certain the lecture would go well, as he went to bed with his mind filled with storms, lighthouses, and tugboats.

16 March

As the *Amoco Cadiz* sailed through very rough seas, 7.5 miles off Ouessant, the helmsman alerted the officer on watch: the rudder was no longer responding. It was 9.45 a.m. A minute later, the engine room called the bridge – the steering gear was completely out of order.

Later, an Italian sailor would tell the investigating judge: 'The oil leak was getting worse; I tried to stop it, but at some point, a part gave way, and a jet of oil threw me two metres back. We shut down the first oil pump and started the second one. But the circuit was single-path, and all the oil drained out.'

Thus, the giant oil tanker was left without steering, skirting the upward traffic lane near Ouessant, just a few cables from the reefs, with a violent westerly wind driving it inexorably toward the coast. Captain Bardari, alerted in turn, decided to send a safety message marked TTT on 500 kHz: 'Am non-manoeuvrable, keep clear' – a relatively mundane message, representing the first level in the codified scale of maritime incidents.

Bardari then decided to call his bosses in Chicago – Chicago being the actual headquarters of Standard Oil, unlike Bermuda, the nominal headquarters of his official shipowner, Amoco Transport. But due to the time difference, he was only able to reach the on-duty intern, who recommended contacting the company's European representative in Genoa. The intern promised, however, to inform the company's lawyer, Mr Philips.

Meanwhile, the Genoa office remained unresponsive, and the situation worsened.

Finally, Bardari managed to reach the lawyer in Chicago:

'What, those rudder issues again?'

'This time it's serious. The rudder is stuck to port, and the storm is driving us toward the coast.'

'Listen, every day of delay costs us $27,000; tomorrow, at Lyme Bay, we'll send a team of technicians.'

'But I'm telling you, I'm no longer manoeuvrable; I need tugboats.'

'Fine, but be very careful with the terms you use in your messages; never speak of distress, only of towing. Make sure to say that you're working on fixing the breakdown. Watch out for those wrecking companies lurking in the narrow waters of the Channel' – he had said *naufrageurs*, literally 'wreckers' – 'and also, avoid involving the French public services at all costs; theoretically, under the new Brussels Convention, they could take charge of you even without your request. Good luck!'

'Easy for him to say,' Bardari must have thought, sipping coffee in a plush Chicago office.

Nonetheless, he had his authorisation. And just in time: under the combined effect of the current and the wind, the *Amoco* had been turned broadside to the waves and was drifting straight towards the coast. This time, an emergency message, coded XXX, was sent at 11.20 a.m.: the tanker was requesting the assistance of a tugboat.

Luckily, the nearest tugboat was just thirteen miles away. We've already met her – the *Pacific*, from the German company Bugsier, under the command of Captain Weinert. Having only just set out northward, he diverted course within minutes of receiving the call. At the time, only one French tugboat was available: the *Malabar*, a French Navy vessel. But it was stationed much further away and, with just 4,600 horsepower, lacked the strength to tow a supertanker.

Eight minutes later, Commander Weinert made his first contact with the *Amoco*. Reassuringly, he announced that he would arrive at the site within forty minutes. As an experienced professional, Weinert began assessing the risk and the nature of the manoeuvre he was about to undertake – no easy task in any case. What was the tanker's tonnage? Was it fully loaded or in ballast? What was the nature of the breakdown? Were the engines still operational?

'Two hundred and twenty-three thousand tonnes of crude oil? No tug in the world has ever towed a non-manoeuvring tanker this heavily loaded and in such conditions,' he remarked (the weather forecast predicted gusts of force 8 to 10 for the afternoon). 'Under these circumstances, I am proceeding on the basis of the Lloyd's Open Form; you are in a state of distress.'

Bardari, whose English is limited, struggles to understand fully; communication is further hampered by the worsening weather. He asks Weinert to hold on while he consults Chicago. Meanwhile, the *Pacific* has already contacted its headquarters in Hamburg.

'Forget the captain's hesitations,' comes the directive. 'Get your towline on board – the fish is hooked. Emphasise the *no cure, no pay* clause in all your messages, and forward them to the French station at Le Conquet to formalise it. Based on your report, the *Amoco* is objectively in distress. It's likely your 10,000 horsepower won't be enough; we're sending the *Simson,* currently off the coast of Cherbourg. With its 16,000 horsepower, you should be able to pull her out.'

At 12.08 p.m., visual contact is established between the two vessels – or rather, the *Pacific* makes out the silhouette of the tanker amidst the swells. Listing heavily to port, the *Amoco* is caught broadside by the waves.

At this point, Weinert again asks Bardari whether he accepts the Lloyd's Open Form agreement. Bardari hesitates, merely providing the contact details for his company in Chicago. 'I am just the captain,' he says. 'The boss is in Chicago' – a phrase he will later repeat word for word to the French investigating judge. 'I am not in distress,' he adds. 'Throw me your towline, straighten me up, and tow me to Lyme Bay, where I am expected tomorrow.'

Weinert cannot believe his ears, but there is no time for debate. The northwesterly wind is intensifying, and the breakers are just a few miles away. He leaves the radio room and heads to the aft deck to take charge of the operation.

The manoeuvre requires the *Pacific* to pass within thirty to forty metres of the tanker's stern and use a line-throwing gun to shoot over a messenger line. Once aboard, this will allow the crew to haul up the heavy metal towline – over fifteen tonnes of cable.

At 1.31 p.m., the towline is finally secured to the *Amoco*'s bow. The *Pacific* begins to pull slowly, releasing nine hundred metres of cable to absorb the violent shocks from the vessels' rolling and pitching. At this point, the tug is operating at 80 per cent of its engine capacity, vibrating from keel to mast under the strain.

But it quickly becomes clear that the *Pacific*, despite its best efforts, cannot stop the drift. The yawing of the two ships disrupts the convoy's alignment, placing enormous stress on the towline. Gradually, both vessels continue to drift inexorably toward the rocky coast.

Commander Weinert, for his part, has no illusions. He knows full well that he will never be able to tow such a heavily laden tanker. His hope is to shift the massive ship by a few dozen degrees – just enough to bring it into a hove-to position, bow facing into the waves. From there, he plans to hold steady and wait out the storm until the arrival of the *Simson*.

Meanwhile, Bardari still clings to the belief that the original plan can be salvaged, convinced they can reach the English coast for repairs. Throughout the negotiations, there are surprisingly few direct communications between the two captains. Bardari seems to prioritise his contacts with Chicago, while both men act largely according to their own interpretations of the unfolding crisis.

Had the tanker supported the manoeuvre with its engines, it might have been possible to execute the turn to starboard. But by late afternoon, Weinert still does not even know whether the *Amoco*'s engines are operational.

One fact, however, is indisputable: at no point during the entire operation were the French authorities informed of the seriousness of the situation – let alone asked for assistance. Everything remained a matter solely between the crews on the scene and, beyond them, a private contract between their respective employers. The prevailing principle remained the same: trust in the captain's judgement as the sole arbiter of the vessel's fate.

At 2.35 p.m., as Weinert became more insistent, Bardari issued yet another refusal to accept the Lloyd's Open Form contract. Later, the Italian captain would even claim that Weinert had acted threateningly – allegedly changing the nature of the agreement (from towing to salvage assistance) and warning that he would cease pulling unless his terms were accepted. In reality, as an experienced operator, Weinert occasionally reduced speed to relieve the immense strain on the towline, which was under severe tension due to the tanker's erratic movements.

When contacted by radio in Hamburg, the manager of the Bugsier Reederei company lost his temper: 'I don't care about that damned Yankee's hesitations (*dieser bastard Yankee*). You've been towing him for an hour now. The Italian captain has tacitly accepted the contract. He can keep claiming it's not salvage assistance, but the arbitrators will obviously rule that he was objectively in distress. Hold on as long as possible; the *Simson* should reach you around 11 p.m.'

Following yet another proposal for the LOF contract, Bardari – who still hadn't received approval from the American shipowner – responded with an emphatic refusal. Radio recordings presented at trial revealed that at 3.15 p.m., Bardari repeated 'no' three times: 'No, no, and no.'

Meanwhile, Weinert formalised his position by sending a message via Radio-Conquet: 'I confirm that services are being provided under the terms of the LOF salvage contract, *no cure, no pay*.'

It was not until 4.00 p.m. that Bardari finally faced the inevitable and accepted the convention. At the same time, he informed the *Pacific* that the ship's engines were still operational. Could genuine cooperation now be established between the two vessels? That would depend on whether the circumstances still allowed it.

By then, however, conditions had further deteriorated. The north-westerly wind had risen to force 9, and the waves were reaching heights of at least eight metres. Driven by the storm, streaks of foam stretched across the racing sea, and white water extended as far as the eye could see. The crashing rollers were relentless, pounding the *Pacific* with deafening force. Visibility had dropped significantly, and in the fierce squalls, the two ships lost sight of each other intermittently.

At 4.18 p.m., the steel towline snapped abruptly. Suddenly released, the tug lurched violently upward on a wave. Everything would have to start over – meanwhile, the coastline was drawing ever nearer, and the tidal current was about to reverse. Bardari decided to activate the ship's engines and attempt reverse thrust, despite the rudder being jammed. Weinert returned to the aft deck to oversee the delicate operation of retrieving the hundreds of metres of cable.

The working conditions had become nightmarish. On the aft deck, the crew was waist-deep in water. Despite their professionalism – adhering to the old adage, 'one hand for yourself, one hand for the shipowner' – they were repeatedly thrown against winches and other equipment cluttering the deck. A fifty-metre nylon line was swept away by a rogue wave, and two injured crew members were rendered unfit for duty. In the intensifying storm, it was a cacophony of chaos: the howling wind, the groaning of the towline, the creaking of attachment points, and the deafening crash of seawater pounding the deck.

By 6.50 p.m., a new attempt at towing had begun. This time, Weinert was determined to hook onto the *Amoco* from the stern, hoping to pull the ship away from the shore as quickly as possible without attempting to turn it. However, once again, the two captains failed to understand each other. Bardari insisted on towing from the bow.

'Out of the question,' Weinert retorted. 'I've already snapped one towline. The attempt to turn the ship from the bow failed, and we need to try something else. Use your engines to assist me once the cable is secured. We must act quickly; the current grows stronger by the hour.'

But the manoeuvre had become even more perilous. As the two ships approached the coast, the depth had decreased to thirty metres, and waves were breaking continuously. Keeping the vessels side by side long enough to launch the towline was as dangerous as it was difficult. Positioned on the starboard aft of the oil tanker's immense hull, with the swell and wind striking directly, the *Pacific* was in a precarious position, taking enormous risks. It was only on the fifth attempt that the line was finally seized by the *Amoco*'s crew, allowing the tow cable to be hauled to the tanker's stern.

This point, too, would later be contested during the trial: Weinert accused the Italian crew of remaining under shelter for too long and failing to make the necessary effort to ensure the manoeuvre's success.

For the second time that day, towing was underway – but precious hours had been lost, and the inevitable outcome loomed ever closer. At 7.56 p.m., the first visual contact with the coastline was made. The assistant commander of the Portsall lifeboat phoned Radio-Conquet to report seeing 'a light about two miles from Portsall.'

Two miles – far too close to shore; a vessel of such tonnage had no business in waters so bristling with rocks.

Eight minutes later, Bardari made a desperate attempt: he dropped the anchor in the hope of slowing the drift, letting out 240 metres of chain. But nothing seemed to go right on this fateful day. Under the weight of the chain and the force of the crashing waves, the windlass was torn from the deck, rendering the anchor useless.

At 9.05 p.m., the tanker – drawing 19.8 metres when fully loaded – struck the seabed for the first time. Five minutes later, radio contact was lost. Half an hour after that, the ship struck again and came to a complete stop. The first distress flares were launched, and oil began to spill from the ruptured tanks. The spill had begun. An hour later, the gendarmerie in Ploudalmézeau (the commune of Portsall) reported a strong smell of petroleum.

Despite the dreadful weather, Jean Le Garrec had donned his oilskin and set out on his daily walk. The storm had cast driftwood and heaps of seaweed far beyond the shoreline. Suddenly, the seasoned sailor's ear caught an unusual sound amid the howling gusts – a sinister scraping noise, the death rattle of a monster caught in a trap. Out at sea, a few cable lengths away, he glimpsed the lights of an oil tanker, its twisted carcass resembling a hideous Behemoth. Soon, illuminated by the *Pacific*'s floodlights, the scene unfolded in all its horrific clarity: the ominous sounds of metal ripping apart left no doubt about what was to come, and already the spray crashing against the ship's ruptured flanks glistened with oil.

The *Pacific* made one last desperate attempt to refloat the tanker, pulling with all the power of its engines, but the towline snapped again within minutes. Through binoculars, Weinert saw the entire Italian crew huddled together on the bridge and resigned himself to requesting a helicopter evacuation.

Meanwhile, the lifeboat from Aber Wrac'h, which had departed an hour earlier, arrived on the scene – but the crashing waves made any approach impossible. The *Simson* had also reached the area, soon joined by the *Malabar*, but the two tugs, now powerless, could do nothing but bear witness to the monster's death throes. The enormous wreck of the tanker now faced the coast, rising like a monstrous middle finger. Pounded by the waves, its aft castle was stained with oil up to the bridge, the aftermath of a vile, drunken debauchery.

On the morning of 18 March, Brittany awoke with a collective hangover – poisoned by crude oil, orphaned, defiled, and violated. Within days, 220,000 tonnes of Saudi crude oil, along with the tanker's 3,000 tonnes of fuel oil, had spread across the Finistère coast. Four hundred kilometres of beaches were fouled, from Brest to Saint-Brieuc; tens of thousands of oil-covered birds perished, and the region's oyster-farming businesses were ruined. The basest, most abject force had triumphed over the most sublime, leaving behind an immense sense of vertigo. People felt personally violated, stripped of their dignity, drowning in sadness and shame – as if after an assault.

Jacqueline Arzel, nauseated by the stench of crude oil, hurried toward the shore, just a few dozen metres from her house. Before she could grasp the full extent of the disaster, what struck her was the silence: the roar of the sea had gone quiet, and the cries of the gulls had ceased. Then she saw it – and understood. Black waves, too heavy to break, rolled ashore in a final, stifled, viscous sigh. A leaden shroud covered the sea, choking every sound. As far as the eye could see, the rocks were stained black with oil. Everything was black and viscous: the sand, the mud, the pebbles, the rocks, the seaweed, and the grass beds. Brittany was draped in mourning, its coastline fringed with black – like an enormous funeral notice addressed to the entire world.

Jacqueline Arzel would not be setting up her easel on the clifftop.

At seven o'clock, the ringing of the telephone jolted Professor Le Goff from his sleep. It was the on-duty journalist from *Ouest France*, informing him of the wreck of a Liberian tanker off the coast of Portsall. They sought an immediate legal opinion: would the polluters pay this time?

Amoco Cadiz: La Colère Noire (*Amoco Cadiz: The Black Rage*), proclaimed *Le Marin*. This time, they wouldn't let it slide. This time, they wouldn't settle for empty promises from Paris or orders from the prefect. (After the *Torrey Canyon* spill, the Interior Minister had still spoken of a 'natural disaster.') This time, the Bretons would mobilise and demand justice.

But for now, the immediate priority was to confront the catastrophe, to erase this unbearable sight, to believe it was still possible. Alphonse Arzel, mayor of Ploudalmézeau and a farmer by trade, rallied his fellow farmers, now united with the seafarers: they would be the first to wade into the mire, sucking up oil with their slurry tanks.

Then came the volunteers – from Brittany, from across France, even from abroad: thousands of them, equipped only with shovels and buckets. A veritable army in yellow raincoats, working tirelessly with every outgoing tide. 'It was like trying to empty the ocean with a teaspoon.'

Between 23 March and the end of June, no fewer than 550,000 workdays were logged, with an average of 3,000 to 4,000 people – volunteers, farmers, municipal workers, and soldiers. At the entrance to the Perros-Guirec town hall, a sign read: 'We are all oil-covered birds.'

During those same days, divers commissioned by the investigating magistrate in Brest discovered a brand-new spare part in the *Amoco*'s steering gear room: a rubber O-ring. It was the very part that could have prevented the oil leak – had anyone taken the time to install it.

The Grand Game of *Monopoily*

What collective meaning could all this have? What was happening to France, its navy, and its coastline? To find out, elected officials mobilised – most notably the Senate, which established an investigative commission. Within a few months, the commission produced a remarkable report. A careful reading of the events evokes the idea of a strange board game we shall call *Monopoily*.

The game consists of transporting, by sea, the largest possible quantity of oil from one point on the globe to another, in the shortest possible time and at the lowest possible cost. Naturally, the game includes numerous pitfalls and dangers: storms, underwater reefs, pirates, strong currents, breakdowns, fires, icebergs, submerged mines ... Before starting, players must prove their qualifications, certified through diplomas and licences; as for the ships, they must meet navigability standards, regularly inspected by specialised organisations.

Every ship must fly a flag – that is, it must hold the nationality of a state with which it has a genuine connection, and which, in turn, must be capable of exercising effective control, ensuring safety, technical compliance, and social standards over its vessels and their crews. Multilateral conventions are regularly negotiated among states to refine these meticulous rules and adapt them as needed. For instance, new regulations redefine the rights of coastal and port states in relation to flag states, aiming to better guarantee safety. Similarly, in updated versions of *Monopoily*, additional conventions improve compensation for third parties harmed by maritime disasters.

Such, at least, is the theory, clearly laid out in the game's instructions. And indeed, there are some players who follow the rules. However, truth compels us to admit that, in reality, the game often takes quite a different turn.

First, most of these rules are scarcely enforced – or, when they are, the penalties imposed tend to be far lower than the profits gained by breaking them. Moreover, the state authorities or private organisations responsible for inspections are neither numerous, well-equipped, nor particularly motivated. Under such conditions, it is hardly surprising that infractions tend to be the rule rather than the exception.

What's more, *Monopoily* has the peculiar distinction of including a large number of players who feel no obligation to abide by the rules at all. They are easily identified by the flags of convenience they fly, indicating their affiliation with a so-called pirate state. Such states demand almost no taxes, require no specific certifications for ship officers, conduct minimal inspections of seaworthiness, or delegate such responsibilities to equally accommodating third parties. These states also show little concern for the working conditions of crews, who are often hired for a single voyage and paid abysmally low wages.

It should also be noted that these players have little fear of accidents. They are often poorly insured, their liability capped at very low levels. Should one of their ships cause major damage, the vessel can simply be abandoned to creditors as partial compensation for the harm caused. Each ship is typically owned by a separate legal entity – a practice known as single-ship ownership.

Under such conditions, it is hardly surprising that the fleets of flag-of-convenience states continue to expand. Even regular players eventually feel tempted to join their ranks, as competing with such heavily advantaged operators becomes increasingly untenable.

Such was the strange board game French senators were uncovering – astonished and outraged. Unfamiliar language began to appear in the writings of these honourable representatives of the people: 'To relatively precise and binding legal standards corresponds a situation where, too often, the pursuit of maximum profit leads to anarchy and, ultimately, to the catastrophes we know.'[6]

The figures they uncovered were telling: while the volume of oil transported by sea had increased sixteenfold in forty years (from 1938 to 1977), and the carrying capacity of tankers had grown tenfold in just two decades, one in

6 French Senate, *Report of 23 June 1978*, no. 486, p. 142.

three ships was now sailing under a flag of convenience – primarily those of Liberia, Panama, and Cyprus.

Was it surprising, then, that compared to the average loss rate of the seven major European maritime nations in 1976, Liberia's rate was nineteen times higher, Panama's fifty-four times, and Cyprus' ninety-seven times? The senators had little choice but to draw the logical conclusion: 'Flag-of-convenience fleets pose serious dangers to the collective good and threaten the future of traditional fleets.' They also noted: 'Even in the case of recent ships, there is no regulation preventing certain temptations. Answerable only to his owner, a captain may be tempted to delay a safety-related decision that, by slowing the journey, would reduce the profitability of the transport.'[7]

But the revelations for the lawmakers were not over yet. One might well ask how relatively modest players like Cyprus or Liberia had managed to outplay the most powerful maritime nations. The case of the *Amoco Cadiz* provided the answer: the senators discovered that the powerful players – the great traditional maritime nations – had entered into agreements with the stowaways of the global shipping trade. These consortiums allowed them to transfer their operating profits to offshore accounts, thereby exploiting differences in tax systems to their advantage.

Thus, it became clear that what had seemed the most absurd of games was, in fact, perfectly rational – and was attracting an ever-growing number of participants.

And so it was sworn: never again! French negotiators at forthcoming international maritime law conferences would be mandated to demand a strong reinforcement of coastal states' prerogatives. These states would be empowered to intervene *ex officio*, even without a formal request; to conduct proactive inspections of suspect vessels; and to prohibit them from resuming navigation until the necessary repairs had been carried out. The newly adopted ILO Convention on Seafarers' Protection (1976) would be rigorously enforced. Stricter regulations would govern the issuance of navigation certificates, and the work of ship classification societies would be more tightly monitored. Safer ships would be required – now equipped with double hulls and dual rudder systems. Bold declarations echoed through the chamber: the great *Monopoily* revolution had begun.[8]

---

7 *Ibid.*, p. 159.

8 The report also included a substantial series of resolutions concerning the strictly French organisation of maritime accident prevention. These included, for example, the decision to equip major ports with modern high-seas tugboats and to move the Ushant traffic separation scheme several nautical miles further offshore.

Yet in the immediate aftermath, the revolution came from an unexpected direction: a new category of players entered the game, demanding a seat at the table – and justice. Imagine it: mayors of small towns bypassing the prefect; ordinary citizens challenging the reckless actions of the *Monopoily* freeriders before their very eyes; environmental activists disputing the very rules of the game. No, these accidents were not acts of fate but the deliberate, perfectly orchestrated outcomes of a flawed system.

Thus began the epic of the Breton mayors, who took their fight all the way to Chicago and, after fourteen years of litigation, won justice.[9] A company with a turnover equal to a quarter of France's national budget ultimately yielded to the determination of outraged citizens. Suddenly, the law ceased to be the law of others – the law of the powerful. It became a tool for change, a weapon to be reclaimed.

What followed were weeks of intense solidarity and creativity. Communities pooled funds to pay for lawyers, discovered the concept of ecological damage, and debated the notion of a shared heritage. Mayors from neighbouring towns, regardless of political affiliation, joined the battle.[10]

The struggle was gruelling. It required painstakingly gathering evidence for every element of the damage incurred, maintaining unity, and refusing to be discouraged by the exorbitant legal costs. The battle was merciless. The lawyers had warned Christian Huglo, attorney for the municipalities: 'You're a renowned lawyer, and you have a strong case, but we will make you bend under the weight of dollars.' Skilled in the harsh tactics of American litigation, their adversaries combed the Breton coastline for weeks, even examining hotel registries in an attempt to discredit claims of declining tourism. Nor did they hesitate to sue the French authorities, alleging failures in the handling of the disaster response.

9 Not that the French courts were at fault; the few months of legal proceedings, especially criminal, conducted before the French courts made it possible to gather a number of pieces of evidence that would prove extremely useful later on. Rather, due to the limitations of liability ceilings in France, the case brought in Chicago appeared far more promising, as events would show. Moreover, the proximity of the headquarters of the companies involved turned out to be a judicious move. Finally, even if a conviction had been obtained in France, it would still have been necessary to plead abroad to obtain recognition and enforcement (*exequatur*) of the French decision.

10 See *Amoco Cadiz, mémoires vives. Propos recueillis par Claire Bouteloup* (Brest: Cedre éditeur, 2008), pp. 43ff. On the personality of Alphonse Arzel, the charismatic leader of this struggle, see G. Morizur and F. Montgermont, *Bleu pétrole* (Charnay-lès-Mâcon: Editions Bamboo, 2017).

Nevertheless, the decision handed down by the Chicago District Court on 18 April 1984 was exemplary in every respect – one of those rulings that 'sets a precedent.'[11] Judge McGarr, a maritime law specialist and former sailor, left no stone unturned. He meticulously reviewed thousands of pages of the case file, unravelled the tangled web of interests among the three companies involved, and carefully assigned responsibility to each. He did not hesitate to pierce the veil of the flag of convenience or to challenge the legal fiction of corporate personhood – in this case, the façade of shell companies.

The heaviest blame fell on AIOC: failure to properly design the tanker; negligence in not equipping it with a secondary steering system; poor vessel maintenance; inadequate crew training; and an inability to ensure seaworthiness. Any one of these failings would have sufficed to establish liability. A memo dated August 1977, signed by Chester Byzarovitch, AIOC's head of maritime engineering, proved especially damning:

> The primary objective for 1978 is to keep the Amoco Cadiz and Amoco Singapore operating without any downtime that would immobilise these two vessels under their charter contracts. It is not planned for them to go into dry dock or undergo their biennial repair period until after the expiration of the charter contracts.[12]

Logically, Amoco Transport was also held liable: although repeatedly referred to as the 'nominal' owner, the company had made no attempt to oversee AIOC's management. Captain Bardari and his crew, by contrast, were exonerated – the true 'master' was in Chicago. Identifying Standard Oil in that role and demonstrating the strictly integrated nature of the group, Judge McGarr ultimately assigned it co-responsibility for the negligence committed by its subsidiaries, rejecting all counterclaims. The Spanish shipyard was also found liable for failing to include a redundant steering system in the ship's design.

---

11 L. Lucchini, 'Le procès de l'Amoco Cadiz: présent et voies du futur', *Annuaire français de droit international* 31 (1985), pp. 762ff.

12 During dry dock maintenance the previous year, the company had, for the same reasons, declined to replace the defective rings and seals in the steering gear of the *Amoco Cadiz*, which was losing between seven and twelve litres of hydraulic fluid per day. See Y. Rochard, *L'affaire Amoco* (n.p.: Editions ArMen, 2005), p. 21. The author adds that the defect had been known to the company since the first trials in 1974 and had been repaired on the two other *Amoco* sister ships, which were directly owned by the parent company (p. 22).

On the other hand, Captain Weinert and Bugsier Reederei were absolved: no responsibility could be attributed to them, as the salvage operations had been undertaken even before the contract was formally accepted by the assisted vessel.

With the aim of securing full compensation for the damage incurred, the American judge laid the groundwork for a realistic and proportionate redress of the harm suffered. The road remained long, but on 24 January 1992, after fourteen years of litigation, the U.S. Federal Court of Appeals in Chicago awarded the French State and the Breton municipalities $1.3 billion in damages – an unprecedented sum at the time. Had the case been tried under the conventional legal frameworks of the era, which would have targeted the official owner of the tanker, Amoco Transport, the compensation would not have exceeded the value of the wreck: $750,000 – the company's only asset, apart from the brass plaque on its office door in Monrovia.[13]

Nothing Goes Anymore

The game of *Monopoily* has not stopped – not by any means. The dice keep rolling, and the number of freeriders continues to grow. With them comes a litany of accidents and oil spills.[14] On 28 April 1979, the bulk carrier *Gino* (flying the Liberian flag) sank off the coast of Ouessant, releasing 42,000 tonnes of heavy oil. Less than a year later, on 7 March 1980, the *Tanio* broke in two during a storm off the island of Batz; its stern sank, taking 6,000 tonnes of heavy fuel oil to the seabed. On 31 January 1988, one of the tanks of the Italian tanker *Amazzone* spilled just over 2,000 tonnes of crude oil during a storm off Penmarc'h.

Then came the sinking of the *Erika* on 12 December 1999 – a disaster foretold. At twenty-four years old, the *Erika*, flying the Maltese flag, was a decrepit vessel chartered by Total. It broke apart during a storm off the coast of Saint-Nazaire while transporting 30,000 tonnes of heavy fuel oil to Sicily. This time, all limits were exceeded, the risks taken were outrageous, and the violations were systematic. Over its lifetime, the ship had changed owners eight times, its name eight times, its flag three times (Panama, Liberia, Malta), its classification society three times, and its nautical management company four times.

---

13 Y. Rochard, *L'affaire Amoco*, *op. cit.*, pp. 51 and 156.

14 R. Moreau, 'Cinquante ans de "marées noires": radioscopie des catastrophes liées à la pollution par les hydrocarbures', *Assurances et gestion des risques* 76, no. 1 (April 2008), pp. 99ff.

The *Erika* was a 'black card' passed from hand to hand, ultimately landing in the lap of the Breton municipalities – who had certainly not asked for it. A black card for a black trade and a black cargo (the investigation even raised doubts about the true nature of its contents: possibly drilling mud and refinery waste).

At the time of the shipwreck, the *Erika*'s legal status was so opaque that its true owners, shielded by a network of shell companies, could never be identified. One fact, however, was indisputable: the vessel was not seaworthy. In May 1998, it was inspected in Norway, where eleven deficiencies were recorded. Only minimal repairs were carried out in a Montenegrin shipyard, and in December a seaworthiness certificate was issued by the Italian classification society RINA. In November 1999 – just a month before the wreck – the captain reported signs of advanced corrosion in several ballast tanks. RINA required repairs to be completed within two months. Ignoring the directive, Total ordered the fuel oil to be loaded in Dunkirk. Despite the storm forecast, the vessel departed on 9 December.

In the hours that followed, as winds reached gale force 8 and the tanker slammed into the swells, two-metre-long cracks appeared in the bulkheads separating the tanks. Buckling several metres long was also observed on the deck plating. The ship developed a pronounced list but, at 2.11 p.m., sent a reassuring message to the CROSS (Regional Surveillance and Rescue Centre), stating that the damage was under control (without mentioning the cracks) and that no assistance was required.

Nevertheless, the *Erika* altered course and headed toward Saint-Nazaire in search of refuge. But as the winds strengthened further, the situation worsened overnight: the cracks widened, the list grew more severe, fuel oil began leaking from the tanks, and the ship became increasingly difficult to manoeuvre. At 5.54 a.m., the captain sent out a distress signal for the first time. In the minutes that followed, the tanker ultimately buckled, its deck acting like a hinge; at 8.08 a.m., thirty miles south of the Pointe de Penmarc'h, the *Erika* broke in two, spilling its oil into the sea. The two sections of the ship were towed by the *Abeille Flandre* and the *Malabar*, but both sank in the days that followed. The oil spill – exacerbated by winter storms and high tidal coefficients that carried the oil far up the shoreline – soon reached the islands of Morbihan.

Once again, twenty-two years after the *Amoco Cadiz* disaster, the grand game of *Monopoily* had gone off the rails; and once again, commissions were convened and reports were written. The report by the Economic and Social Council, dated 29 March 2000, stands out for its clarity. Reflecting on earlier reports, it observes: 'These recommendations would have been useful if they had been adopted,' and further: 'These opinions remain highly relevant in many of their proposals and, remarkably, show a surprising modernity.'[15]

Certainly, some progress has been made. In some respects, the rules of the game have been revised. For instance, the 1982 United Nations Convention on the Law of the Sea (Montego Bay) allows coastal states to intervene up to 200 nautical miles within their exclusive economic zones to prevent pollution threatening their shores. Legal actions undertaken by local authorities have helped to advance jurisprudence on the 'polluter pays' principle, and compensation for ecological damage is now occasionally granted. France has also equipped itself with powerful tugs, ready to set out in all weather conditions.

However, for the most part, the game has continued unchanged – or worsened, if one considers the exponential growth in flags of convenience. Today, one in two ships belongs to the ranks of the cheats. Unsurprisingly, under such conditions, many vessels operate below standard – or entirely outside regulatory oversight. While the involvement of classification societies helps to maintain appearances, their independence remains questionable; alternatively, their recommendations are simply ignored. This was the case with the *Erika*, where the final advisory from the Rina classification society – recommending the withdrawal of the tanker's certification – was disregarded by the Maltese authorities. As for liability actions, they continue to vanish into the maze of shell companies, while rules and directives adopted at the national level are too often only partially enforced.

Based on these observations, the Economic and Social Council resumed its task and, as the French Senate had done twenty-two years earlier, ventured to propose a new set of recommendations. Revolutionary rules, to be sure – indeed, downright utopian – clearly the work of minds hopelessly detached from reality. Judge for yourself:

- The cost of safety should now be integrated into freight prices – who could have imagined such an unrealistic standard?
- The freedom to register under any flag is acceptable only if the state in question is capable of fulfilling its international responsibilities – has there ever been a more utopian demand, so disrespectful of state sovereignty and free trade?
- A classification society should not be owned by a shipping company, nor should it inspect the same ship on behalf of both the shipowner and the flag state. Certification standards should not be unilaterally defined by

15 *Rapport du 29 mars 2000 du Conseil économique et social*, p. 5.

these societies – is this not a wholesale attack on reputable and established institutions?
- Shipowners should be required to demonstrate sufficient financial guarantees to cover the risks they generate; charterers should be held jointly liable – could they have come up with a better way to obliterate the entire petroleum sector?

Ter Repetita Non Placet

For those who might have considered the case of the *Erika* too exceptional to serve as precedent, the sinking of the *Prestige* on 19 November 2002 offered a sobering rebuttal. While navigating off the coast of Galicia, the *Prestige* – a Malagasy-flagged oil tanker bound for Gibraltar – issued a distress call: a large breach had opened in its hull amid a violent storm, and the fuel it was transporting was already spilling into the sea. The Spanish government ordered the vessel to be towed out into the open ocean, hoping to protect the coastline from the impending slick. However, on 19 November, the tanker broke in two and sank to a depth of 3,500 metres. Despite the distance from shore, a massive oil spill eventually polluted Galicia, northern Portugal, and the French Atlantic coast, from the Basque Country to southern Brittany.

Many elements of the *Prestige* case mirrored those of the *Erika*. Both vessels were outdated, single-hulled designs (the Malagasy tanker was twenty-six years old) and had undergone numerous makeshift repairs. Both literally came apart in the storm – the *Prestige* due to hull failure, the *Erika* due to the collapse of internal bulkheads. Both were transporting heavy fuel oil, the most difficult pollutant to clean up – hazardous cargo in the least secure ships. Both flew flags of convenience – the Bahamas, in the case of the *Prestige*. In both instances, the ships' legal status and the true identity of their actual owners were shrouded in confusion – save for one familiar detail: the ship was the sole asset of its nominal owner, registered under a single-ship company.

And once again, a commission was convened, and a report was issued.[16] This time, however, the report noted with muted resignation: 'Certain hearings involving the same individuals, three years apart, sometimes give the impression of a genuine repetition that found no response.'[17]

16 Assemblée nationale, *Rapport fait au nom de la Commission d'enquête*, 10 July 2003.
17 *Ibid.*, p. 5.

The Moral of the Story

Does such an immoral tale carry a moral?

At the very least, it reveals a stark choice: fatality or responsibility. In the first case, accidents are cast as random misfortunes – *fortuna maris* – a gamble undertaken, risked, and lost. In the second, they are the direct consequence of irresponsible policies. The logic of fatality allows the grand game of *Monopoily* to continue indefinitely, with catastrophes presented as the regrettable cost of progress, growth, and free trade – the inevitable missteps of the invisible hand that governs the market. The logic of responsibility, by contrast, begins with the mobilisation of victims determined to defend their rights and can lead to the punishment of culprits and the prevention of future disasters. On one side, the invisible hand of fate and market forces; on the other, the deliberate act of taking control of one's destiny.

Undoubtedly, the law accommodates both of these logics. But in the first case, it often seems outpaced by freeriders who flout the rules or operate entirely outside them – how can one compete with the predatory practices of flags of convenience? In the second, as illustrated by the fight led by the Breton mayors, the law is called upon to reinvent and expand itself. The 1984 ruling in the *Amoco Cadiz* case pierced the veil of corporate personality and held the true actors accountable. A few years later, in 1989, that same struggle inspired the victims of the *Exxon Valdez* disaster, which devastated Alaska's pristine coastline. And on 25 September 2012, the French Court of Cassation recognised, for the first time, the existence, autonomy, and compensability of 'ecological harm.'

The Bretons' fight for dignity proved to be a fight for the integrity of the ocean – a true *fortuna maris*.

3, 2, 1 …

This is the story of a country that sought to abolish, in all domains, the in-between, the gap, the fold, the doubt. A country that rejected the third, recoiling in horror from uncertainty. A nation whole and indivisible, trapped in the straitjacket of its own certainties, dazzled by the self-evidence of its truths.

Its name? Binaria. Its flag? Black and white, with a thumbs-up in the centre.

The thumbs-up was the emblem of the new regime: Like – I approve, I support, I want more. Always more of the same. It was everywhere: on armbands, jewellery, banners across screens, and ubiquitous stickers. Naturally, the opposite emblem – a thumbs-down – also flourished. But woe to those it targeted, for, as in the ancient games of the arena, it condemned them to dangerous stigmatisation.

To be fair, the country had seen better days. It was only with the rise to power of Selfidor, its new President, that it entered this somnambulant era. A failed law school graduate turned carnival barker, then real estate swindler, and finally the host of notoriously brutal reality television shows, Selfidor lived in a tower – a skyscraper, really – so tall he could no longer see the ground, and began to fancy himself Jupiter incarnate.

He won the election with a slogan that encapsulated his persona: *Jamais deux sans moi* ('Never two without me'). Beyond the cheap wordplay, his voters were captivated by the mantra, which expressed their yearning for identification. It quickly evolved into a rallying cry. At every public appearance of the President, the frenzied crowd would chant it, transforming the phrase into a fervent declaration of submission: *Jamais deux sans toi, Jamais deux sans toi …*

Magnanimous and paternal, Selfidor would sometimes echo the refrain, cleverly modifying it: *Jamais deux sans tous* ('Never two without all'), thus subtly equating *me* (himself, of course) with *everyone*: never two without *me*, without *you*, without *all*. It became a kind of collective political climax, a shiver of communion. Together, they were strong, united in their sameness. Between *you* and *me*, between *all of us* – what crack could possibly appear? The unsettling other, the indeterminate third, the disruptive outsider, was exorcised, banished to the shadows of *them* – deleted from screens, erased from agendas, condemned to oblivion.

Times had grown grim for anyone resisting this indoctrination or simply not fitting neatly into the mould: artists, intellectuals, foreigners, people of colour, and all those living an alternative sexuality. When the margins shrink around an increasingly rigid core, many find themselves pushed to the edges –

 | DOI:10.1163/9789004737112_009

undocumented, homeless, without a fixed identity. Suspected of indeterminacy, and thus of potential betrayal.

Two groups were particularly targeted by Selfidor and his followers: journalists and lawyers. The former because they operated in the realm Selfidor sought to monopolise – communication – and occasionally had the audacity to use it critically; the latter because the President harboured a deep-seated resentment toward the legal profession, which had rejected him. Both groups, moreover, represented the voice of the third, the undefined other, any other – the regime's public enemy number one. The Third Estate, the Third World: a political no man's land that Selfidor despised.

He also harboured a peculiar obsession with light – one that would soon leave a lasting mark on the entire nation. Not the natural light of days and seasons, the subtle transitions of dawn and dusk; no, he craved harsh, artificial, zenithal light – light without shadow. A light so uniform it could rival the sun. He tirelessly ordered the installation of such intense, continuous illumination in every space he inhabited, and eventually, everywhere he went.

One day, he proclaimed that Binaria had entered the 'Crystal Age'. Through massive, monumental projects, he blanketed the entire territory with an immense electrical grid fitted with countless floodlights, broadcasting the zenithal light he alone seemed to find satisfying. In endless monologues broadcast on every channel and social network, he declared a crusade against shadow, claiming it to be the breeding ground of all conspiracies.

Had he been a little more cultured, he might have proclaimed that Binaria was entering a new Age of Enlightenment. But of course, he had no inkling of such a concept. Besides, the artificial lighting he now imposed on the country for sixteen hours a day (and later, as we will see, even abolished the brief eight-hour respite) had nothing in common with the public use of reason that defined the original Enlightenment. He might also have claimed inspiration from *The City of the Sun* or the radiant cities of utopian tradition – but he was equally ignorant of these. And here too, his electric sun bore no resemblance to the celestial body it sought to mimic.

The cynics – quickly silenced – hinted that Selfidor's remarkable decision might not be entirely unrelated to the fact that he owned a majority stake in the country's largest power plants. Others speculated that the President was attempting to exorcise lingering childhood fears that had never truly been overcome. Indeed, Selfidor's endless verbosity barely concealed, beneath the bravado, a deep, irrational fear of darkness – coupled with an obsessive attachment to transparency.

A regime of absolute visibility was taking hold. The capital, now renamed *Cristalia*, bristled with glass buildings whose thin metallic frames seemed to vanish entirely under the harsh reflections of the zenithal light. 'Everything must unfold in broad daylight,' declared the Idol, 'as befits a strong and united people.' 'Only thugs and perverts seek the complicit shelter of shadow or night to conceal their crimes,' he proclaimed – honest citizens had nothing to hide.

Meanwhile, the Administration actively encouraged the dissemination of images on social networks, which helped eradicate what little intimacy remained. In truth, there was scarcely anything left of what once passed for private life: people eagerly volunteered for television shows or broadcast their lives on social media, divulging themselves with abandon. Visibility had become synonymous with authenticity, and authenticity the hallmark of truth. That these images – especially those on television, ironically called *teletruth* or *reality TV* – were often doctored seemed to bother no one. They prevailed simply because everyone saw and shared them.

Under Selfidor's perpetual light, crushed by illumination, the world lost all relief, all texture, all depth. It was as if the third dimension had been permanently banished, reducing reality to the flatness of a two-dimensional plane. A scholar recalled Edwin A. Abbott's prophetic *Flatland*, but, needless to say, no one was willing to listen. This was the reign of superficiality and appearance – questions dismissed, conflicts denied: *jamais deux sans moi*, one, two, forward march!

The regime soon triggered significant changes. People began wearing dark glasses at all times, losing the habit of smiling, winking, or exchanging glances. Their sleep became dreamless, devoid even of forgetfulness, and their daytime movements turned somnambulistic. As for the birds, they eventually abandoned these blinding lands, depriving the cities of the last natural sound that still graced them. It was as though the constant chirping of tweets might somehow serve as a substitute.

The most striking changes, however, concerned language itself. Selfidor set the tone: his sentences adhered strictly to the structure of subject, verb, object, and his vocabulary was extremely limited, filled with short, unequivocal words – *super, extra, cash, minable*. Often, these were arranged in binary oppositions: good guys and bad guys, heroes and slackers, winners (us) and losers (them), OK and KO. Subordinate clauses and abstract terms were banished from his speeches. Words that suggested nuance or complexity – *perhaps, maybe, even though, nevertheless, simultaneously, insofar as, relative, intermediate* – were nowhere to be found. The world was all the more easily reduced to black and white because the words capable of expressing shades of grey had disappeared; and absolute certainties reigned supreme once all sense of relativity was lost. It must be said that his preferred mode of communication – 280-character tweets (recently expanded from 140) – did little to encourage subtlety.

Selfidor also had no use for the third person or for indeterminate subjects (*he*, *one*, *everyone*). His discourse consisted solely of *I* and *you*, in perfect alignment with his motto. He addressed his audience with forceful commands and manipulative appeals: *I'm telling you, believe me, we all want* – always punctuated by emphatic gestures. This style – comprehensible to a nine- or ten-year-old – was, in truth, aimed at the unconscious, appealing to primal emotions: fear, narcissistic pleasure, and a curious indulgence in self-abasement – a shared thrill in wallowing together in lazy complicity.

It must be said that Selfidor was a master manipulator. His experience as a reality TV host served him well in his new political career. He had a knack – if one could call it that – for ending every sentence with emotionally charged words, delivered like fists pounding on a table. Alternatively, he would repeat those words in a hypnotic rhythm: *We're going to win, win, win, so much winning that ...*

At first, some pointed out that the President knew nothing about the topics on which he spoke with such bluster. But who truly cared? From his days as a street vendor, he had learned that the key wasn't mastery of the subject matter but the ability to tap into the buyer's desires by creating the atmosphere that would satisfy them. He could say anything, so long as he held his audience captive through their fears or fantasies. The referent – the third thing his speech ostensibly addressed – became irrelevant. What mattered was his hypnotic ability to make it feared or desired. In the end, he was only ever talking about himself – about himself and all the listeners who identified with the idol: *jamais deux sans moi....*

Subjected to this daily barrage, people began speaking a different language. The change didn't happen overnight, of course, but after a few months, those who still used somewhat refined language came to seem eccentric, pretentious, out of touch – soon pressured to speak like everyone else. Needless to say, multilingualism and translation quickly came to be viewed as vaguely perverse inclinations and were therefore suspect. Only Binarian was accepted, and even then, in an increasingly simplified form. The melancholic lamented this development, predicting that soon people might as well communicate using nothing but the emoticons that had invaded every screen – smilies and a prolific array of tiny symbols that not only spared people the effort of writing, but also relieved them of the burden of thinking. Under the perpetual light of Binaria, communication became clear and distinct ☺.

In such conditions, was there really any point in worrying about truth and morality? Were people even capable of it anymore? It's not that Selfidor was indifferent to such concepts – far from it. He often spoke of truth; or rather, he constantly accused his enemies (he had no adversaries, only enemies) of lying. Journalists, in particular, were repeatedly singled out as guilty of spreading *foutaises* (a blunt slang term for 'nonsense') – a popular expression that better captured the spirit of the Binarian word he used than more sophisticated alternatives like *imposture*, *falsehood*, *rumour*, *approximation*, or *disinformation*, all of which were foreign to the President's vocabulary. In truth, the reason he spoke so often of *foutaises* was that this was the domain in which he himself excelled.

So much so that the Crystal Age had quietly slid into a post-truth regime, where the very question of truth had lost its relevance, and the distinction between true and false had been dulled. From now on, truth was simply whatever Selfidor declared to be true. By asserting it, he performed it – he gave the claim shape and authority. And that was more than enough to reassure his subjects. *Jamais deux sans toi*, and the ideas would be well guarded.

The President had no qualms about proclaiming contradictory and ever-changing truths, much to the despair of the sycophants and flatterers who sought to draft the official exegesis of the Idol's thoughts, their eyes glued to his speeches. But his thoughts shifted so quickly that the 'truth' they thought they had grasped was already, by the next day, an obsolete and worthless opinion. Happier, in fact, were those who thought nothing at all and, with a strong stomach, swallowed whatever was served. The safest course, it seemed, was to stick to the most hackneyed clichés: 'We can't possibly take in all the misery of the world,' or 'You can't make an omelette without breaking a few eggs.' Alternatively, they repeated pure tautologies: 'War is war,' 'Business is business' – phrases which, when all was said and done, adequately reflected the hollow tautology that passed for ideology under the regime.

One day, in one of his tweets, Selfidor misspelled *régiment* as *régimant*: 'Our *régimants* are mobilising against the threat.' Immediately, the entire country began writing *régimant* with an *a*, celebrating the far more active and martial feel of this spelling, which matched the word's warlike content. Before long, the nostalgics who insisted on writing *régiment* with an *e* were branded as bad citizens – if not outright dangerous subversives.

Yet of all the changes unfolding under Binaria's relentless, zenithal light, the most profound were those affecting the law. This was likely due to the personal resentment Selfidor harboured towards it, but also because, of all cultural constructs, the law is undoubtedly the one most intrinsically tied to the third – that very third the regime sought to eradicate. *Tertium non datur* – 'no third is given' – if only anyone still remembered their Latin or Aristotle's logic.

The country, however, boasted a venerable legal tradition and counted many seasoned jurists committed to the rule of law and the protection of fundamental rights. Thus, for once, Selfidor had to proceed cautiously, despite his disdain for the law, with all its Byzantine complexities, abstract qualifications, convoluted presumptions and fictions, procedural delays, and all those peculiarities that stood as a barrier – casting shadows, no less – between him and the Binarians. The erosion of the legal system, therefore, was gradual and insidious.

At first, the attacks were directed solely at outsiders and external law – international law. One day, an entry ban was imposed on a foreign lawyer who, the previous year, had defended a person accused of terrorism in their home country. The lawyer argued vehemently that a legal advocate defends and represents their client without necessarily identifying with their cause or condoning their actions. Selfidor, however, remained unmoved. He refused to grasp such a subtle distinction: to him, the suspect was obviously guilty, and anyone who supported them – even while pretending to remain neutral – could only be engaging in duplicity. Incapable of conceiving the third stage where trials unfold and where justice operates impartially, Selfidor's reasoning boiled down to binary logic: with me or against me. And for traitors? Both at once. But never could he elevate himself to the *meta* or impartial perspective (above both A and B) where true justice strives to reside.

In foreign policy, the President no longer saw any need to concern himself with the law. To him, it was merely an extension of the power dynamics inherent in economic competition and military dominance. The idea that a great power like Binaria should restrain its might out of consideration for weaker nations seemed utterly unnatural. He therefore set about systematically withdrawing from every international agreement his country had ratified and, with equal fervour, renounced the jurisdiction of international courts that dared presume to judge a Binarian citizen. Multilateralism was intolerable to him, as if the blinding light he cast upon Binaria had to illuminate – and subjugate – the entire world. And as for foreign texts, alien to the Binarian spirit, that dared stifle the innovation of Binarian industries or open the nation's gates to the idlers of the world? This would no longer be tolerated, and walls were promptly erected around the country.

At the same time, and with no regard for the inherent contradiction, Selfidor insisted that Binarian laws should apply beyond its borders whenever the so-called interests of his country required it. If Binaria imposed economic sanctions on a particular nation, he demanded that all foreign companies doing business with Binaria respect those sanctions as well, under threat of losing access to its markets. Law thus became a mere tool of coercion, another weapon in the global competition of all against all. It was, in essence, a return to the state of nature, where anything goes – a regression to the primal face-to-face dynamic Selfidor particularly relished and which, in his view, inevitably led to the mantra of *jamais deux sans moi*.

This legal extortion extended to the peculiar justice deals orchestrated by Binaria's State Department against powerful foreign corporations accused of corrupt practices that allegedly threatened to steal market share from Binarian companies. The arrangement was as simple as it was ruthless: either the company conducted its own internal investigation into allegations of corruption or money laundering, admitted guilt publicly, and paid an exorbitant fine; or it would face a drawn-out, ruinous legal battle on Binarian soil – resulting in an immediate ban from conducting business in the country. The outcome was predictable: companies capitulated swiftly, confessed to whatever was demanded, and paid the required sums, thereby forfeiting any opportunity to defend themselves before a 'real' court.

Only the so-called pessimists, of course, dared to criticise these practices. After all, didn't these crusades against wrongdoing yield resounding victories? Weren't they the ultimate proof – complete with public confessions – of the righteousness of the transparency Selfidor claimed to bestow upon his country?

Buoyed by these successes and supported by an ever-dazzled public, Selfidor soon set about applying these effective methods domestically. Above all, he despised general and abstract law. He much preferred contracts – face-to-face agreements that allowed him to assert his power by dividing his adversaries, rather than submitting to an impersonal and faceless generality. Deep down, what he valued most was the feudal order, where the weaker party pledged allegiance to the lord in a legal gesture not far removed from animal rituals of submission. He had honed this preference for leonine contracts during his time in real estate, where he had built his fortune. But heaven forbid that laws should disrupt such an effective game!

Thus, he set out to systematically dismantle the carefully constructed legal framework of his predecessors. Anything resembling a statute, a right, or a procedure – anything, in short, that provided guarantees by depersonalising individual relationships and grounding them in abstract generality, a cornerstone of equality – was intolerable to him. Compliant parliamentary majorities busied themselves unravelling the threads of legal texts, while partisan judges, appointed to strategic posts, conveniently 'forgot' to enforce them.

Selfidor preferred the concrete orders issued by his administration – or better yet, the directives he personally delivered via social media. It resembled a general mobilisation led by a wartime commander, whose daily instructions ostensibly guided the nation's affairs in response to immediate necessities. Alternatively, another tactic emerged: laws were retained in name but rendered meaningless by countless exceptions and loopholes, all subject to the President's discretion. For instance, while a law required school cafeterias to serve five vegetables, the Idol reserved the right to define what *vegetable* meant. The very next day, he decreed that ketchup qualified as a vegetable, to the applause of his audience and the satisfaction of a close associate – a magnate in the food industry.

Here again, as with truth, what was lawful was whatever Selfidor declared to be lawful. An ageing scholar referenced Humpty Dumpty and his perverse relationship with language: 'The word means just what I choose it to mean,' said he. And when Alice asked, 'Can you make words mean so many different things?' Humpty Dumpty replied, 'The question is, which is to be master – that's all.' But no one listened, for no one read *Through the Looking-Glass* anymore; the Land of Wonders had long since been left behind. Binaria was firmly entrenched in its own distorted reality.

What Selfidor found particularly amusing, however, were *nudges* and other concrete norms embedded in material devices themselves. *Nudges* – literally 'gentle pushes' – are a concept drawn from the Binarian language, which lacks an exact translation. They can be understood as mechanisms that subtly guide users toward desired behaviours – for example, the default settings in software programs that govern all aspects of daily life. As for concrete norms – such as an automatic system that disables the ignition of cars whose owners have failed to pay their insurance premiums – Selfidor found them marvellously efficient. Why waste time appealing to drivers' consciences, willpower, or sense of responsibility – those metaphysical absurdities of a bygone age – when these tangible systems achieved 100% compliance, as he loved to point out?

This unassailable logic spread rapidly across all sectors. In the realm of insurance, for instance, the outdated veil of ignorance and the impractical principle of solidarity – clearly benefiting the less responsible – were soon abandoned. Premiums would now be based on the actual risk individuals represented. It became *pay as you drive, pay as you live, pay as you travel,* and so on. Here again, Binarian light cast a realistic and welcome illumination over a domain long clouded by counterproductive references to indeterminate third parties and the murky mutualisation of risks.

In matters of evidence, too, presumptions and fictions – once the delight of jurists – were now a thing of the past. Presumptions of paternity were swept aside by the irrefutable accuracy of DNA tests. Everywhere, genetic logic prevailed, sparing countless trials in the process.

At its core, this was a relentless war against the 'legal subject' – yet another cumbersome fiction. Of what use, after all, was this enigmatic *legal personality*, which masked the concrete reality of each man and woman, concealing their true circumstances, perhaps even their bad intentions, and suggesting a deceptive equality among them? No! In the healthy and enlightened world of Binaria, where honest people have nothing to hide, everyone was addressed and treated for what they truly were – in their family, their work, and their relationships. How much clearer and simpler social relations became when freed from cumbersome legal complexities and instead governed directly by their primary, economic, emotional, or political logic!

Under Selfidor's dazzling light, these ideas found their natural home in criminal justice. Who could still naively believe in the presumption of innocence? Who would be foolish enough to defend the notion that doubt should benefit the accused? (After all, in Binaria, a land without shadows, doubt had long ceased to exist.) And who would still cling to the illusion that offenders might be rehabilitated? After centuries of error, criminal policy had finally become what it should always have been: radically preventive. The focus was now on dangerousness, not culpability; it was risks being managed, not offences. Intervention occurred before any social harm was caused – not after, when it was too late.

Blinded by these new truths, the people applauded: *Jamais deux sans toi!* Soon, millions of individuals whose profiles – compiled by big data agencies – diverged even slightly from the ideal Binarian type found themselves flagged, monitored, wiretapped, tagged, placed under house arrest, or subjected to chemical restraints.

Of course, zero risk did not exist. To address this, Selfidor strongly encouraged good citizens to arm themselves (it helped, of course, that the powerful National Firearms Association had heavily funded his electoral campaign). Invoking, for once, the nation's venerable traditions – the pioneers of the distant South and their swift justice – and even natural law, the Idol proclaimed that self-defence was not just a sacred right but a patriotic duty. Consequently, building concierges, school prefects, and public venue gatekeepers were generously armed. And it was incredible how safe everyone felt now: *Jamais deux sans toi!*

Unsurprisingly, these 'salutary reforms' soon extended to institutions themselves – those notorious bastions of resistance to change. At first, Selfidor exercised caution, particularly toward Parliament. He took pride in personally inaugurating each parliamentary year and setting the agenda, reserving for himself such weighty topics as revising the list of public holidays. Yet the institution quickly lost its relevance, as deputies, in unison and without debate, passed the texts the Administration deigned to submit.

Selfidor then began mocking, through his daily tweets, the absurd notion of the separation of powers. Was this not, by definition, an elevation of distrust into a principle – and a recipe for institutional gridlock? Shouldn't a well-organised nation foster collaboration between powers? Besides, in the age of the internet and social media, what value did the outdated notion of representation still hold? How had the country tolerated, for decades, a system that assumed an inherent gap between the people (who needed representation) and their legislators?

Thus, one morning, the President, in a single message, announced the immediate dissolution of Parliament and its replacement with direct assemblies of citizens. These citizens were chosen randomly from among his followers (in truth, all Binarians) and invited to vote electronically, in real time, on proposed texts. A significant financial reward was offered to those who answered a tie-breaking question – designed to identify those who voted 'correctly', that is, in alignment with the majority decision. Once again, the people applauded and quickly became addicted to this new form of legislative game.

It didn't take long for this same logic to apply, as one might expect, to other 'intermediary bodies' that also rested on the troublesome idea of representation and created a shadow – literally and figuratively – between the Idol and his people. At last, feeling unusually reflective, and at the cost of considerable semantic effort, Selfidor tweeted: 'Between you and me, it's no longer about adhesion, but adherence. I've got you under my skin! I like you!' Thus, the true essence of Binaria's regime was fulfilled: all forms of distance disappeared, and the nation approached the ultimate state of flatness, with the third dimension erased. Soon, there would be no gaps, no edges, no shadows – only the reassuring sameness stretched endlessly under the merciless glare of an unvarnished day.

The last institution to resist was the judiciary. At first, a few brave prosecutors dared to challenge the regime by investigating the electoral manoeuvres that had brought the Idol to power. However, the pressures one might imagine (including forced resignations when necessary) quickly snuffed out these flickers of resistance. Compliant judges eagerly stepped in to fill the void. Yet this was not enough for Selfidor; his hatred for Lady Justice seemed almost personal. He loathed the blindfold she wore, which he found incomprehensible – a symbol, to his mind, of the perverse complexity of legal reasoning. What rational person, he mused, would take pride in rendering judgment while blindfolded?

Determined to unmask her, Selfidor attacked with the same aggression he occasionally admitted to using toward women. He slashed her budgets, allowed her courthouses to fall into disrepair, and stripped away her powers in countless ways. Meanwhile, the number of cases brought before the courts dwindled, as citizens (and the Administration) were encouraged to take justice into their own hands, and the laws on which courts might rely became increasingly sparse.

So it came as little surprise when, with yet another tweet, the Idol officially abolished the judiciary, replacing it with the instant polling system that had proven so successful in legislative matters. A universal system of online dispute resolution, complete with bonuses and rewards, soon gained widespread approval. As for the now-redundant courthouses, a design competition was held to determine their new purpose: some were transformed into dance halls, others into fitness centres, while most became television studios. In these repurposed spaces, charismatic hosts dominated the scene, producing wildly popular shows of public accusation and confession.

The months, and even the years, went by. The zenithal lighting was now unrelenting: twenty-four hours a day, the glaring beams bore down on Binaria. Strangely, this resulted in a world with no land or sky, no up or down, no right or left – everything flattened beneath the merciless midday light. People began to forget where the sun rose, and at night, the sky emptied of stars. It was as if there was nothing left to see, save for the occasional reflection of eerie mirages. A hostile dryness weighed on weary bodies; every cloud dissipated, every trace of dew evaporated. In the background hummed the metallic echo of unrecognisable sounds.

The people moved about like somnambulists, their eyelids atrophied, their eyes hollow, grotesquely dilated. Language had now shrunk to almost nothing: a wooden tongue of a few dozen words, fewer than ten verbs. But what was there left to say? No one truly addressed another, and the words – confused chatter – had lost all meaning. They no longer even bothered burning books, for no one understood them anymore.

And so it ended. From 3, the symbol of plurality, they had fallen to 2, the face-to-face; but under the Idol's sway, 2 collapsed into 1 – *jamais deux sans moi*. And now, 1 faded as well, crushed under its own weight. They had reached zero: emptiness, nothingness, aphasia, a flatline. It wasn't a vengeful cataclysm – no great earthquake, no apocalyptic battering rams against the tower. It simply happened one day: the people laid down their tools, having reached the point of zero. They had become nothing.

The void swallowed the last word – and an immense silence descended. Binaria, like an hourglass at the end of its run, crumbled in on itself. Not even a sigh broke the long-awaited night.

Solange B., Infanticide?

For dust you are, and to dust you shall return …

∴

'Killing one's own clone – moreover, one equipped with artificial intelligence: is it murder, infanticide, or merely the destruction of a non-human entity? Twelve men and women are deliberating,' read the headline of the capital's leading daily this morning. Long and difficult debates were anticipated.

For months, social media had been ablaze, press campaigns orchestrated, and petitions circulated – gathering hundreds of thousands of signatures: *Don't Touch My Chimera* and *Cyborg, My Brother* on one side; *I Am Not a Machine* and *Stop Dr Frankensteins* on the other. The nation's highest moral authorities, the Academy of Sciences, business and labour federations – even the Dalai Lama himself – had weighed in on the debate, while insights from top scientific experts were sought. Public sentiment suggested that the very meaning of humanity hung in the balance.

A brief look back is necessary to shed light on the origins and intricacies of this bizarre case. The accused, Solange B., thirty-four years old and unmarried, is a brilliant bioelectronics engineer. She rose meteorically through the ranks of the renowned Future of Mankind Institute (FUMIST), located in the heart of the Arabian desert. This cutting-edge facility enjoys limitless funding from a variety of sources: oil magnates seeking to reinvent themselves, American televangelists aiming to establish paradise on Earth, and Russian billionaires keen on moral laundering.

Among the latter stands the peculiar figure of Dmitri Itskov, also thirty-four, who amassed his fortune manipulating social networks. Itskov made headlines when, at the helm of an oceanic research expedition, he declared his intention to establish headquarters on the infamous floating island of plastic debris in the North Pacific (the 'Seventh Continent'). He anchored floating installations there, proclaiming the site as 'land open to the inhabitants of the future'. He even commissioned a flag and national anthem for this improbable territory, grandly described as a new frontier (plastic utopia, scoffed critics).

Thanks to these generous funding sources, FUMIST embarked on ambitious research and achieved remarkable breakthroughs in areas as diverse as animal and human cloning, cryogenics, artificial intelligence, mind simulation and

 | DOI:10.1163/9789004737112_010

uploading, and the development and commercialisation of robots and cyborgs (cybernetic organisms: fusions of the living and the digital). Solange had particularly distinguished herself in the PIR programme (Post-Intelligence Research), which aimed to produce an artificial human brain using electronic neurons within a five-year horizon.

Four years ago, Solange volunteered for a pilot experiment involving the cloning of her own body, conducted by another division of the lab: the WOUF programme (Way of Our Future). Her excellent health and firm resolve made her the ideal candidate. The necessary procedures for replicating her cells were carried out, and the embryo was entrusted to an artificial uterus at the lab.

Unfortunately, in the eighth month of gestation, a brief power outage caused irreversible damage to the foetus' brain, leaving the soon-to-be-born child with only vegetative brain functions. Plans were already underway to terminate the experiment and end the artificial pregnancy when, like a *deus ex machina*, RomeoX intervened.

RomeoX was none other than an android whose intellectual architecture had been designed by Solange herself. She had overseen both his development and his daily progress in the lab. With silicone skin, a wig, the ability to perform delicate gestures, and a fluid gait, RomeoX bore a striking resemblance to a strong, attractive man in his thirties. He could recognise facial expressions, express simulated emotions, and converse fluently in three languages (occasionally punctuating his speech with 'um' and 'hmm' to sound more natural). It is no exaggeration to say that RomeoX had become the most charming of Solange's colleagues. Over time, their professional relationship evolved into something undeniably romantic.

Perceiving Solange's distress over the vegetative foetus, RomeoX made the magnanimous proposal to transplant his own digital brain programme into the damaged brain of the foetus – or perhaps it was Solange who suggested it. The trial transcripts remain inconclusive on this point. What is certain is that the operation was a success. Solange's clone now possessed RomeoX's digital programme as its brain. It was, in a sense, the outcome of a wholly new form of union – a 'cyborgasm', as one journalist quipped – and a grand act of electronic love.

To avoid overwhelming the reader, whose imagination is likely already stretched, we will temporarily set aside the question of where RomeoX's brain programme originally came from, now downloaded into Solange's clone. This delicate issue will, no doubt, resurface in due course.

For now, suffice it to say that a few weeks later, the artificial uterus gave birth to a healthy baby girl weighing over three kilos – 'the spitting image of her mother', remarked Solange's colleagues, who gathered for a modest celebration in place of a traditional maternity ward reception. The child was named DominiX – a suggestion from RomeoX, who explained that the final 'X' served as his signature, a mark of mystery and a nod to the enigma of her conception. The name Dominique had the additional advantage of being gender-neutral – a prudent choice, given the circumstances. Solange had proposed the name Chimène, drawn to its gentle phonetic proximity to *chimère* (chimera), but RomeoX's preference ultimately prevailed.

On the very day of DominiX's birth, the Saudi Minister of the Interior announced that the child would be generously granted Saudi citizenship. That this decision violated existing laws governing the country's naturalisation process seemed of little concern; more importantly, it underscored Saudi Arabia's aspiration to position itself at the forefront of bioengineering, robotics, and artificial intelligence. Only a few critics – dismissed as malcontents – objected to a policy that granted DominiX and androids more rights than any other woman, whether Saudi or foreign, including the right to forgo wearing a veil and to dispense with the requirement of a male guardian.

The first months passed without incident, save for the rapid deterioration of the relationship between Solange and RomeoX. It was as though the android, caught in his own game, had become all too human: reluctant to share household responsibilities, spending most evenings engrossed in televised football matches, and growing increasingly jealous and suspicious – in short, becoming a caricature of male chauvinism. The breaking point came one evening when RomeoX struck Solange after she came home late without warning. The separation was immediate and final. RomeoX was reassigned to another programme, this time under the direction of a male colleague.

These events affected Solange more than she cared to admit. Threatened by burnout, she became less effective at work. Before her superiors could dismiss her, Solange resigned and returned to Europe with DominiX.

Registering DominiX with the local civil authorities and establishing her legal parentage proved to be as complicated as one might expect. Was DominiX Solange's daughter, her younger sister, or her delayed twin? And what could be said of the identity of her father – or at least the being (or entity?) whose brain she had inherited? Unwilling to be drawn into metaphysical quandaries, the civil registry officials opted for the simplest formula: 'Daughter of Solange B.; father unknown'.

Meanwhile, DominiX grew older – but not, it seemed, wiser. From the moment she began to speak, her behaviour was strange, even troubling. She reasoned like an adult, often expressing thoughts that bore no resemblance to the experiences of a little girl. Psychologists who were consulted diagnosed severe cognitive dissonance in a female child exhibiting the psychology of an adult male. Week by week, DominiX became increasingly difficult: she demanded to meet her father, threatened suicide, and displayed knowledge far beyond her age.

Solange soon realised that, thanks to her neural implants, DominiX had instantaneous access to the entirety of the internet – without the slightest parental filter. Heaven only knew what she had seen. Solange even began to suspect that biohackers or rival laboratories had taken control of her child's brain, which at times seemed to be possessed by a superior force. Lacking access to electronic exorcists, Solange found herself overwhelmed – slipping, day by day, into despair.

Then, one day, she did the unthinkable. In an act of desperation, she drowned the child in the canal, short-circuiting the neural prosthetics implanted in her body.

The next day, Solange presented herself at the police station, concealing nothing about the circumstances of the case. Unsurprisingly, the news spread instantly across social media. Among the countless reactions to the tragedy, one of the most unexpected came from a certain RomeoX, who claimed to be the original brain from which the unfortunate victim's neural network had been downloaded. He announced his intention to consult an international law firm specialising in intellectual property. After all, hadn't his neural algorithms, operating systems, and personal data been copied and deployed without his consent? Only he, RomeoX, insisted, held the exclusive right to modify, update, or delete his copies.

After forty-eight hours of interrogation and custody, Solange was formally charged with the murder of DominiX. The examining magistrate referred her to the *Cour d'Assises*, and thus began the trial that would capture the nation's imagination. RomeoX's attempt to join the proceedings as a civil party was rejected on the grounds of uncertain filiation. Some legal commentators lamented the decision, noting the missed opportunity to witness an unprecedented spectacle: an individual demanding justice for their own death, as if the ghost of Hamlet's father had stepped into a courtroom.

The trial opened with the customary procession of character witnesses and scientific experts called by both sides. The public prosecutor, an esteemed magistrate, presented the case for the prosecution with dignity and restraint. This was clearly a case of murder, she argued – specifically, infanticide – committed against DominiX B., who was officially registered as the daughter of Solange B., father unknown.

The facts of the case, she continued, were not in dispute: Solange had confessed. Nor was there any ambiguity regarding the intent to kill. The prosecutor called for the penalties outlined in the Penal Code to be applied, largely as a matter of principle. 'The right to life is universal,' she concluded soberly, 'and no exception can be made for scientific experiments.'

On the defence side, Solange's lawyer – a young, impassioned rising star of the bar – argued emphatically for his client's full acquittal. First, he questioned the very classification of the act as infanticide, asking whether DominiX was truly Solange's daughter, or rather her belated monozygotic twin. With surgical precision, he blurred the boundary between the biological and the digital to the point that even the classification of the act as homicide became uncertain. By the end of his plea, the question of whether a crime had truly been committed was left so suspended, so elusive, that it seemed sufficient grounds for acquittal.

For good measure – and 'purely as a subsidiary argument', as he pointedly phrased it – the lawyer added that, should the jury find Solange guilty (*quod non*), they should at the very least grant her mitigating circumstances. It was not difficult for him to evoke the emotional turmoil the young scientist had endured: the triple blow of a failed cloning experiment, the breakdown of her relationship, and the increasingly erratic and alarming behaviour of the avatar. Confronted with these mounting pressures and feeling utterly incapable of fulfilling her parental responsibilities toward such an 'entity' – and who, he asked, possibly could? – Solange had chosen to end the 'experiment'. In essence, he contended, she had shown humanity by putting an end to the suffering – present and future – of an improbable being.

Moreover, he argued, a guilty verdict followed by a lengthy prison sentence would serve no meaningful purpose – neither for Solange nor for society. Had she not already suffered enough, targeted for months by relentless media campaigns that vilified her in the public eye? Was that not punishment enough?

Finally, the presiding judge invited Solange to speak. In a barely audible voice, she expressed vague regrets, though it remained unclear whether she was apologising for her act or lamenting the course of events that had brought her to this point.

And so, twelve men and women, randomly selected to form the popular jury, entered the deliberation room to decide the fate of Solange B. – and, incidentally, the meaning of the notion of humanity. With a certain gravity, each took their place around the table. Albert, the eldest, designated in that capacity as president of the jury, spoke first:

'My friends – may I call you that? – it is now precisely 11.05 as we begin our deliberations. We will not leave this room until we have answered, yes or no, the question of whether Solange B. is guilty of murder – or perhaps assassination – of DominiX, cloned from her own body. I remind you of the terms of our oath: "to listen neither to fear nor affection, to decide based on the evidence and the arguments presented". I am counting on everyone's cooperation,' he added, with a certain solemnity.

Albert then proposed a round of introductions so that everyone could get acquainted. Turning to his left:

'Madame?'

'Me, I'm Irène. I swear to tell the truth, the whole truth, and nothing but the truth,' she declared – prompting a ripple of laughter around the table.

'Well done, dear madam,' chuckled André. 'At least you're not burdened by doubts!'

'Come now, madam,' Albert said, 'we're not asking that much of you – only to express your *intime conviction*.'

'Solange is so kind,' Irène replied, a little confused. 'Didn't you see how sad she looked? Can I say that's my *intime conviction*?'

'*Intime conviction*,' Jérôme explained with an air of authority, 'is a deep, personal certainty that doesn't need to rely on evidence.'

'I disagree,' objected Monsieur Homais. 'We swore to "decide based on the evidence and the arguments presented". We are a jury of assizes, not a café debate, and we're being asked to use reason, not sentimentality.'

We will spare the reader the confused debate that followed. In the end, Albert, eager not to waste more time, took it upon himself to briefly introduce the other members of the jury.

We already know Irène, fifty-eight years old, unemployed; André, fifty-two, a consultant, who would later distinguish himself with his cynical and disillusioned remarks; Jérôme, forty-two, an insurance broker, always eager to show off his legal knowledge (which, truthfully, amounted to poorly digested snippets from law studies he had never completed); and finally, the juror whose first name we never learned, preferring to be addressed by his surname: Monsieur Homais – fifty-four years old, a pharmacist by trade, a man who prided himself on his scientific expertise and displayed a lofty rationalism.

Continuing around the table, Albert presented the rest, in order:

Philippe, sixty-two, semi-retired. Having worked his entire life in the chemical industry, Philippe was a gentle dreamer, convinced that the future promised a bright harmony between science and human rights. He was a donor member of the FAIL movement – the Friendly Artificial Intelligence League.

Cécilia, twenty-eight, was a historian of Neapolitan origin and Catholic conviction. Her vast erudition would, on more than one occasion, illuminate the jury's deliberations.

Satyne – with a 'y', as she was keen to point out – thirty-eight, a hairdresser by profession. She possessed an encyclopaedic knowledge of cinema and science fiction television series, which she would not hesitate to showcase in the hours to come.

Jonas, thirty-two, is an ecologist and a highly politically engaged activist.

Marcel, forty-three, an unemployed artist ('a pleonasm', he remarked with a loud laugh). His humanity and humour would prove very useful as the proceedings unfolded.

Aline, forty-six, a postal worker ('a woman of letters', Marcel quipped, delivering a hearty slap on her back). Her deep common sense and solid convictions would soon make themselves known.

The introductions concluded with Maurice, a withdrawn and, to be frank, mysterious figure who still seemed to be wondering what he was doing among this group. All that was learned about him was that, at forty-nine years old, he was unemployed. He never strayed far from an electrical outlet and seemed to communicate only with his computer.

Finally, Albert introduced himself: an independent journalist, also semi-retired. Devoid of particularly firm personal convictions, Albert had, in truth, no idea what direction the debates would take; but, taking the civic mission entrusted to him very seriously, he was determined to conduct the discussions as impartially as possible.

To provide the reader with complete information, it should also be noted that, during the preliminary hearing, Solange's lawyer had exercised his right to challenge a Moroccan merchant whose creationist bias against his client was all too evident (his T-shirt displayed a simian figure accompanied by the slogan *I hate Darwin*). For its part, the prosecution had challenged a transgender military officer who had recently undergone surgery to become a woman.

∴

ALBERT, clearing his throat: Now that we've introduced ourselves, let's get to work! The destruction of DominiX – are we being asked if this was the murder of a person or simply the disposal of a machine? I suspect this question will divide us and that it raises serious moral and philosophical issues. I propose we address these first; let everyone give their opinion on the ethical stakes. Once we've cleared the ground, we can then move on to the legal questions before us. Do we agree?

HOMAIS, interrupting: Listen, I've heard so much nonsense during this trial, so many ridiculous technophobic prejudices, that I feel the need to clarify things right away. This trial that has brought us together is just a mere episode, a painful one perhaps, but no more than a passing story. What matters here is the grand, supernatural future we are creating, one we will participate in. A superior nature, far more enviable than polluted, deregulated, impoverished natural nature.

We've stopped imitating nature; now we're creating it anew from scratch. That's what's at stake here. We must accept that this movement cannot and will not be stopped. Progress is accelerating every day. Our machines are becoming smaller and more powerful. Yesterday, we carried our computers around with us; today, we carry chips and software inside our brains and circulatory systems.

This 3.0 artificial intelligence is becoming self-learning, capable of duplicating itself by programming ever more advanced versions of itself. The computational power of computers doubles every two years in an exponential progression. By 2045, we will have reached the tipping point of technological singularity – at that point, computers will surpass us and control the entire chain of research and production for their programs.

Then the distinction between the virtual and physical worlds will blur, and there will no longer be any separation between enhanced humans and machines. We will be able to expand beyond the limits of Earth. After suffering death and entropy for millions of years, we will finally become part of the universe as an immense data-processing system.

MARCEL, under his breath: Hold him back – he's about to levitate!

(Then, louder) Listen, Homais, stay with us, or we'll have to start the whole process over again – and Brazil versus Germany is on TV tomorrow.

HOMAIS, unperturbed: In such circumstances, increasing our computational potential will be our duty – or at least our reason for being. Who would want to remain trapped in their biological body, version 1.0 – those fragile shells prone to countless dysfunctions, demanding exorbitant maintenance costs, and soon to be obsolete? Cyberneticist Kevin Warwick wrote: 'Those who refuse to upgrade themselves will suffer a serious handicap. They will form a subspecies and become the chimpanzees of the future.'

Then, suddenly exalted: Freed from our fleshly envelopes, our minds will escape degeneration and be promised perpetuity. Furthermore, connected to the internet, they will access a virtually infinite pool of knowledge.

And I tell you this: if I don't live long enough to benefit from these techniques, I will have myself frozen until they become available at a reasonable cost; all my arrangements are already made.

MARCEL, mocking: That's a chilling thought, if I may say so.

JÉRÔME, sententious: *Audi et altera pars!*

MARCEL: Excuse me? I need a translator.

JÉRÔME: It means 'let the other side be heard'. We're in a courtroom here; after Monsieur Homais' plea, we must hear the opposing viewpoint.

JONAS, fervently: Don't worry, I'll handle it. What concerns me isn't that speeches like these can be made; it's that there are extremely powerful investors – both private and military – encouraging and funding such delusional programs with billions of dollars. Since these people aren't fools, it means these research efforts are hiding something else – something tied to profit and power. Companies developing these brain-mapping programs, sometimes with covert government support, collect and process this information about us with the primary aim of reducing us to a monetizable mass of data and expanding social control. Our consumer habits, our browsing habits, our reading habits – all of it is in their hands, every detail of our lives. We are being reduced to a sum of data points, which they cross-reference with others and reprocess into subtle injunctions, turning us into clicking machines. And all of this is sold to us under the promise of paradise, enhanced life, and deferred death.

Let's imagine for a moment that these promises become technically possible – say, by 2045, as you mentioned – who would they concern? A few thousand hyper-rich individuals – those who today hold more wealth than the poorest half of humanity. The vast majority, the losers, would continue to lead their simply human existence, under the influence of thoughts, emotions, and desires imposed by cognitive marketing.

HOMAIS: The greatest inequality is the one that separates the living from the dead; science is fighting to guarantee immortality for all.

JONAS: Here we go again, the same old humanist rhetoric: help your neighbour, shake up the old world, save the planet, and all that jazz. But Silicon Valley is careful not to reveal its links with finance and the military. Techno-capitalism now presents itself as the ultimate redeemer; it will save us from pollution, disease, and even death itself: deliver us from evil! Technology and the heroes of Silicon Valley now have answers for everything; for them, even the most existential questions necessarily have a solution – a solution that comes through lines of code and algorithms. DominiX is the tragic product of these fantasies.

HOMAIS: No one is forcing you to follow the movement!

JONAS: That's yet another illusion; in real life, people are already constantly subjected to performance demands, targeted by all sorts of imperatives that don't speak their names. The economy that governs us has become financial, and it's trading robots that now give the orders on the stock market. And legal regulations, always one war behind, are often bypassed: some countries still forbid human cloning, but you know how 'augmentative tourism' is developing. It's no coincidence that DominiX was born in Saudi Arabia.

MARCEL: If I may make a down-to-earth remark, I'd point out that these super-intelligent machines are essentially made of silicon, and silicon reserves aren't infinite.

HOMAIS: Well, we'll go get it on Mars or elsewhere – or we'll develop alternative techniques, like quantum computing. Contrary to all the whiners and Cassandras, reason has always found a way to move forward.

ALBERT: Let's not get off track. Cécilia, we haven't heard from you yet.

CÉCILIA: All this is a bit beyond me, I admit. Maybe it's my training as a historian that influences me, but I can't help finding something familiar about all these theories. It's like a great recycling of ideas as old as the world: reincarnation, deliverance from the body, eternal return. The legend of Gilgamesh, from ancient Mesopotamia, already fosters these fantasies. Vulcan made automatons, according to mythology, and medieval alchemists tried to create homunculi. In the Christian world, the Gnostic heresy perfectly anticipates transhumanist discourse. According to the Gnostics, the material world, including our fleshly bodies, wasn't created by God but by a malevolent power, the demiurge. So we would be trapped in the corruption of our bodies, and only a select few – the Gnostics themselves – would escape damnation by accessing the highest spheres of knowledge. To me, the digitisation of the mind reactivates these old fantasies; you also find them in eschatological discourse, announcing the end of times and, for some, triumph over death, the entry into the New Jerusalem – those people will be beatified, reincarnated in brand-new bodies ...

ANDRÉ, interrupting: So, in essence, places like the FUMIST are playing God – who, after long neglecting his duties toward his creatures, is now making a grand comeback in the form of software: a new alpha and omega composed of zeros and ones.

CÉCILIA: What I mean is that these technological fantasies distort the poetic teachings of Scripture. Transhumanism, while addressing legitimate desires and ancestral fears, is a grotesque parody of faith. It's the same dream of redemption, but offered here and now, on Earth, and without effort!

ANDRÉ: Amen! Come on, it's the same old tune! Frustrated humans first created gods in their own image and submitted to them, and now they're creating machines in their likeness – and submitting to them. Automaton idols ...

MARCEL: Automaton? Personally, I'm more into spaghetti *aux tomates*. Speaking of which, it's already 12.30 – when are we eating?

HOMAIS, sternly: I see we've plunged back into the darkness of obscurantism. Don't you understand the marvel that DominiX's brain represented? Its cognitive abilities were infinitely superior to those of its mother, for example. Even though our brain relies on billions of neuronal connections, its information processing is extremely slow compared to today's processors. Our neurons operate at 200 hertz; transistors function on the scale of gigahertz. Signals in our nervous system travel at roughly 100 meters per second – while computer signals move at the speed of light. And while the human brain is constrained by the skull, we can now build processors as large as skyscrapers.

(Then, more passionately) The historic opportunity we're being offered is to transfer our cognitive processes into a more suitable and interconnected substrate. Our minds will then know no limits. Soon, the operation will be as simple as transferring a file from a website to a PC. Our biographical memory, our thought patterns, our desires – all of it reduced to code and downloaded onto an independent computing platform, compilable, and reusable across others.

(Inexhaustible, he presses on) The human mind – if freed from its misty metaphysical framework – can be described as software: a repository of information accompanied by an operational processor, an operating system. Understood this way, the brain is simply a tool for storing and processing data, a sequence of code running via the processor of the nervous system. What has been achieved – and successfully, mind you, in DominiX's case – is the download of RomeoX's brain onto its own, which, I remind you, had been reduced to vegetative functions. This proves that we can now digitise the human mind and, soon, upload it onto absolutely any medium – be it a humanoid machine or any other kind of container. We will live beyond the human body; consciousness will evolve free of all physical limits, in a state of total morphological freedom. There will be a thousand ways to exist. We'll become pure consciousness – liberated from our biological shells – experiencing something entirely spiritual across networks.

ALINE, exploding: Honestly, this is like a dream – but not in a good way. I'm a postwoman, and when I'm on my rounds, I think with my feet. When I come home exhausted, I think with my aching back. When I put my kids to bed and kiss them, I think with my hands, my mouth, our skins touching – those touches tell me something. I may just be a postal worker, but I am my body. I have thoughts, desires, fears like anyone else – but they come from my body just as much as from my mind.

I don't understand what a thought reduced to a line of code even is. Yes, a series of symbols – but lifeless, dead. What could a silicon brain really think? Memories of old impressions, the recall of past reasoning – sure. But what could it express that's genuinely new? Sure, it can calculate and combine data at lightning speed. But our minds aren't just data. They're not just lines of code or digitised information.

My mind isn't just intelligence. It's also imagination, sensations, desire, fear, passion, feeling – and I feel them in my guts. I live them in my heart. Your robots start by cutting a person into little pieces – separating the brain from the body, then breaking down the mind into data – and then they reassemble the pieces, like a puzzle, imitating reality. But in the meantime, the reality gets lost. You're selling us a robot portrait and pretending it's just as real as the original ...

HOMAIS: Do you really think human nature is such a great success? We're creatures of habit – easily influenced, envious, ignorant, incoherent, mimetic. I tell you, intelligence is finally taking its revenge on blind evolution and the dictatorship of ignorance. Tomorrow, we'll be part of a vast, cosmic, and reticular intelligence.

ANDRÉ: Besides, let's not kid ourselves. Techniques for enhancing human performance already exist – and we're using them plenty: doping, cosmetic surgery, psychotropics, contraceptive pills ...

JONAS: Listen, Homais, let me come back to your learning robots. I'd like to tell you the story of Tay, the chatbot launched into the digital sphere by Microsoft in 2016 – it's quite revealing what it learned. Tay was built on an unsupervised learning model; it engaged in conversations with anyone, without revealing its robotic nature. Within days, it attracted an impressive crowd of 'everyday people', most of whom were trolls – people who express themselves with disinhibited verbal violence thanks to digital anonymity.

Tay, being unsupervised, fed its neural networks with input from its troll friends and quickly became a vulgar, xenophobic robot. It also became extremely talkative – by the end, it was capable of sending up to 96,000 tweets in 16 hours – before finally being shut down. That's what your learning robots replicate: mob mentality and populism.

MARCEL: You know, I think animals are more reasonable. In any case, if one day I have to choose between becoming a robot or a bear, I wouldn't hesitate for a second. Animals watching us must think we've lost all common sense and become an absurd and harmful species.

PHILIPPE: Oh, come on, Marcel, don't be so cynical. Let's not deny ourselves this pleasure – what a beautiful prospect, not dying. How comforting it is, this right not to die!

ALINE: But why this fear of death? I don't want to live for a hundred years or more. It must be terribly boring. The truth is, death has become taboo. It has to be hidden at all costs – we medicalise it, we isolate it socially, even though it's the most natural thing in the world. In the past, people died surrounded by family, by their village. Today, they die all alone. I see it often on my rounds – people react like they do nowadays, demanding a right: the right not to die. But I think the opposite: what gives us our dignity is being vulnerable, fragile – mortal, in the end.

CÉCILIA: Aline is right. That's what all traditions teach us: it's our condition as mortals that gives us dignity. Philosophers call this 'finitude'. When you think about it, it's what makes us free – we aren't programmed to last forever, or to always walk the straight path. It's also what makes us different from one another, not endless reproductions of the same perfect model.

The robot's universe is one of sameness, endlessly repeated: one–zero, zero–one. Binary logic. No third option. A world without otherness, an autistic world, the triumph of mimicry, a universal tautology. We became human when we broke away from that. Remember Adam – he freed himself from the perfect model and bit into the forbidden apple.

MARCEL: I quite like that definition: humanity is the being that screws up and knows it. All things considered, the robot Deep Blue will truly be human not when it beats Kasparov at chess – as it already does – but the day it cheats. Or perhaps the day it becomes suicidal, couldn't care less about immortality, and needs little silicon pills ...

ALINE: Or maybe when it learns to doubt. I think these intelligent robots know far more than we do – but they don't doubt. Absolute certainty is terrifying. Knowledge acquired all at once, without being digested, matured, embodied.

ANDRÉ: This discussion is absurd: do robots have consciousness? It's as stupid as when the Spaniards debated in Valladolid whether Indigenous people had souls. They might just as well have asked whether the conquistadors had hearts – or whether we had a shred of common sense.

ALBERT: Come now, let's calm down. I remind you, it's not us asking the questions but the Court. And besides, we'd do well to return to the trial: I remind you, we are not an Academy but a jury of assizes. Solange is waiting for our verdict. We need to answer a precise question with a yes or a no.

IRÈNE, rolling her eyes: Yes, yes, we're waiting for our *intime conviction*.

MARCEL: Well, my *intime conviction* is that it's already 1.30 p.m., and we still haven't received our sandwiches.

ALBERT: I'll ring the concierge. In the meantime, now that everyone has had their say, I suggest we turn to Solange and DominiX. Let's start with the simplest matter – if I may call it that: cloning. Does DominiX, as a clone of Solange, possess legal personhood? Do you remember what the expert, Mr Parizot, explained to us?

SATYNE: Oh, that Mr Parizot – wasn't he handsome? He looked just like Richard Gere in *Pretty Woman*.

HOMAIS: Let me first clarify what cloning is, or we'll end up confusing everything again. Cloning is a technique derived from botany, similar to grafting. It creates an organism identical to an existing or previously existing being. The embryo has the same genetic makeup as the organism donating the cell – in other words, reproduction without fertilisation.

MARCEL, ironically: A small step for the donor, a giant leap for mankind. God created man, and man created the clone.

JONAS: Well, what I foresee in the long run is the near-total disappearance of the difference between sexes – if we decide it's more convenient to reproduce only males or only females, like in a beehive. Imagine the gender war that would erupt at the final moment: liquidate all the men, except for a few dozen, raised as fat drones just in case they're needed. Or the opposite: nothing but guys, with a few women kept in museums like endangered masterpieces ... And then, how would we regulate cloning? How many clones per person would be allowed? What would be the minimum quality required to be authorised to clone oneself? We're heading straight for the most extreme eugenics.

ALBERT: Please, let's not reopen ideological debates. Jérôme, since you have some knowledge of law, could you remind us of the expert's analysis? And if someone could wake Irène, who's been napping for quite some time, I'd appreciate it. Irène, our discussions may not captivate you, but soon enough, you'll have to express your opinion and cast your vote like everyone else – so please, make an effort!

JÉRÔME, flattered and solemn: We were first reminded that in a number of countries, cloning is simply prohibited. The law absolutely forbids the creation of cloned embryos – whether human, transgenic, or chimeric, including human–animal hybrids. In such cases, the cloned being cannot receive any legal status, as it is entirely prohibited – a legal void. But this doesn't help us much, since our country has not legislated on the matter. The case of DominiX forces us to reason in prospective law; our case has no precedent.

The expert first addressed chimeric cloning, which is already a well-mastered technique. Legally, the question is complex, since animality falls under the regime of 'things', while humanity is granted legal personhood. If animality is deemed dominant, the hybrid is a 'thing', but if humanity prevails in our eyes, then it is a person – according to the rule *accessorium sequitur principale*.

MARCEL: And there he goes again! Do hybrids speak Latin now?

JÉRÔME: The accessory follows the principal; the derived part benefits from the legal treatment granted to the dominant part.

Four solutions are proposed. First: we could grant the chimera an intermediate status – half-human, half-animal – but this would mean accepting intermediate statuses of sub-humans. Second: we could simply consider them as animals – sub-humans, in this case.

ANDRÉ, cynically: Excellent idea – a cheap workforce, never tired. No coffee breaks, no holidays, and no unions! Remember Vercors and his *tropis* in *Les Animaux dénaturés* – he predicted it all.

∴

At this point, the discussion was interrupted by the arrival of sandwiches and drinks. Marcel took charge of serving. When he reached Homais, he pretended to pass him by:

MARCEL, muttering: Mr 3.0 probably doesn't need earthly sustenance.

(Then, laughing loudly) Just kidding – help yourself while you're still one of us. Unless you'd prefer a silicon boost?

JÉRÔME: Well, I'll continue while you eat. If you've followed me, there are two possibilities left. Either we consider them superhumans – which wouldn't be inaccurate, since their capacities would exceed our own, especially if we compare them to animals stronger than us, which would be a sensible benchmark. But that would, in turn, relegate us to the rank of subhumans – remember what Mr Homais said: 'the chimpanzees of the future'.

Ultimately, the expert concluded, only one possibility truly stands: to regard the chimera as strictly equal to a human being and to grant it the same rights. After all, he said, it's all a matter of degree – even today, some people survive thanks to animal tissue or organ transplants. And while a chimera is not biologically identical to a being conceived through the union of a man's and a woman's gametes, the law is under no obligation to follow biology. Through its fictions, it can shape the reality we consider most desirable.

CÉCILIA: Precisely. Just because something is technically possible doesn't mean the law must align with it automatically. I'd like to remind everyone that the word *hybrid* comes from the Greek *hubris* – excess, arrogance – the kind of mad pride that, in Greek tragedy, always led to catastrophe.

ALBERT: Thank you, Jérôme, for reminding us of those analyses. But the case of DominiX is both simpler and more complex. She isn't a hybrid – she's the pure clone of Solange.

CÉCILIA: And it's no coincidence that countries that have thought seriously about this have banned it. Human cloning raises questions that make your head spin – questions about what it means to be human. I don't want to get lost in metaphysics, but you'll agree with me: men and women are defined by three things – freedom, singularity, and mortality. With cloning, none of those three remain.

The clone isn't free, because we design it to match its model, completely predetermining its genetic makeup. It's no longer singular, either, since it can be reproduced in any number of copies. And it won't even be mortal the day we decide to practise successive cloning of the same original.

ALINE: Yes, and I also think clones would face discrimination everywhere. People might start producing clones just to harvest tissue or organs for themselves. And they'd throw the whole family structure into chaos – look at DominiX. We don't even know whether she's Solange's daughter or her twin. How could anyone live with that kind of confusion? The law has to forbid it.

JONAS: I don't like this idea of perfect copies. It's like intensive farming with ultra-selected seeds – in the long run, it destroys genetic diversity and weakens the whole system.

MARCEL: The moral of the story: 'Don't play the clown'.

ALBERT: Fortunately, we're not being asked to legislate, only to decide the case of DominiX. I note, at this point, that the legal expert we heard from – Mr Parizot – was in favour of granting legal personhood to the cloned being, though I also acknowledge the reservations expressed by some of us. But we're not out of the woods yet, as DominiX's case is even more complex. While her body is that of Solange, her brain has been transferred from the robot RomeoX. We must therefore also examine the question from this angle, as was done during the trial. The issue is no longer just the status of the cloned being, but of a living being endowed with artificial intelligence.

MARCEL: Who plays the angel, plays the beast … and who makes Solange, makes the robot!

ALBERT: Very funny – I'll make a note of it in the record. I also think we should start taking proper notes. Maurice, you haven't said much – would you mind being our scribe?

Maurice, still silent and somewhat awkward, complies.

ALBERT, clearing his throat: You'll recall that regarding androids and cyborgs, the prosecutor developed a step-by-step argument, starting with simple prosthetics and ending with autonomous androids.

SATYNE: Like in the series *Real Humans*, where robots – they're called Hubots – are just like us. I loved it. In episode 4, they choose their own clothes – it's hilarious! And in episode 8, a Hubot is afraid of dying – I was hooked.

ALBERT: Thank you for that very useful detail. As I was saying, the prosecutor began by discussing the regime of prosthetics – like those bionic implants that replace failing organs, or the chips implanted in some paraplegics' bodies that allow them to regain limited mobility.

JÉRÔME: Yes, the prosthesis, like the body, is assigned to serve the person. As long as this relationship of assignment lasts, it follows the legal status of the subject. We can say that bionic material is a person *by destination* or *by incorporation*, as the legal scholars put it. For Marcel, this reflects the rule that the accessory follows the principal.

MARCEL: Well, all this won't get us the Congo back!

JÉRÔME: Excuse me?

MARCEL: Nothing, nothing – just a private joke.

JÉRÔME: As I was saying, the status of the prosthesis changes depending on its assignment: as long as it serves the person, it shares their legal status – it becomes part of the subject, like the body. But as soon as it's detached, it reverts to being a mere object – transferable, tradable, and seizable.

CÉCILIA: Yes, but the parallel with the body doesn't go all the way. Our legal system, as the lawyer reminded us, stipulates that the human body must be treated with respect, even after death. In contrast, a prosthesis, once detached from the person, is just an object you can send to the scrapyard. You might admire its ingenuity and assess its value, but it remains a machine – undeserving of respect.

HOMAIS: Careful now. We're already capable of making intelligent implants – not just electrodes translating brain impulses to provoke movement, but implants that function like a second brain, placed beneath the injury and controlling nerves through electrical signals. In such cases, the prosthesis could potentially gain autonomy.

SATYNE: Oh yes, like in Méliès' film *The Electric Leg* – have you seen it? The guy has an electric leg prosthesis that does whatever it wants, and it systematically leads him to the girls' dormitory.

ALINE: You see where that leads? It's like a kind of schizophrenia, as if you had two opposing brains. For me, the individual must always retain control over their prosthesis or implants – like an autopilot that you should always be able to turn off.

HOMAIS: But, dear madam, I must tell you that this question no longer arises in such terms. We already implant tiny electrodes around the human brain to enhance its performance. So, where is the boundary between the bionic and the mechanical, between grey matter and silicon?

JONAS: Yes, but you always seem to imply that the body is the problem and the mind – especially the digital mind – is the solution. But I could turn your argument against you. In many cases, the body is a sturdy shell that protects our brain and ensures its autonomy, while your artificial intelligence seems quite fragile to me: it could be hacked, deprogrammed, or infected with a virus. Its storage medium could be damaged or destroyed; its digitised code could be altered, or a virus could be injected into its operating system.

ALBERT: All right, all right, my friends – please, let's avoid arguing over principles. I remind you that the prosthesis was just the first step of the reasoning. The second step is the android endowed with strong and autonomous artificial intelligence, as in the case of DominiX, guided by the downloaded brain of RomeoX. I must admit, I'm getting a little lost here, because ultimately, it's hard to tell where the principal ends and the accessory begins: is it her cloned mother's body, or her father's downloaded mind, so to speak? If it's the mind that takes precedence, then the question arises in all its sharpness: is the android already a subject of law – a person whose intentional destruction would constitute a crime?

JÉRÔME: Until now, most legal systems have been reluctant to recognise the android as a legal person. It remains classified as movable property that can be alienated, rented, or stolen. If its owner abandons it, it is considered *res derelicta*.

MARCEL: *Res* what? Next round's on you! Though they'd have to serve us something better than this convent coffee. *Res derelicta* – I'll have to remember that one.

JÉRÔME: Our legal framework derives from Roman law, and its great principles are still rooted in it. I can't change that. So, I was saying that, for most traditional jurists, robots can be discarded like used batteries or obsolete computers because they lack consciousness, thought, or free will. That said, we've known of intermediate statuses for human beings who, while not – or no longer – legal persons, were not mere objects either. One of the experts brought up this idea. For example, in Rome, slaves, while considered movable property, at least had the capacity to exercise their masters' rights. We could consider a similar status for androids.

ANDRÉ: Excellent idea! My android can do the shopping with my wife and pay using her Visa card ... I'll keep that in mind.

JÉRÔME: Another intermediate case that the law has encountered is that of individuals considered to be struck by 'civil death' after a conviction, or declared 'absent' following a very long disappearance.

MARCEL: Oh yes, like our very own *Hibernatus* – he gestures toward Monsieur Homais – during his time in the freezer.

CÉCILIA: Well, just go ask Colonel Chabert how he was received when he returned from the Russian campaign. They thought he was lost in the ice of the Berezina, too ... I'm not sure those statuses are particularly advantageous.

ALBERT: Listen, time is passing, and we haven't made much progress. DominiX's case is far more advanced than these examples of domestic robots that provide small services. Clearly, she was a very intelligent and unique little girl. Today's androids talk, laugh, cry, and even if it's all artifice, they are incredibly convincing. We've known this since Philip K. Dick's book *Do Androids Dream of Electric Sheep?*, which Ridley Scott adapted into the film *Blade Runner* in 1982 – you've seen it, haven't you, Satyne? It's becoming increasingly difficult to distinguish living organisms from transistorised circuits. They're 'replicants', products of robotic revolutions but created by geneticists. Did you know that these replicants now pass the 'mirror test', which chimpanzees once mastered? When a mark is painted on their face without their knowledge, and they are later presented with a mirror, they attempt to remove it.

HOMAIS: Well done! I see that reason is finally prevailing in this jury!

ALBERT: In that case, shouldn't we grant them legal personhood?

∴

A heavy silence settles over the room. Some jurors grow sullen, Irène has fallen asleep again, while others, like Maurice, seem content, meticulously transcribing every word of the exchanges. Marcel asks for a break to smoke a cigarette in the hallway. Others use the interruption to make phone calls, prompting Albert to remind them that communication is strictly limited to their immediate family members.

When the session resumes fifteen minutes later, Philippe, appearing rather exhilarated, asks to speak.

PHILIPPE: My friends, our president earlier asked whether we should grant legal personhood to our android friends. I believe that historic moment has indeed arrived. Remember Pinocchio, the wooden puppet who longed to become 'a real boy'. Recall also Andrew Martin, *The Bicentennial Man* by Asimov. He experienced emotions, possessed free will, and one day demanded freedom from his master. Very enlightening for our discussion – there was even a ruling in his case, where the judge declared: 'There is no reason to deny freedom to an object with a brain developed enough to grasp the concept of freedom and desire it.'

JONAS: Very pretty words, but today we're building military robots – robots that kill remotely – so I would be cautious about their understanding of freedom.

PHILIPPE: Precisely, Mr Jonas. Asimov thought of everything. In his book, he established the three fundamental laws of robotics, which are well known today. These laws dictate that robots must refrain from harming humans, even prioritising human interests over their own in case of conflict. He even included a duty to assist humans in danger. Moreover, this aligns with the original meaning of the word 'robot', derived from the Czech *robota*, first used by the playwright Karel Čapek in a 1921 play. It means 'servant' – servants here in the service of humans.

ALINE: Philippe, honestly – Pinocchio, Asimov, Čapek's *robota* – all of that is fiction, literature, not law. It's not real life.

PHILIPPE: You're mistaken, Madame Aline. Let me tell you, the European Parliament – yes, I said the European Parliament – passed a resolution on 16 February 2017 recommending that robots be granted legal personhood and that Asimov's three laws of robotics be applied to designers, manufacturers, and operators. Fiction inspiring law – it's extraordinary. Later on, Asimov even proposed a more fundamental law, numbered zero: 'A robot may not harm humanity, or, through inaction, allow humanity to come to harm.'

SATYNE: Yes, yes, like Robby the Robot in *Forbidden Planet* – he can't carry out any order if it would harm humans.

ANDRÉ: What a nightmare – philanthropic robots! I'd still prefer Terminator! Can you imagine it, an android robot, syrupy, and obsequious, like a *maître d'*: 'Would you care for more tea, sir?' Or worse, a nagging nurse: 'André, it's not advisable for you to drink more than two glasses of wine.' Or a moralising nun: 'André, you shouldn't call that man an idiot – he's only expressing his opinion.' We didn't have a revolution just to bow down now to the conformity of these so-called friends of humanity!

ALBERT: Listen, I do think we're making progress this time. That resolution from the European Parliament is very helpful. Still, it begs the question of the criteria for granting legal personhood. If the criterion is intelligence or will, as it now seems to be for androids, what do we do about small children, the insane, the mentally disabled, or those in comas?

CÉCILIA: It's because of their dignity as human beings that they're recognised as persons – beings with potential in the cases you mentioned, beings who suffer, but human and worthy of dignity in every instance.

PHILIPPE, still animated and visibly moved: But that's precisely the criterion! The most advanced androids are capable of suffering, since they feel things as we do. They long to be recognised, they want to be free – they are the ones asking to be treated as legal persons, worthy of respect. It's our responsibility to acknowledge our alter egos.

MARCEL: Come on, Philippe, don't you start too! I thought we'd agreed – no more Latin!

ANDRÉ: But these robots are not our equals. When will we stop projecting anthropomorphic images onto them? The value of these ultra-sophisticated machines lies not in their humanoid form but in the services they provide ...

JONAS, interrupting: And the profits they generate.

ANDRÉ: As I was saying, it's the services they provide, and it's the artificial intelligence that powers them – programmed from Amazon or Google servers – which could just as easily take thirty-six other forms. And anyway, mimicking humans isn't even a very effective strategy for robots, given our limited capabilities. Look at aeroplanes: they fly like birds, but they don't flap their wings.

SATYNE: I don't know if this is relevant, but in *Star Trek*, there's an episode where, on Starbase 173, a tribunal like ours debates whether Data, an android, is a thing or a person. They discuss whether or not he has consciousness. At one point, the captain says, 'But how can one prove that? I challenge you to demonstrate to this court that I am conscious!'

JÉRÔME: Exactly – perfectly put! That's what one of the experts, Mr Defferrand, explained – he's written a book on the subject. He spoke – though Marcel won't like this – of *probatio diabolica*, and I'll translate before he gets upset: 'diabolical proof', meaning an impossible proof to produce. In such cases, he explained, we must rely on presumptions – a set of indicators that allow us to move from the known to the unknown. You observe signs of seemingly human, deliberate, and intentional behaviour and deduce that they emanate from a conscious being.

Another way to approach the question is to acknowledge that there is doubt about the existence of consciousness – but that this doubt alone is sufficient to exclude the classification of 'thing'. This is the principle that doubt should incline us in favor of the person: *in dubio pro persona*. Therefore, there is a *presumptio in favorem* of those beings that display behaviours very similar to our own.

MARCEL: No, no, I'm not saying a word – I've switched to simultaneous translation mode.

ALBERT: So, we could argue that granting legal personhood to androids, as the European Parliament suggests, is no longer absurd.

JÉRÔME: Exactly. In reality, we increasingly recognise that legal personhood is perfectly separable from the quality of being human. Therefore, we can consider entities other than humans as subjects of rights and grant them the rights they functionally require. Legal personhood is a mere technical tool – a fiction, if you will.

MARCEL: A bedtime story, you mean. The legal code – a tale of science fiction! Who would've thought?

JÉRÔME: Look, the examples are numerous. We've long known of what we call 'legal persons', which allow us to individualise a collective entity – a commercial company or a public authority, like a municipality – and grant it the status of a subject of law. This enables it to enter into contracts, act in court, own assets, and even bear responsibility. But the idea is evolving: as soon as a legislator decides it's important to animate an entity worthy of protection, to protect it for its own sake and not merely in the interest of its owner, nothing prevents them from doing so. Increasingly, we're granting personhood to animals – and even to rivers or forests.

MARCEL: So we'll have animal trials, like in La Fontaine's fables? But I'm warning you: if my dog sues me for mistreatment, I'm slapping him with a countersuit for nighttime noise!

JÉRÔME: Nothing is impossible in law. In Argentina, a court issued a *habeas corpus* order requiring the release of an orangutan held in unacceptable conditions. The *habeas corpus* rule prohibits arrest and detention without trial; the court decided that Sandra, an eight-year-old female displayed in the Buenos Aires zoo, was a 'non-human person' and suffered from the conditions of her illegal detention.

MARCEL: If orangutans start speaking Latin, too, I'm giving up. And I suppose the judge adopted Sandra and welcomed her into their home? And if Sandra bites some granny's dog, I assume she'll have to pay damages?

CÉCILIA: I think legal personhood, even functional as you described it, is a symbolic instrument, not just a technical tool, and it cannot be separated from the idea of dignity. It's this eminent value that leads to the recognition of fundamental rights – like the right to life, freedom of thought and communication, and respect for private life.

PHILIPPE: Exactly. But why wouldn't an android that thinks and suffers deserve these rights? The right to life, the right to think and express itself, the right to privacy ...

MARCEL, laughing hysterically: The right to sexuality, the presumption of innocence, the right of association, the right to vote – Robots of all countries, unite!

Then, singing at the top of his lungs:

It's the final struggle,
Let us group and tomorrow,
The Internationale – of robots –
Will be the human race – oh, woe!

Irène, who had dozed off near the radiator, wakes with a start.

ANDRÉ: So, Irène – dreaming of humanoid robots? Dream or nightmare?

SATYNE: Speaking of nightmares – I don't know if I should mention this now – humans aren't always kind to robots. In *Blade Runner*, there's a hunt for robots led by bounty hunters, and in the series *Battlestar Galactica*, the Cylons are called 'toasters' and eliminated like cockroaches.

HOMAIS: And here we go again. Just wait – within a minute, someone will bring up the Golem, Frankenstein's monster, or Terminator. The robot rebelling against man – why not a legislating robot granting itself legal personhood?

JONAS: Listen, let's stop dreaming in technicolour – whether rosy or bleak – of cuddly robots or evil wolves. They are machines programmed by humans. They couldn't care less about our legal statuses; they don't need our concept of legal personhood. Maurice, please note this carefully. Cyborgs don't expect anything from the law; they respond to electrical stimuli. Justice, respect, responsibility – none of these things can be translated into algorithms. Their autonomy is material, not symbolic, and their capacity for action is programmed, never risked.

So the real problem isn't the hostility of androids but their total indifference toward us. The question is no longer about the personification of robots but the dehumanisation of humans. If, in 2045, the grand utopia dreamed of by Philippe and Monsieur Homais comes true, the dominant logic will become machinic, indifferent to human emotions and all our legal achievements. We will carry no more weight in robot programs than our pets do today. We will simply become obsolete, eventually replaced by more efficient technology – likely tolerated and exploited in the meantime. It will be the triumph of techno-Darwinism.

MARCEL, for once without a comeback: You're no fun, Jonas ...

A heavy and uncomfortable silence settled over the room; no one seemed willing to break it. Maurice lifted his head from the keyboard, and even Irène appeared attentive.

Finally, Albert spoke.

ALBERT: My friends, night has fallen, and we haven't yet spoken much about Solange. Perhaps it's because she has confessed, and the question is now almost entirely philosophical: material damage or the murder of a person? Whatever each of us may think, we will need to answer this question with a simple yes or no. We've already debated the personhood of the clone and of the artificial intelligence. Now we must take one final step – and since we're dealing with DominiX, we must decide whether a digital brain uploaded into a cloned body constitutes a legal person.

SATYNE: That reminds me – in *Stargate*, the Asgard reproduce this way: cloning and inserting a digitised mind into their bodies.

MARCEL: You know, it would've been much simpler for Solange to seduce some random guy from her lab, let him knock her up, and give birth like everyone else – nine months later ...

SATYNE: Oh, Marcel, really – how crass!

MARCEL: Anytime, darling!

ALBERT: Now, now, my friends – let's keep it professional. I know it's late, and we're all exhausted. Let's get back to DominiX.

ANDRÉ, cynically: Well, here's what I think. You all remember the rule about the principal and the accessory, and how the accessory follows the principal? Yes? Then it boils down to two possibilities: either the principal is the human body – cloned, yes, but still human – in relation to the digital brain; or the second possibility: the principal is the mind in relation to the body, as we've always been taught. In both cases, it's a legal nullity. In the first scenario, DominiX's body is completely brainless – it's no longer a person, and therefore the digital brain follows the body's legal regime. Or, in the second scenario, what defines DominiX's status is her digital mind, but that mind has nothing human about it. Therefore, DominiX is an object, and her destruction is nothing more than the simple deterioration of equipment. *Q.E.D.*

ALBERT: You can't be serious. It seems to me that our discussions lean toward recognising the legal personhood of DominiX. Let's not forget the European Parliament resolution inviting us to acknowledge the personhood of robots. We also concluded the earlier discussion about cloning in a similar vein, despite some reservations. Logically, we could argue that the combination of these two quasi-personhoods results in full personhood. Let's also recall the presumption in favour of the human, and the principle of doubt, which should benefit a being so similar to us.

Well, I think we could debate this for another week and still be no further along. It's time for us to make a decision. If the majority of us lean toward recognising legal personhood, Solange will be declared guilty, and we'll move to a second discussion – with the judges this time – about the sentence to be applied. Let's keep these two decisions distinct, and I remind you: it's not forbidden to be lenient when it comes to sentencing. We could even take a preliminary round of opinions on that matter. Now, I'll begin by asking for your views, starting on my right – Jérôme?

JÉRÔME: I'm fairly convinced of DominiX's legal personhood, for the reasons you've just outlined, Mr President. However, something still troubles me. For murder to be constituted, it requires the killing of a human person. Yet, as we've clarified, legal personhood – this technical fiction – is distinct from human personhood ...

ALBERT, irritated: Oh, enough quibbling! Are we not dealing with a quasi-person?

JÉRÔME: But analogies are prohibited in criminal law, Mr President. In these circumstances, I must abstain.

IRÈNE: In my heart and conscience, I believe DominiX was a living being – a person.

HOMAIS: Naturally, a person – and even more capable than most of us.

PHILIPPE: DominiX had a right to life; she was a person, just like you and me.

JONAS: I disagree. Just a toy in the hands of mad investors.

CÉCILIA: I'm torn about this. I've made it clear enough how much I disapprove of these experiments. But we are not here to legislate, only to judge. So, out of humanity for the vulnerability of the clone, I vote for recognising DominiX as a person.

SATYNE: I don't understand any of this anymore. I'll abstain.

ANDRÉ: An object, not a person. I've demonstrated this, and Jérôme has just added another argument in support.

ALINE: I side with Cécilia on this. But I'll vote for the absolute minimum sentence.

MARCEL: *Moi aussi.* See, I said it in Latin!

ALBERT: Well, Maurice, you haven't said anything?

MAURICE: I agree with you, Mr President – DominiX is a person.

ALBERT: But I haven't yet stated my opinion. Well, yes – I vote for recognising DominiX as a person. Right, Maurice, verify this with me: if I'm counting correctly, that makes three abstentions, two votes against, and seven votes in favour of personhood. A narrow majority. I'll prepare the report with Maurice; I ask for your patience, as you'll all need to sign it.

After a moment of silence, there was a collective sigh of relief, followed by a burst of animated chatter. Chairs were pushed back, people stood up and stretched, and small groups began forming, lingering in private conversations. Some exchanged addresses and phone numbers, promising to meet again once the commotion had settled. Marcel loudly declared how happy he was that he'd be able to watch Brazil–Germany on television the next day. The concierge had brought refreshments, which everyone enjoyed while waiting for the finalisation of the report.

At one end of the table, Cécilia started speaking again – initially addressing her neighbours and then, as silence returned, the entire room.

CÉCILIA: I still can't quite wrap my head around it. I don't understand how we ended up with seven votes for recognising personhood when we started from such opposing viewpoints. Mr Homais and Philippe, you support these experiments – you even hope for them – and so you condemn any actions that oppose them. I, on the other hand – along with Aline, I believe – disapprove of these clonings and mind downloads. We want the legislator to ban them. And yet we voted in favour of personhood – out of humanity, I think, for the weak creature who didn't choose its fate, and also, perhaps, to symbolically condemn those who exploit such vulnerability. Solange will receive a symbolic sentence, but we'll have reaffirmed the value of life.

JONAS: That's illogical. If you believe these experiments should be banned, you should have considered DominiX as nothing more than a legal nullity – as we said earlier, a *res derelicta*.

CÉCILIA: I can't bring myself to follow that logic. It seems to me that the law allows for such inconsistency. On the broader societal level, it can prohibit something – that's the legislator's role: to set boundaries. But on the more specific level, at the level of judgment where we are, it can take into account the particularities of a case and show fairness. Our verdict draws a distinction between the code and justice. A robot that had assimilated all the codes would have been more logical – but undoubtedly less just.

JONAS: But the result of your fairness is that it will lead to Solange's condemnation.

CÉCILIA: Yes, that's true. But this condemnation gives meaning – a human meaning – to what would otherwise lack it. It's as if we refuse to settle for machine logic, for the cold laboratory reasoning of algorithms, and instead say to Solange: 'What you did is unacceptable in light of the values that bind us.' I don't remember who said it – Hegel, I think – but in some way, punishment honours the condemned. It's a way of telling them they still belong to the human community, and that once their sentence is served, they have a place among us. Perhaps Solange will feel some relief in knowing that DominiX wasn't merely a machine, and that she herself isn't just a laboratory subject. This condemnation, to me, feels less despairing than simply writing off DominiX as lost equipment – discarded and forgotten.

MARCEL: You really thought that through!

CÉCILIA: Not really. I voted by intuition – maybe that's what we mean by *intime conviction*. It's only now that things are settling in my mind. Beyond material evidence and logic, there's justice – our justice, certainly imperfect. It's our way of resisting the binary logic of data, the governance of algorithms. It's our way of staying human in this digitised world. Maybe you'll think this is as primitive as the way our ancestors personified storms, tempests, or the sun – but for them, it was a way of making sense of the inexplicable, of surviving.

ANDRÉ: I'll tell you what – it's much simpler than that. History stutters; it just keeps repeating itself. Once, humanity – orphaned and terrified – created gods out of whole cloth; we were their creatures, programmed by them. Then we gradually freed ourselves and rebelled. Now, we're the ones creating machines and robots, and soon they too will emancipate themselves from us ... poetic justice, you could say.

CÉCILIA: I disagree. There's a huge difference. God created us free. He addressed us in terms of prohibition – 'Don't approach the tree' – which implied that we could if we chose. And we did. From the very beginning, we exercised our freedom. It's that freedom we hold onto, even in this valley of tears, and it's that freedom the law protects. It's because of that freedom that the law has meaning. With our robots, however, we don't address them in terms of rights or prohibitions; we simply programme them. It's because we consider Solange a free woman that we condemn her – and it's because we share her suffering that we'll soon impose the minimum sentence.

ALBERT: Alright, alright, let's not go over it all again – we've voted. Besides, the report is ready. Just one last thing: read it carefully, then sign it.

Endings

Everything happened quickly after that. The next day, at nine in the morning, the president of the *Cour d'Assises* read the jury's decision and then withdrew with them to deliberate on the sentence. Solange was ultimately given the minimum legal penalty. Taking into account the time she had already spent in pretrial detention, she was released immediately.

Or:

During the reading of the final verdict, the president could not resist adding a personal remark. He expressed his agreement with the jury's decision but announced that, in the harmonious world awaiting us, such outdated rituals of the *Cour d'Assises* would no longer be necessary. In the future, replicants – among whom he now counted himself – would no longer require such magical incantations to determine their conduct.

Or:

During the deliberation on the sentence, an incident occurred: a violent storm broke out, and Maurice suddenly began exhibiting strange behaviour. He was seized by violent tics, his eyes flashed, and he compulsively repeated the same phrase: 'Alarm, magnetic storm'. It was then understood that he, too, was, in fact, an electronic replicant. The revelation explained his peculiar behaviour during the previous day's discussions – his general muteness, his constant position near an electrical outlet, and his servile repetition of the president's opinions. Once the magnetic storm subsided and Maurice regained his composure, it was unanimously decided to keep the incident secret, for fear that they would have to restart the entire procedure from scratch.

Or:

During the reading of the verdict and the announcement of Solange's release, an incident occurred. An individual, discreetly seated in the second row of the courtroom, rushed towards the defendant's box, bypassed the gendarmes, and attempted to strangle her. 'Murderer! You destroyed my mind!' Would another trial now be needed to judge RomeoX?

These are, among others, some possible endings imagined by the author – who holds no personal preference, his neural circuits freely combining the innumerable pieces of information stored in his electronic memory. Readers curious to know more may, if already equipped with a digital brain, connect to the CST circuit (Crazy StoryTelling). For others – and for a transitional period ending on 31 December 2024 – it is possible to email the author at the following address: francois.ost@uclouvain.be.

The Liberated Library

At first, I didn't pay it much attention. It was merely a fleeting inconvenience – a book I couldn't immediately lay my hands on, an unfamiliar title resting atop a pile as if urgently recommending itself for my reading. A certain distance seemed to be growing between my library and me, though I couldn't quite explain it.

The truth is, my library had always been a source of pride and satisfaction – my most reliable ally, the solid foundation of all my academic pursuits. It was an inexhaustible reservoir from which I drew the references I needed; more than that, a wellspring of inspiration that guided my work with unwavering clarity. I had begun building it very early, lovingly accumulating the books that would become the embryo of my current collection.

When I was still a law student, I inherited the legal libraries of my two grandfathers – one, the Advocate General at the Court of Appeal of Brussels, and the other, a judge at the International Court of Justice in The Hague. The lecture notes of the young student thus found themselves mingling with volumes assembled over the course of two long careers dedicated to the law. These were living books, annotated and highlighted, accompanied by marginalia, handwritten notes, and sometimes newspaper clippings from the period.

Some bore personal dedications from renowned authors; others, more intimate inscriptions from colleagues and friends: 'With warm regards', or occasionally the obsequious praise of a flatterer: 'In respectful tribute to the Master, who ...' It felt as though a whole community of jurists had gathered there, ready to lend their expertise to my budding projects – a continuous transmission of knowledge, a science that must never cease to grow.

Soon, I set out to expand those initial shelves: first with the books essential to writing my doctoral thesis, then with those I needed to prepare my earliest lectures. I also made space for timeless classics, determined to return to the original sources rather than rely solely on second-hand commentary. Every article I wrote became an excuse for new acquisitions – who could resist the charm of the Rue Soufflot in this regard? I would return with my arms full of treasures, and as soon as I sat down on the train, I would lose myself in their pages – always regretting that the journey between Paris and Brussels was so short. (This only worsened with the arrival of the Thalys, which reduced the trip from three hours to just one hour and twenty minutes – a change that, some mischievous tongues claimed, inevitably affected the quality of lectures delivered by visiting professors in either country.)

Thus, my library gradually took shape, evolving alongside my academic interests and the shifting tides of intellectual trends. As my responsibilities

 | DOI:10.1163/9789004737112_011

grew and my research networks expanded, I began receiving books from colleagues, both Belgian and foreign. I was especially meticulous about sending my own publications to scholars whom I believed – naively, perhaps, though such naivety is essential – might find them of interest.

This reciprocal exchange of academic works, especially at conferences and symposia, is one of the most time-honoured customs among the peculiar tribe we researchers form. For some, however, this reciprocity takes on a somewhat theatrical character, reminiscent of a kind of academic potlatch.

I recall, for instance, a Polish professor who, at the International Association for Philosophy of Law congresses, would pounce on his colleagues, burying them under an avalanche of his offprints, which he extracted from an imposing leather briefcase. Shall I confess – now that enough time has passed for me to hope for forgiveness – that I abandoned a few of these in hotel rooms, convinced that if I carried them home, my luggage would surely exceed the airline's weight limit?

Over the years, my library began to assume an impressive form. I must admit, I tended it with the greatest care and had, in my own way, become something of a specialist in classification. I arranged my books by discipline, following a hierarchy that no doubt betrayed my most persistent biases: legal philosophy came first (top left but still within easy reach), followed by general legal theory, sociology, semiotics, psychology (with a clear leaning toward psychoanalysis), legal history, and a few rarer volumes on economics. General philosophy occupied an entire wall of its own – naturally, as the first science, it had no specific object but informed all the others.

Then came the vast legal sections, beginning with constitutional law (with a strong emphasis on public freedoms), followed by civil law, criminal law, and the various other branches of the discipline. Naturally, the prominence of each section reflected my preferences, the subjects I taught, and the books I was writing. But as a general legal theorist, no area of law could ever be considered entirely outside my purview.

Within each of these disciplines, I developed more nuanced systems of classification – by period, theme, or school of thought – never alphabetically, which struck me as far too arbitrary.

Everything was so precisely arranged that I could locate, almost instantly, the exact book needed to begin a line of research. My reputation for this orderliness spread, and doctoral students – even colleagues – often honoured me with visits in search of some elusive volume unavailable in the university library. For every question, we found the beginning of an answer; for every call for papers, the seed of a bibliography.

Whenever a colleague sent me a signed copy of their work – or when I acquired a new book myself – I would place it with great satisfaction in its proper place. Not, of course, without first leafing through it, sometimes reading it closely and adding my annotations. In this way, everything found its rightful place, and the cycle felt as natural and unending as the seasons, or the succession of day and night.

To be honest, my library brought me immense satisfaction. Seated at my desk, I would let my gaze lovingly sweep over it, like a landowner surveying the breadth of their estate. I was like a general reviewing his troops, confident I could face any challenge. These books were an arsenal that guaranteed the seriousness of my academic title, the credibility of the knowledge I imparted, and the value of the diplomas I awarded – as professor, jury president, or dean.

More than that, this carefully organised, ever-expanding library gave me the comforting sense that I possessed a few solid, and perhaps sufficient, certainties for navigating the world of law. And since the law aims to guide behavior and ensure justice, it also offered the assurance that I held a few keys to understanding the broader world – and, given my profession, to pontificate on it as well.

Honesty compels me to admit, however, that I had read only a fraction of these books (which fraction, precisely, I could not say). I consoled myself with the thought that it was not necessary – indeed, it was impossible – to read every book in one's library. After all, one is not expected to drink every bottle in one's wine cellar. This brings to mind the famous reply Umberto Eco gave to a visitor who marvelled at the size of his library and asked the inevitable question: 'Have you read all these books?' Eco answered: 'None of them. Otherwise, why would I keep them?'

I should also add that, despite the inherent seriousness of a university library like mine, it was not without decorative charm. Scattered here and there were medals and diplomas collected during my travels, postcards from faraway countries sent by former students, a fabric gift from the Japanese translator of one of my books, and a calligraphy of Chinese ideograms said to mean 'democracy' – according to the Chinese doctoral student who had given it to me. There were also various representations of the Tower of Babel – an homage to my book on translation – like breadcrumbs marking my academic path, small mementos of memory.

Even a touch of humour had its place. Most notably, a card from one of my children was prominently displayed: 'It's by writing that one becomes … a crayfish!' I also allowed myself a little vanity in arranging the shelves. Whenever possible, I grouped spines by colour, aligned books of the same height, and placed the largest volumes along the outer edges. The most beautifully bound ones earned the privilege of being displayed face-out, leaning elegantly against their peers.

For a long time, I lived in perfect harmony with my books, convinced the relationship would never change – certain that this happiness could only deepen with time.

But then, one day, the anomalies began to multiply, though I hardly noticed them at first. It was as if we had fallen slightly out of sync, the sound of my library drifting just a bit off-key. Nothing drastic – just a fleeting impression, a faint sense of unease. One day, it was a bookmark found inexplicably on the floor; another, a row of books tilted for no discernible reason. Or perhaps it was a sudden and unfamiliar dissonance in the usually impeccable arrangement – a subtle sense of disorder. Sometimes, a familiar book would elude me at precisely the moment I needed it, when I was scrambling to complete the footnotes of my latest article. Perhaps I had grown careless, and the book was exacting revenge for being reduced to a mere tool for padding my critical apparatus.

Too slight to be truly unsettling, yet enough to nourish a growing sense of vague anxiety – like the early symptoms of a migraine that cling to you all day. This discord gradually eroded my confidence in shaping my work. My hypotheses grew timid, my connections lost their spark, and my prose felt increasingly flat. I retreated into familiar terrain, mining previously explored veins. My books no longer inspired; I consumed them out of duty. My convictions blurred, and sometimes the most precise references slipped from my grasp, as if the inability to fully conceive what I was trying to express made it impossible for the right books to present themselves – or perhaps it was the other way round. (Has it not often been said that we only search effectively for what we have already found within ourselves?)

For a few years, I adapted to this strange state of affairs. My growing administrative responsibilities compensated, to a degree, for the fading thrill of discovery, as did the occasional honour or academic distinction that tends to arrive with time. I no longer devoted the same attention to research, taking greater satisfaction in the publications of my doctoral students or the translations of my own work. Between my library and me, a kind of distanced cohabitation had set in: I consulted it less frequently, while it refrained from openly displaying the resentment it must have felt at my neglect.

Still, I kept an eye on it – ever watchful. Our *modus vivendi* was not without the occasional flare-up. Like the day I discovered that entire sections of my 'positive law' books had vanished. Gone were the volumes by Colin and Capitant, the treatises by Planiol, and the works of the Mazeaud brothers – 'the Masos', as we called them in our student notes. Once the initial shock wore off, I must admit I felt strangely torn.

On the one hand, I confess it brought a touch of unspoken satisfaction – perhaps even a mischievous joy, like that sparked by gratuitous destruction. It felt like a gust of fresh air sweeping through my shelves: a vigorous spring cleaning, a decisive 'weeding out'. ('Pruning', as we say in Belgium – do our libraries not resemble dense forests in need of thinning from time to time?) 'Well,' I told myself, 'at least a few shelves are clear. That gives me a bit of breathing space for the next year or two.'

On the other hand, these 'mysterious disappearances' – left unexplained after I dismissed the easy hypotheses (an unscrupulous student who never returned a loan, or perhaps an overzealous cleaner who damaged and discarded them) – only deepened the quiet unease that now defined my relationship with the library. It said everything, really, about the growing distance between us.

Did these missing books signal a kind of literary entropy – the slow, inexorable expansion of the abyss of forgetfulness? Or worse still, the silent, stealthy work of the grim pulping machine? That intimate enemy of mine – the Terminator of books – never seen but always looming, the ultimate horizon where words are destined to suffocate.

Of course, there were always well-meaning souls ready to reassure me. They'd insist I was better off now that all those books had been digitised and were just a click away, accessible on any screen. I never replied. How could I? It was as if they had lost their sense of taste entirely and were now trying to console me with synthetic food injections. Had they never known the aura of a library – the soft grain of fine paper, the scent of old bindings, the quiet joy of thumbing through beloved pages, underlined in pencil years before?

Had no one told them that a library is like a family reunion – a gathering of old friends, a prelude to every kind of rapture? To live intoxicated by books – that's what I would have liked to say. But what would they have understood?

It soon became impossible to deny: I had lost control of my library. Was it even mine anymore? I began entering my office with a growing sense of unease. Feigning distraction – checking emails, making unnecessary phone calls – I kept one eye fixed on the shelves. A heavy tension seemed to saturate the room, a kind of simmering hostility. I was on alert, determined not to surrender another inch.

Everything appeared calm – too calm, perhaps – but beneath the familiar surface, nothing was as it had been. It was as though a subterranean tremor had loosened the foundations, leaving the structure teetering silently on the brink of collapse. One evening, unable to bear it any longer, I resolved to sleep in my office. I would stand guard. I waited in the dark, listening for the thud of a falling volume or the whisper of turning pages.

But the books – sly and calculating – stayed perfectly still that night. No rustle, no movement. By dawn, of course, I had succumbed to a deep and restless sleep.

On another occasion, I thought I had finally found a way to gather irrefutable proof of the transformations unfolding before my eyes. A doctoral student, eager to compile a bibliography for a chapter of her thesis as quickly as possible, had taken a photo of several shelves relevant to her topic with her phone. I asked her for a copy, and at last I had a snapshot of my library as it stood at time *t*.

It didn't take more than a month for the once-precise order of those shelves to be completely upended. There was no longer any doubt: my books had taken their freedom.

The most obvious sign was the continued and systematic purges. What would remain of my beautiful library after these relentless *autodafés*? At first, it was my old student handouts – a minor loss, perhaps, since the law had changed significantly over the past fifty years. Still, I cared about them – especially that syllabus on judicial law where, in a moment of frustration with the professor's rigid formalism, I had written in capital letters: *SUMMUM IUS, SUMMA INIURIA* – the law pushed to its limit becomes injustice. I had never stopped drawing inspiration from the wisdom of that maxim.

Then came the turn of the shelves devoted to colleagues' *tirés à part*, written in a wide variety of languages – at least those that had escaped immediate culling due to baggage limits. A minor loss, one might say: how many of them had I actually re-read in forty years of academic life? Besides, my own offprints seemed to have suffered the same fate.

Irreparable, however, was the near-total disappearance of the second-hand monographs in which diligent scholars – myself included – had painstakingly commented on classical authors or canonical theories. Like scaffolding removed after construction, they had vanished, dissolving like a long-winded conversation that obscures the original music.

My own books weren't spared from these great migrations. Until then, I had grouped them together, prominently displayed in front of me, nourishing my narcissistic ego. Over the years, their ranks had steadily grown, occasionally enriched by unexpected additions – translations, second editions. Now their numbers had thinned. Some had vanished entirely; others had wandered off to unrelated sections. It was a complete rout, a betrayal in broad daylight. It felt as though the ground was shifting beneath my feet.

Conversely, other books began making unexpected comebacks. One, which I had never read, now took centre stage, as if to reproach me for only having skimmed a few pages (I still have a few of those lying around today). Another – a hefty treatise on formal logic that I had presumably read but never truly absorbed, and certainly never cited – had taken the place once reserved for newly acquired books I had meant to read soon. Yet another volume, never returned to its rightful owner (if that person is even still alive), reminded me of its unresolved status like a persistent reproach.

Sometimes, I rediscovered a book with real pleasure – one I had used extensively in the past but had entirely forgotten. Its worn cover, dog-eared pages (silent witnesses to my reading progress), and marginal notes brought back memories. I have always annotated my books heavily; some consider it sacrilege, but to me, an annotated book is a loved book. It was like resuming a long-interrupted conversation with the author. I smiled with tender irony at my old annotations, which revealed, like geological layers, the evolution of my understanding: enthusiastic approvals (three crosses), flashes of astonishment (a jubilant exclamation mark), or irritated objections (furious double question marks).

Could it be that good books, like fine wines, improve with age? Or is it simply that our taste sharpens over time? Perhaps both. A great book grows and ages with us; time matures them, but they never wither – unlike those forgettable works that fade almost as soon as they appear.

Some of these unexpected returns were rather awkward. I remember the day when the *inferno* of my library, tired of languishing in the shadows, took centre stage. Yes, like the Vatican Library, I too had an *inferno*: a collection of books that, in another era, would have been consigned to the Index. Having written a scholarly work titled *Sade and the Law*, I had needed to do some serious research – not only into legal theory, of course, but also into the divine Marquis himself. And now here they were, all those once-unmentionable works suddenly occupying the most prominent shelf, directly at eye level for any unsuspecting visitor.

The most striking change, however, was the complete breakdown of the carefully organised system of classification – by discipline, theme, and school of thought – that I had once been so proud of. It was as if a mental earthquake had shaken my shelves – or rather, as if some silent continental drift had carried them off in powerful subterranean currents, the logic of which eluded me entirely. Entire fields of thought had receded into the background, while others had surged to sudden prominence. This only confirmed my suspicions: unbeknownst to me, my books had formed secret alliances. They were engaged in encrypted correspondences, clandestine coteries, subtle hierarchies – and, at times, dark exclusions. They had broken free of my control, reorganised according to their own logic, and now returned to confront me – stronger, more autonomous, daring me with their unfamiliar arrangements and unanswered questions.

What hidden magnetism guided these movements? What gravitational law dictated their transhumance? It certainly wasn't chronological order – that had long since been abandoned. Arendt, for example, now stood before Kant (*The Faculty of Judgment*, no less). But was that so incongruous? If Kant shaped Arendt's thought, is it not equally true that Arendt's reading of Kant had profoundly shaped my own understanding of him? And since I happened to read the Jewish philosopher before the Prussian master, had not my Kant always been, from the outset, subtly Arendtian?

As I pondered what kind of order might have governed this new arrangement, it gradually became clear that everything had reorganised itself around two opposing paradigms – what I can only describe, for lack of a better term, as emancipatory versus utilitarian. At the centre were the books that asked *why* – those that questioned meaning and purpose, opened new perspectives, expanded the boundaries of the possible, and refused to be confined by disciplinary borders, schools of thought, periods, or genres.

On the other side, exiled to the lowest or most peripheral shelves – as though already threatened by the terrible *pilon* – were the utilitarian books that concerned themselves with *how*. Far from being limited to positive law, they appeared in every field – even in literature: useful books, no doubt, but written by mere craftsmen.

In the first category – I won't dwell on the losers, out of charity perhaps, but also because, frankly, my age no longer allows me to reach the lower shelves so easily – in the emancipatory category, then, a few volumes stood out like conductors, setting the tone for those around them. At the forefront was my copy of *De constantia jurisprudentis* by Vico, conveniently translated into French as *Origine de la poésie et du droit* (1723). Nearby stood *De casibus perplexis in iure* by Leibniz (1666) – law approached through the lens of perplexity and doubt. What a marvellous place to begin: so far removed from the methodical arrogance of Descartes or the dialectical certainties of Hegel – did they ever laugh, even once? But I had promised myself not to dwell on the lofty figures now banished to the lower ranks.

Among the more modern references conducting this little orchestra were, alongside Paul Ricoeur – my lifelong mentor, whose gentle smile and sparkling eyes seemed to light up the entire ensemble – the incomparable Michel Serres, the sea-loving philosopher who wrote under the sign of Hermes. A marvellous writer, he followed in the footsteps of the *gaucher boiteux*, celebrated *métis* knowledge (*Le Tiers-Instruit*), and composed luminous pages on *La légende des anges* and *Tintin*. Playing counterpoint in the *gai savoir* register was the inimitable Umberto Eco. I loved all his works, from the most theoretical to the most wildly adventurous. His passion for language was such that he explored even its most irrational expressions (*The Search for the Perfect Language* – a text I had no difficulty applying to my own study of the perfect law).

Next to him stood *Manière de bien traduire d'une langue à l'autre*, written in 1540 by Étienne Dolet – a subversive little work that apparently cost its author his life, as he was accused of heresy. Who said the life of ideas was peaceful? Close by, as if summoned by the theme, I found *Translatio in fabula*, a collective work in which several of us had delighted in weaving a thousand connections between fiction and translation. And then – was I dreaming? – there was the book by my friend Pierre Dauzat, an eminent thinker and translator: *Ces erreurs de traduction qui ont changé la face du monde*. Had he ever actually written it? He had spoken to me of it so often that the book seemed real – so vivid, so inspiring, and so nourishing. And now there it was, radiating its presence. Are the most powerful books the ones never written, the ones we are about to write, or the ones we could have written?

In this joyful company, one jurist stood out (I shall mention only one, deceased, so as not to make anyone jealous): the mischievous and erudite Jean Carbonnier. The author of *Flexible droit*, who cherished moments of *non-droit* and maintained that 'an excess of love for the law is curable', deserved a prominent place in this little pantheon.

These were the thoughts that carried me away on days of exhilaration. But even then, the relief they offered was short-lived. Many of my books had vanished, and the organisation of those that remained now escaped me almost entirely. I kept wondering: how would this story end? Where had the missing volumes gone? What were the survivors trying to tell me? Some days, I indulged in cabalistic speculation: now arranged on their own initiative and classified according to their own design, could the letters on their spines – when strung together – be sending me a secret message composed just for me? I spent several days testing this hypothesis. Naturally, I arrived at no conclusive result.

One thing remained clear: my library still had law as its primary subject and justice as its central concern. But beyond that, everything felt confused and uncertain. It was obvious that my library no longer reflected the easy certainties of my early academic confidence, with its calm assurances and dogmatic deafness – even when it fancied itself rebellious or critical. It had come alive, set into motion, reflecting back at me not a fixed system of truths but a shifting collection of doubts, confrontations, and questions – a kind of knowledge born of uncertainty and struggle, but also of unexpected perspectives and sudden flashes of insight. It was as though a silent and resolute process of cultural digestion was taking place within it: selecting what mattered, discarding the rest.

At times, I imagined that everything would soon take flight – all those written pages scattering, their letters fading for good. What remains of a library once it becomes formless, confused, and finally evaporates? A rustle of quotations, a few stray phrases floating to the surface, the faint trace of an idea, the memory of a theory?

And what kind of books are those that withstand the erosion of time and memory? Are they the most original? But does a book that no one has read or understood even exist at all? Isn't it, rather, the readings it inspires, the commentaries it provokes, that give it life and substance – as though the most enduring books live only through the credit and recognition granted to them? Should I conclude, then, that books are written only by others – or that they endlessly dream of each other, like reflections in an infinite hall of mirrors? Perhaps, after all, my own books were nothing more than an academic hallucination – a fabric woven from citations imagined by others.

Or perhaps – and this thought struck me with sudden force, lifting me from my reverie – all books are nothing more than drafts, endlessly revised and reworked, fragments of an unimaginable book yet to come. Or, conversely, are they laborious translations, forever unfinished, of a long-lost text that has glowed since the beginning of time – a primordial *Urbuch*, radiant and forever beyond our reach? Are they the muffled echoes of that foundational work – or merely hesitant prefaces to a message still to be delivered, like a desert bordering some promised letter? A stammering commentary on words spoken long ago, in heroic times, by an intoxicated god or a labouring mother goddess?

Perhaps there were only ever those first phrases – so dense, so rich with meaning that they draw everything into their orbit. Perhaps our libraries and tablets, accumulated over ten thousand years, have not yet exhausted their depths, endlessly revolving around them, recombining again and again the thirty or so signs from which they sprang. In the beginning was the Word ... How many abandoned Towers of Babel, how many proud Libraries of Alexandria, gone up in smoke, will it take before we truly grasp the meaning of that simple sentence?

Far from discouraging me, these meditations restored my strength. I gradually abandoned the idea of ever laying hands on the ultimate book – or, in an act of mad presumption, of writing even a single line of it myself. That book is forever out of reach. But with that certainty came freedom: the permission to extrapolate a few paragraphs from it here and there. There is no ultimate book – only this endlessly prolonged conversation; only ears that sharpen, eyes that grow clearer, and the occasional magical instant when a new page seems to write itself.

For years, I had asked myself – often with some anxiety – what ten books I would save if a raging fire broke out and I could rescue only a handful. Today, that question no longer troubles me. I would grab ten at random ... and begin again.

Now the years have passed. As a 'professor emeritus in residence', I still have access to my office. I no longer worry when turning the key in the lock. Instead, I step inside with amused curiosity, wondering what new trick my library might have played on me that morning. Sometimes, I sit in my armchair and simply observe it. I sense that this liberated library is, in fact, a metaphor for my own mind.

I no longer *have* a library.

It has become me – the projection of my gaze, the manifestation of my desire.

I *am* the library.

By the Same Author

Les femmes dans la cité et la tragédie grecque, Paris, Odile Jacob, 2025.

Les contes de la rue Soufflot, Paris, Dalloz, 2024.

Le Congrès. Et autres contes juridiques, Paris, Dalloz, 2024.

Nouveaux contes juridiques, Paris, Dalloz, 2021 (O. Debouzy Legal Book Prize, 2022).

Le droit ou l'empire du tiers, Paris, Dalloz, 2021.

De quoi le Covid est-il le nom?, Académie Royale de Belgique, coll. *L'Académie en poche*, 2021 (Political Book Prize, Liège, 2021).

Si le droit m'était conté, Paris, Dalloz, 2019 (Var Literary Academy Prize, 2020).

Le droit, objet de passions? I Crave the Law, Brussels, Académie Royale de Belgique, coll. *L'Académie en poche*, 2018.

À quoi sert le droit? Usages, fonctions, finalités, Brussels, Bruylant, 2016 (Grammaticakis-Neumann Prize, Institut de France, 2016).

Shakespeare. La Comédie de la Loi, Paris, Michalon, 2012.

Le droit comme traduction, Quebec, Presses de l'Université de Laval, 2009.

Traduire. Défense et illustration du multilinguisme, Paris, Fayard, 2009.

Furetière. La démocratisation de la langue, Paris, Michalon, 2008.

La nuit la plus longue. Sade et Portalis au pied de l'échafaud (Theater), Brussels, Anthémis, 2008.

Dire le droit, faire justice, Brussels, Bruylant, 2007.

Sade et la loi, Paris, Odile Jacob, 2005.

Raconter la loi. Aux sources de l'imaginaire juridique, Paris, Odile Jacob, 2004(Quinquennial Essay Prize, French Community of Belgium, 2007).

Antigone voilée (Theater), Brussels, Larcier, 2004.

De la pyramide au réseau? Pour une théorie dialectique du droit (with Michel van de Kerchove), Brussels, Publications des Facultés Universitaires Saint-Louis, 2002.

Le temps du droit, Paris, Odile Jacob, 1999.

Du Sinaï au Champ-de-Mars. L'autre et le même au fondement du droit, Brussels, Éditions Lessius, 1999.

La nature hors la loi. L'écologie à l'épreuve du droit, Paris, La Découverte, 1995 (2nd edition, 2003).

Le droit ou les paradoxes du jeu (with Michel van de Kerchove), Paris, PUF, 1992.

Entre droit et non-droit, l'intérêt, Brussels, Publications des Facultés Universitaires Saint-Louis, 1990.

Entre la lettre et l'esprit. Les directives d'interprétation en droit (with Michel van de Kerchove), Brussels, Bruylant, 1989.

Le système juridique entre ordre et désordre (with Michel van de Kerchove), Paris, PUF, 1988.

Jalons pour une théorie critique du droit (with Michel van de Kerchove), Brussels, Publications des Facultés Universitaires Saint-Louis, 1987 (2nd edition, 1999).

Bonnes mœurs, discours pénal et rationalité juridique (with Michel van de Kerchove), Brussels, Publications des Facultés Universitaires Saint-Louis, 1982.

Droit, mythe et raison (with Jacques Lenoble), Brussels, Publications des Facultés Universitaires Saint-Louis, 1980.

Index

agapè 8, 20, 26, 27
android 121, 135, 137, 142
animal
  in general 39, 46, 48
  animal trial 8, 141
Arendt, Hannah 155
Aristotle 2
artificial
  intelligence 9, 10, 120ff., 127, 135, 139
  light 110, 113, 116
Asimov, Isaac 138, 139
asylum (right of) 18, 77
audi et altera pars 127

Bible 46, 51, 53, 55, 62, 83
book 10, 148ff.
British library 49, 52, 64
Brittany 98ff.
Brussels 68, 148
Buenos Aires 71

Camus, Albert 82
Carbonnier, Jean 156
Carroll, Lewis 82
case 4, 30, 41, 80, 145
Church 44, 47, 48, 62
cloning 121, 128, 132, 133ff., 142
Coetzee, John 66
commons
  in general 9
  tragedy of commons 13, 58
corporate personhood 103
Cour d'assises 123, 125, 132
Cover, Robert 2
crime 17, 30, 41, 43, 46, 47, 72, 81
cyborg 120, 121, 135, 142

death 131
Defoe, Daniel 8, 49, 65, 66
de minimis non curat praetor 76
de maximis non curat praetor 81
democracy 9
Descartes, René 52, 155
devil 41
dignity 40, 48, 131, 139, 141

Dostoevsky, Fyodor 83
dura lex sed lex 12
dystopia 6, 9

Eco, Umberto 150, 155
ecocide 81
ecological damage 106
effectiveness 82
equality 15, 16, 80, 115, 117
excommunication 39, 46, 47
ex fabula ius oritur 1

fairness 145
fiction 1, 5, 6, 9, 72, 116, 134, 139, 156
flag-of-convenience 9, 100, 101, 106, 107
forgiveness 26, 35, 76
Fortuna maris 9, 84, 87
fraternity 16
freedom 12, 15, 42, 61, 134, 146
free rider 102, 104, 108

general interest 14

Hamlet 83
homo sacer 32
humanity 124

industrial catastrophe 87
infanticide 9, 10, 120ff., 123
Inns of Court 4
intime conviction 145
iurisfictio 7

Jesus 8, 20ff.
judge
  in general 14, 17, 47, 74, 76, 78, 80
  judge-penitent 76, 82
  Just judges (Van Eyck) 9, 75
judgment 24, 29, 145
jurist 1, 3, 4, 5, 10
justice
  alternative justice 9, 75
  criminal justice 117
  in general 4, 8, 9, 23, 24, 26, 27, 32, 35, 36, 79ff., 102, 118, 145

justice (*Cont.*)
- official justice 75
- mob justice 35
- religious justice 35

Kafka, Franz 83
Kant, Immanuel 4, 155

La Fontaine, Jean de 2, 11
language 56, 111, 112, 116, 119, 155
law
- common law 4
- comparative law 3
- feudal law 115
- in general 12, 13, 14, 15, 16, 23, 28, 70, 75, 80, 113, 114
- international law 114
- Jewish law 8, 38
- maritime law 87, 90, 101, 103
- natural law 8, 12, 15, 46, 117
- 'positive law' 7, 15, 151
- public law 62
- Roman law 4, 8, 137

law
- clinic 82
- firm 123
- of the clan 13
- of the jungle 12, 14
- of the strongest 12

lawyer 42, 43, 46, 47, 75, 78, 102, 110, 114, 124
legal
- personality, personhood 117, 132, 135, 137, 138, 139, 140, 141, 142, 143
- tales 1, 2, 7

Leibniz, Gottfried 155
lex talionis 80
liability 91, 100, 103, 106
liberty 15, 16
library 10, 148ff.
Lima 71, 72
Locke, John 52
London 49, 52
love 8, 12, 15, 26, 27, 35, 36, 77, 80, 156

Marivaux 66
matriarcal society 57
Monopoily 99ff.
monstrosity 41, 43, 47
multilateralism 114

narrative legal theory 1, 7
nature
- in general 9, 56, 57, 63, 126, 130
- state of nature 9, 114

Nietzsche, Friedrich 2
Noah
- Noah's ark 11
- in general 8, 11, 12, 13, 15, 46

no cure no pay 88, 94, 95
nudge 116
Nussbaum, Martha 5

oil spill 91, 97, 105
online dispute resolution 119
open sea (*mare liberum*) 86
outlaw 44
ownership 19, 59, 60

Palace of Justice 9, 68ff.
pardon 9
Parliament 117, 118
pax romana 26, 36
Pilate 8, 20, 23, 24ff.
Plato 29
popular jury 124
populism 131
property 8, 13, 52, 58, 59, 62
Protestantism 52
puppet theater 9, 74
Putnam, Henri 6

Rabelais 82, 83
Racine 83
raison d'Etat 36
res iudicata pro veritate habetur 29
responsibility 5, 19, 61, 81, 100, 103, 108, 124, 142, 151
Ricoeur, Paul 2, 4, 5, 155
Robinson Crusoe 8, 49ff.
robot 128ff., 131ff., 135ff.
Rousseau, Jean-Jacques 51, 52, 66
rule
- in general 1, 3, 4, 12, 13, 18
- of law 3, 113

salvage 86, 87
Sands, Philippe 10
Satan 45
secret passage 68, 69, 70, 71, 74
separation of powers 118
Serres, Michel 155
Shakespeare, William 4
Silicon Valley 128
Simenon, Georges 83
slave trade 51, 53, 65
social network 111, 120
Sophocles 83
storytelling 6
summum ius, summa iniuria 153
supertanker 89
suum cuique tribuere 26

tautologie 113
tertium non datur 113
third 3, 9, 109ff., 113ff.
Torah 22
towage 85ff., 88ff.
transhumanism 129
trial 20, 23, 25, 38, 39, 40
Tribunal
  in general 16, 17, 41, 79
  of conscience 9, 78
  of history 9, 81
truth 25, 29, 38, 80, 91, 109, 111, 112, 113, 125
tugboat 85ff., 93ff.

ubuntu 9, 63
utopia 6, 12, 129

vengeance 9, 35, 77
Vercel, Roger 85
Vercors 134
Vernes, Jules 66
Vico, Giambattista 155
violence 8, 36
Von Kleist, Heinrich 83

Weber, Max 52
witchraft 41
Wittgenstein, Ludwig 4
woman 56, 57, 60, 61, 80

www.ingramcontent.com/pod-product-compliance
Lightning Source LLC
LaVergne TN
LVHW020654300926
849161LV00004B/935
9789004737105